TEACHING ARCHERY

Running a Recreational Archery Program

TEACHING ARCHERY

Running a Recreational Archery Program

by Van Webster

Library of Congress Cataloging-in Publication Data

Teaching Archery / Van Webster.
 p. cm
 ISBN 978-0-9913326-4-9 (softcover)
 1. Archery. 2. Teaching. I Van Webster, 1946-

ISBN: 978-0-9913326-4-9

Copyright © 2015 by Watching Arrows Fly

All rights reserved. Except for use in a review, the reproduction or utilization of this work in any form or by any electronic, mechanical, or other means, now known or hereafter invented, including xerography, photocopying, and recording, and in any information storage and retrieval system, is forbidden without written permission of the publisher.

The web addresses cited in this text were current as of January 2015, unless otherwise noted.

Writer: Van Webster; **Copy Editor**; Steve Ruis; **Proofreader:** Michèle Hansen; **Graphic Artist:** Steve Ruis; **Cover Designer**: Steve Ruis; **Photographers** (cover and interior): Van Webster unless otherwise noted; **Illustrator** Steve Ruis

Printed in the United States of America 10 9 8 7 6 5 4 3 2

Watching Arrows Fly
3712 North Broadway, #285
Chicago, IL 60613

Dedication

This book is dedicated to Brain and Stefan.

Van Webster
Spring 2015

Brian and Stefan Webster

Contents

	Acknowledgements	1
1	Introduction	3
2	The Importance of Volunteers	5
3	Archery Class Instruction for Teens and Adults	9
4	Youth Programs	25
5	Instructor and Coach Certifications	37
6	SafeSport Certification	49
7	Tournament Programs	51
8	Fundraising and Grants	69
9	Building Archery Participation and Club Membership	75
10	Range Location and Maintenance	79
11	Archery Equipment Choices and Maintenance	97
12	Business Operations	103
13	Communications and Outreach	113
14	Recognition	121
15	Some Thoughts on Coaching Archery	125

Appendices

A	Safety and Orientation Class Script	139
B	Eight-Meeting Archery Program Instructor Class Syllabus	143
C	Four-Meeting Archery Fundamentals Class Syllabus	157
D	Olympic Recurve Archery Class Syllabus	163
E	Compound Archery Class Syllabus	171
F	Traditional Archery Class Syllabus	181
G	Two-Hour Training/Practice Schedule	185
H	Camp Archery Program Equipment List	187
I	The National Training System	189
J	Glossary of National Training System (NTS) Terms	195
K	Making and Using PVC Pipe Bows as Archery Training Aids	199
L	Archery: A Numbers Game	203
	About the Author	207

Acknowledgements

An email arrived in my in box about a year ago from Steve Ruis asking me if I would be interested in contributing to a series of books he was publishing under the title "Coaching Archery." A quick glance at the other addresses on the "to" line showed that Steve had extended this invitation to a number of the key archery coaches and educators in the field. Their accomplishments and contributions to the sport of archery are substantial and I was not entirely sure that I belonged in their august company. Fool that I am, if Steve thought enough of my potential to extend the invitation to write, I felt that I should honor his request with my best effort. If you find value in these chapters, it is thanks to Steve that this book is in front of you.

Six-time Pasadena Roving Archers President Michael Burnham got me back into the sport after a very long layoff. He met with me and my son Stefan at the range, got Stefan shooting right away and got me into teaching and then coaching archery. Mike is very knowledgeable about shooting archery as well as the setup of archery equipment. His influence is felt throughout these pages.

Six-time PRA President Gary Spiers has skillfully directed the path of the club through ardent and fierce political opposition within the city of Pasadena. The club, as it enters its 80th year, owes its and the Pasadena Archery Range's very survival to the efforts of the club members under his leadership. I am grateful for his many efforts on behalf the sport of archery and PRA that provide me with a venue to practice my coaching and teaching skills.

Teaching children takes a particular talent and uses a set of skills that I do not possess in any substance. PRA Coaches Terri MacQuarrie and Jim MacQuarrie head up our youth archery program which includes beginning youth archers under the age of 10, returning youth archers under the age of 10, and our Junior Olympic Archery Development (JOAD) competitive archery program. They both have special skills that make our program for younger archers a success.

There are more than 30 certified instructors and coaches at Pasadena Roving Archers and I learn from each of them every day. I also learn from the thousands of archery students that come through our program each year. While most participants come once, have a fun time and then go on to other activities, the ones who stick with the sport provide inspiration for all of us to do our best to nurture the sport of archery.

In the early months of 2005, Coach Mike Burnham and I attended a presentation by Don Rabska at the corporate offices of Easton, Inc. on a new, scientific approach to instructing and coaching Olympic Recurve archery. He called it the Biomechanically Efficient Shooting Technique, or the BEST method. The ideas were a revelation. Here was a way to teach archery shooting form that was based on research and facts, not just hearsay and personal experience. PRA contracted with Don to give the same presentation to our instruction program staff. We published a handbook on the BEST method that was the first documentation of the technique here in the US. That book became the foundation of the article on the BEST method that was published by USA Archery in the December, 2005 issue of *Archery* magazine. Don is a terrific teacher and a supporter of the sport of archery. I've learned a lot from him.

In April, 2007 the US Olympic Committee

sponsored a symposium at the Olympic Training Center in Colorado Springs, focusing on Training Design. Coaches Eric Schindler, Dee Falks, and I attended this conference and came away with a ton of great ideas. Many of the coaching principles that Coach Falks wrote into the then Community Coach Course came from this event. I left with a strong impression that archers are athletes and to maximize their performance, coaches need to respect and treat them as athletes. I was also particularly impressed by the presentation of Coach Sue Enquist, coach of the 11-time national champion UCLA women's softball team, on Creating a Culture of Excellence. It was Coach Enquist who really personified for me the character of a successful athletic coach.

I've also had the opportunity to work with some of the leading coaches in our sport including Coach Dee Falks, Coach Steve Cornell, and USAA National Head Coach Kisik Lee. All have been generous with their knowledge and insights.

Chapter 1
Introduction

When Steve Ruis first proposed that I write a book on archery coaching, I felt that there were lots of successful archery coaches, including the ones on his proposed author list, who had more experience than I've had in working with top athletes. Many of these coaches have written about their coaching techniques. I had written some articles for *Archery Focus* magazine on a range of topics in and around archery, but Steve's invitation posed the question of what could I present in book form that would represent a contribution to the literature of the sport and be of value to archery program leaders? There are many books and articles on coaching competitive archers to top form but the vast majority of archery participants are not competitors and never will be. So this book is aimed at instructors, coaches, and program administrators who do the day to day work of teaching the sport of archery to the recreational public.

I teach and coach archery at Pasadena Roving Archers. Pasadena Roving Archers (PRA) will celebrate its 80th anniversary as an archery club in the city of Pasadena, California in 2015. PRA is one of the oldest field archery clubs in the country and the roving range in Lower Arroyo Seco Park is the oldest field archery range in the U.S. that is still in its original location. The founder and chief benefactor of the club at the beginning was Henry A. Bitzenberger (yes, that Bitzenberger). The PRA logo was designed by California Archery Hall of Fame member Stewart Foster who also designed the National Field Archery Association logo.

As with any all-volunteer organization, the club has had its ups and downs. Currently we are in a record high growth period. During the past decade plus, the club's programs have experienced rapid expansion, especially its archery instruction program. The club has offered free, introductory archery classes to the public since the mid 60's. By the year 2000 about 25 people a week were showing up to learn the sport of archery. A dedicated staff of volunteer certified instructors and coaches provided a quality experience for new archers and the word spread throughout the community and Southern California.

PRA saw a jump in interest in our programs with the release from 2009 to 2014 of a number of Hollywood theatrical motion pictures featuring archery as part of the story. With an established archery instruction program already in place, a top reputation and free introductory classes, PRA found that the participation in its archery classes quickly filled to capacity. Currently we are serving more than 10,000 people per year from over 125 Zip codes, introducing more than 4000 people a year to the sport of archery. PRA provides a wide range of classes for archers from first timers to competitors.

All of this growth has happened on an archery range located in a public park where the club is allotted, by the City of Pasadena, only seven hours of range time per week on a Saturday for all of our class activities. In 2006 PRA became a 501(c)(3) non-profit charitable organization and we have been the recipients of grants from a number of Southern California foundations. PRA has produced fund raising events benefitting charitable organizations within the City of Pasadena and the Los Angeles County area.

This kind of success comes as the result of the dedicated efforts of a team of volunteers who take on the many tasks that are needed to keep a major program running. I have been fortunate enough to serve in a number of capacities with PRA including eight terms as Vice President (I'm better at vice than at presiding), recording secretary, and for the past six years as Director of Instruction. So, it seemed to me that I should write about what I know, primarily how to build and sustain a high volume public archery instruction program.

While many of the ideas for programs are presented here in the context of an all-volunteer archery club, a commercially run archery pro shop, martial arts school or shooting range can easily adapt these concepts to their business models. Being a business, it is unlikely that you will find volunteer labor. Factoring in labor expenses can raise the cost and thus the price to the public for an archery program. In pricing your offerings, think of instruction as not only a source of revenue but also as a marketing tool for building your business.

It is unlikely that any purchaser of this book will read it through from cover to cover. Rather the contents should be thought of as a handbook, a reference, a source of information and a guide to successful class planning and operations. While PRA is referred to often in the book, this is not an official PRA document and represents the opinions and experiences of the author alone and not the PRA organization. Not all of the ideas expressed herein are things that are currently implemented in the PRA program. Some ideas are not practical for PRA given operational restrictions imposed by the City of Pasadena. Some are ideas that I have seen work in other contexts. And some are ideas that I would like to implement under ideal circumstances. In any case, there are a bunch of thoughts in here that you may find useful as you develop and grow your own program.

Because of my teaching experience, I have come to view my role in the sport as primarily one of coaching other instructors and coaches. I have trained hundreds of archery instructors and scores of Level 3 coaches. Many of the participants in my classes have gone on to make a significant contributions to the sport of archery, initiating programs, earning higher levels of certifications, and coaching competitive athletes. This book reflects that direction in providing ideas and information for new as well as experienced archery leaders to adapt and employ in their own programs. If I have any long term influence in the archery world it will be through the efforts of those students.

Not all the topics in this book are archery-specific. You'll find that I wander off into other areas of discussion as I have found them to be relevant for not just teaching archery but for building and sustaining an organization that can produce reliable and repeatable results over a long period of time. Such topics are aimed at club and business leaders who have an interest in the administrative side of running a organization.

There are a number of appendices with forms, curriculum plans, references and support materials at the back of this book. Use these resources as they fit your program.

While the major emphasis of this book is public archery classes, I do have the occasion to coach individual athletes. You may find some of my thoughts on coaching and developing archery athletes useful for you. You will also find a lot more information about archery coaching in the Watching Arrows Fly Coaching Library from some of the top and most experienced coaches in the sport.

My thanks to Steve for giving me the opportunity to put these ideas into print and to you, the reader, for taking the time to use these resources in order to build your archery program.

Van Webster
Los Angeles, CA
2015

Chapter 2
The Importance of Volunteers

Nearly all club and recreation-based archery programs are managed and run by volunteers. While pro shops may operate their instruction programs with a paid staff, it is volunteer organizations, instruction, coaching and support staffs that operate most recreational and competitive archery programs.

Club leaders are always on the lookout for potential volunteers to do the many tasks that keep a program running. Recruiting and nurturing volunteer talent is an ongoing process that is vital to the success of recreational and many competitive programs. So, how does one go about building and maintaining an all volunteer staff?

Recruiting Volunteers

The first step in attracting volunteers is to run the best program that you can with the staff and resources you have. People are attracted to successful programs that offer fun and interesting experiences. If your program and the marketing efforts to promote it are working well, you will have a constant influx of new participants from which to find new volunteers.

When you have a staffing need in your program, don't be shy about asking for volunteer help. Many people want to become more involved and are just waiting to be asked. When you do ask for help, be specific about the tasks that need to be done. A potential volunteer wants to know that their skills will be used and that they can make a positive contribution to the group effort. The more organized the program director is about the tasks to be done, the more likely that a person with the skills and interest will step up. Potential volunteers are often frustrated and discouraged when a call for volunteers for a work day is met with confusion, uncertainty, and even apathy from the organizers on the day of the event. Be direct about what you want and you're more likely to get it.

Motivating Volunteers

There are lots of reasons why people choose to volunteer. In youth programs, parents are the prime source of volunteers and their motivations are typically to support their own child. Retirees often look for volunteer opportunities to keep busy and share their knowledge. Working people may find that there is more satisfaction in the work of volunteering than in their day jobs.

For archery, the ideal volunteer is one who is motivated by a love of the sport. Archery can be addictive and people who are hooked on "flinging arrows" make terrific volunteers. Each volunteer candidate brings their own set of skills to the tasks at hand. Some may have a talent for teaching. Some may like archery crafts and be good at equipment maintenance. Others may have a flair for graphics and public relations.

Volunteers with web design and web site maintenance are very valuable to an organization. In the ever expanding "e-world," people with Internet, social media, and web site construction skills are very valuable. Keeping the organization's public image fresh and up to date is critical to success, so finding a team of qualified web people can be a big asset.

People with professional skills such as attorneys, accountants, and financial mangers can be a big asset for keeping an archery program running on an ongoing basis. Clerical skills and journalism skills can be helpful for keeping the minutes of meetings and publishing a newsletter.

What may not be apparent in early contacts with potential volunteers is the range of personal motivations that are fulfilled by participating in an archery program, Social contacts and friendships within the group are a strong motivator. So are senses of recognition and appreciation for efforts made. In our increasingly depersonalized workplaces, many people feel unfulfilled in their professional lives. Volunteer activities provide fertile ground for expressing one's constructive/creative impulses.

Managing Volunteers
(as Contrasted with Managing Employees)

Managing a volunteer staff is quite different from running a commercial business. In a commercial business, you can recruit for the talent you want and, especially in today's labor market, you can be very selective about potential job candidates. Once hired, employees can be directed to perform specific tasks with metrics for performance and consequences for a failure to meet the required job standards.

In a volunteer organization, your staff is made up of people who are working because they want to and not because they are being paid. Volunteers thrive on recognition and the freedom to use their skills in productive ways. For managers of volunteers, you *ask* people to do things, rather than *tell* them do them. Volunteers need to feel that the choice is theirs.

For some kinds of activities, such as a range work parties, the volunteers have made the choice to participate. Once at the site, the organizer can assign specific tasks to individuals without feeling that they have crossed the line into becoming a boss.

Organizers can set standards of knowledge or training when accepting volunteer help with skilled tasks. For example, all instructors and coaches in an archery program should have earned an appropriate level instructor or coach certification by attending and passing the requirements for their certification. As a guideline for an archery specialty program (as opposed to a "summer camp style" recreational archery program) we believe all instructors should hold a minimum Level 2 certification. If a competitive program is operated, at least the lead coaches should have a Level 3 coach's certification. Additional requirements for first aid, CPR and other safety training courses may be required for program leaders.

USA Archery requires a criminal background check for all instructors and coaches at or above Level 2. Starting in 2014 USA Archery will additionally require that all instructors and coaches complete the free on-line course in "Safe Sport," aimed at educating staff on protecting athletes, learning the signs of athlete abuse, and the appropriate responses for organizers.

Although tough to implement, writing down volunteer job descriptions and tasks goes a long

---

"When you do ask for help, be specific about the tasks that need to be done. A potential volunteer wants to know that their skills will be used and that they can make a positive contribution to the group effort."

---

way to directing potential volunteers to their own areas of interest and expertise. Examples are lists of weekly/monthly maintenance activities, public relations and outreach, class schedules and topics to be taught, tournament tasks, responsibilities and due dates. It is very helpful to a busy organizer to have a catalog of tasks at hand to show to a volunteer when an offer of help is made.

Running an all-volunteer organization requires a level of patience not usually found in the business world. There may be a long list of skills needed or tasks to be done for which here are no qualified or motivated volunteers to actually do the work. Organizers can ask the membership for specific needs but if no one steps up the choice is to either leave the task undone or to do it yourself. In other cases, the job may be done but not in the way that an organizer would do the task themselves. In almost all volunteer organizations, it is a small handful of devoted volunteers who do most of the work, with the remainder of the membership voicing support but not actually doing anything. The 80-20 rule applies to volunteers as much as it does in many other enterprises.

That being said, it is important for organizers to continue to ask the membership for help when needed. It is also important to recognize that some potential volunteers may be shy about stepping up to help. You should be very sensitive to any offers of help from the membership by paying attention, asking questions and offering tasks to be done. New members may be intimidated by the confidence of established member/volunteers. Doing your best to invite new member help goes a long way to keeping a program running smoothly.

With time, you will learn which volunteers can always be relied on, who will help if directed, and who are not able to take on tasks. For the organizer, having a Plan B (and Plan C and Plan D) is essential to assure that necessary tasks are completed. Some tasks are desirable whereas some are required. Concentrate on the required tasks and fill in the desired tasks as possible.

While running a volunteer organization is different from running a commercial business, there are certain qualities in an organizational leader that are common to both enterprises. Organizers need to be organized themselves. Nothing creates disorder more effectively than the lack of clear direction. The same can be said for failing to complete organizational tasks that have been promised to the group. The organizations that are successful are the ones with a clear mission, established practices, and continuing communications among the membership.

> "Volunteers are repaid in personal satisfaction with a job well done and the recognition of that success by organizers, colleagues, and the public. It is important to thank volunteers often for their efforts."

Keeping Records and Paperwork

Almost nobody likes to keep records but record keeping is essential for tracking the activities of the organization and for logging volunteer hours. If your organization has a requirement for a minimum number of hours of volunteer work per year, it is important the records are kept so that volunteers know their efforts are known. Often the keeping of volunteer hours is coupled with the duties of the membership chairperson. Have an on-site log book for members to log their work hours and then transfer the records into electronic form on a regular basis. If you need to you can send tickler letters to members who are short on hours early in the last quarter of the year to give the members time to fulfill their work hour's obligations.

Recognizing Volunteers

Volunteers are repaid in personal satisfaction with jobs done well and the recognition of that success by organizers, colleagues, and the public. It is important to thank volunteers often for their efforts. Acknowledgement of a day's work at the end of the day will make volunteers feel appreciated. More formal recognition at an annual banquet

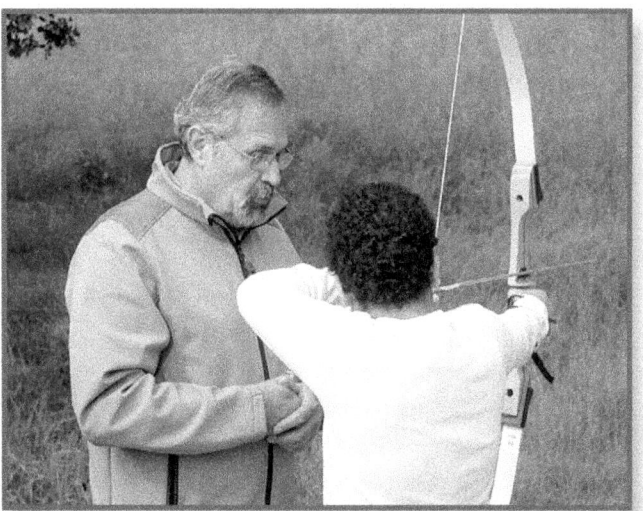

Teaching Archery

or meeting with certificates of appreciation is also a welcome form of gratitude. You may want to award pins or certificates for volunteers serving a certain number of hours during the year. I would avoid naming a "Volunteer of the Year" as singling out individuals may create resentments among the group.

Publishing photos and stories about the efforts of volunteers in the organization's newsletter, web site, Facebook page and/or local news paper brings attention to your programs and rewards volunteers for their efforts. Organizers can decide if end of the year thank you gifts are appropriate.

Dealing with Problem Volunteers

Occasionally you may find a volunteer who may be motivated to help but is lacking in skills. Pairing such a person with one of your more reliable volunteers can provide a basis for skills training and will reassure your newbie volunteer that they are important enough to be so treated.

Sometimes a person wants to join a group and volunteer to satisfy a personal agenda that is not compatible with the organization's goals. The leadership needs to keep a weather eye on anyone who they feel may be detrimental to the group's activities. If the volunteer is unable or unwilling to agree with the group's mission, it's time to ask them to leave.

Persons with problematic mental illnesses or sociopaths need to be directed to appropriate health and support systems and not be brought into the group until they are emotionally stable. It's always hard to turn someone away but there are times when a re-direction is necessary.

Dealing with Volunteer Turnover

Like the rest of us, volunteers live complicated lives. The situations and motivations that make a person want to volunteer for an organization may change over time. Parents, whose primary motivation is to support their child, will often leave a program when their child moves on to something else. People get new jobs, move out of town, retire to a new location or simply burn out.

When a volunteer leaves the program, be sure to thank them for their time and work as well as provide a means for people to keep in touch if they choose. You never know when conditions may change and they will come back to serve again.

Organizers also need to constantly be on the lookout for new volunteers to fill vacancies.

There is a social component to volunteering. People working towards a common goal will bond into groups that extend beyond the boundaries of the organizational structure. These social bonds become motivators in themselves and help to reward volunteers for their efforts. Such bonds spring up spontaneously and are not usually guided by the organizations leadership or the group's activities. Successful organizers will recognize the benefits of social bonding and create an environment where social interaction may flourish. The group will be the better for it.

Chapter 3
Archery Class Instruction for Teens and Adults

On the first day of each first lesson at Pasadena Roving Archers we tell the participants that we have three goals for their class: to be safe, to teach basic archery shooting form, and to have fun. That formula has been hugely successful. Our program has grown to serving over 200 people a week in a single, six-hour Saturday session for a total of more than 10,000 participant interactions per year. We annually introduce over 5,000 members of the general public to their first archery experience. Our numbers could easily double if we had more access time at our range, located as it is in a city-owned public park and controlled by the city's park administrators. There will be more about city relations in another chapter.

There are many factors that contribute to the success of such a program, not the least of which is the dedicated service of your instructor/coach volunteers. Our instructors volunteer their time and expertise every week to serve the public and the sport of archery.

An important component of the instruction program success is the organization and structure of the classes and the class content. Having a class structure and a path to progress in archery shooting form and technique gives participants the sense that they can grow in their skills and accomplishments. Class structure supports the instructors as they know where their efforts fit into the overall scheme of classes.

Creating a class structure starts by putting yourself into the mind of an archery student and designing programs that reward success and build towards more distant goals. There's a lot to learn in becoming a successful archer. The process of learning takes time, requires guidance, and requires lots of supervised practice. A sequence of structured classes interspersed with guided practice sessions lets athletes develop their talents from beginners to fully competent archers.

First Time Archers

In addition to the three goals stated for first time archers above, the first timer class is a sales opportunity, an opportunity not just to introduce newcomers to the sport but also to encourage them to return for subsequent lessons. This additional sales goal is realized through supportive encouragement of the archer's efforts and getting archers shooting arrows as soon as is possible. It is the flight of the arrow and the hitting of the bale that is most exciting to new archers. Designing the initial class to have students shooting within the first 15 minutes of stepping up to the shooting line is a critical aspect in enticing participants to return to the range for more lessons.

Getting archers shooting early is contrary to the training techniques used by internationally successful competitive archery programs. While there is much to be said for beginning archery training using mimetics (miming) and low load training aids before picking up a bow, first time archers have not yet made the commitment to the sport, let alone to a competitive program. In the United States, participants are culturally oriented to immediate gratification. A first timer class should meet that expectation with the shooting of arrows on the first day. If the participant is willing to make a commitment to learning to shoot well, there will be time enough later to use training aids and form work to develop archery skills.

At Pasadena Roving Archers, we have found that offering the first time archer class for free is a big incentive for the public to try archery. There is always a natural resistance to trying new activities. By providing all of the equipment and the instruction for free, the only obstacle to participation is just showing up. The free archery class has been a key to the success of the instruction program and to the membership growth of the club.

No matter what the subject, every teacher who teaches the same topic over and over again, will develop a script of words and actions to convey the ideas to the students. The first timer archery class is no exception. Experienced instructors have developed their own scripts through experience and repetition, saying the same things and doing the same actions with each group of new archery students. For new instructors who have just completed a Level 1 or Level 2 certification class, personal scripts have not yet been developed. I have found that it is very helpful to have new instructors learn a prepared script that takes them through all of the steps of teaching a first time safety class (*see **Appendix A** Safety and Orientation Script*). By using a prepared script, beginning instructors will have the confidence to know that they will cover all of the necessary topics and that there will be a minimum of fumbling for words. In time and with practice, each instructor will modify the script into their own words but starting from a prepared script really smoothes the initial teaching process for instructors.

Every class session should have a start time and a finish time. Learning the steps of shooting requires a sequence of instructions. Students need to be in the class from the start. Latecomers are very distracting to the class, slow the progress of instruction, and force the instructor to repeat steps that have already been covered for the others.

I have seen class programs organized with an "open" format where there is a block of time, say 9:00 AM to 1:00 PM open for instruction and students wander in any time they want. Such a schedule is an inefficient use of instructor's time and reduces the number of new students a program can accommodate in a session. It is much better to have a defined start time for the beginner class (or any of

Plastic poker ships are used as recyclable tickets. The archer's eye dominance is tested and the archer is issued a red chip for right eye dominance and a white chip for left eye dominance. The staff person issuing equipment use the chips for reference and the chip is turned into the person issuing the bow. The number of chips matches the number of available bows of each type so that we can know when we will run out of equipment before issuing it to the archers.

the structured classes). The class members gather, and then the instructor can take them as a group.

With a large number of students, try to limit the number of teen/adult students to eight per instructor. It will take, therefore, multiple instructors to handle large numbers of participants. The number of classes that you can run simultaneously depends on your range setup. If you have a Field Range, you can hold classes at any of the targets that have a relatively flat target presentation (as opposed to uphill or downhill targets). On an outdoor Target Range, you may be able to run multiple classes if there is enough room to provide adequate separation between targets for safety and to avoid confusion from crosstalk from adjoining classes. In most indoor ranges, it is only possible to run one class at a time. Your scheduling of classes will be determined by the number of prospective students, the number of available instructors, the amount of equipment and the number of range positions available.

Running a First Timer Class

When first time archers arrive at the range, the first step in the process is the filling out of paperwork. A waiver and release form must be signed by each participant and a parent if the participant is under 18 years of age. The text of the waiver and release of liability will usually be provided to you by your insurance company. Be sure that the form specifically names your organization, its officers and agents, the landlord and any relevant municipality. It is also a good idea to include text in the waiver form that releases any images made of participants to the organization for use in publicity and promotion. The waiver and release form is filled out only once per participant. It need not be filled out on return visits.

Additionally, a class roster form must be filled out with name, address, contact information, age, gender and any other demographic information that you may feel is necessary. Each page of the roster form should include a general waiver statement at the top of the page. Archers must sign the roster and archers under the age of 18 must have a parent signature on the roster. The class roster form needs to be filled out completely for each class session.

The next step in the process is performing an eye dominance test. Once the test is performed by an instructor, each participant is given a "ticket" in the form of a colored poker chip (*see photo*)—Red–adult right-handed, White–adult left-handed, Blue–child right-handed, Yellow–child left-handed.) The poker chips are shown to the instructors along the equipment line so that the correct gear may be issued to the student. Finger tabs and arm guards are put on each first time archer by an instructor with a brief explanation of the function of the safety gear. All armguards for first time archers should be long arm guards. If you don't have long arm guards, put multiple armguards on the bow arm, shingling them down the arm until the arm is fully protected. No one should leave a first time archery class with a bruised bow arm for lack of proper protection.

Arrows are measured for length from the base of the neck on the chest to at least two inches (2″) beyond the tips of the outstretched fingers, palms together (*see photo below*). With student archers, the only concern about arrow size is adequate length to avoid overdrawing the arrow. Matching arrow spine to the bow's draw weight is irrelevant at the beginning stage. There is no such thing as too long an arrow for first timers. Safety is always the foremost goal. If you use hip quivers, a quiver is issued with the arrows. If a ground quiver is used, the archer is instructed in how to safely carry the

Range Rules

- Know the Waiting, Shooting, and Target Lines
- Bows must be kept on bow racks except when actively shooting
- Bows must be held straight up and down on the shooting line
- Arrows must point at the ground or at the target
- Know the Whistle Commands
- When recovering arrows, only two archers at the bale at a time, archers approach the bale at the side
- Only instructors may go behind the bales to recover missed arrows.

Personal Safety

- Long hair must be tied back
- Only closed toe shoes are allowed on the range, no sandals or "foot gloves"
- Wear your arm guard and finger tab
- Obey the whistle commands
- Rotate the bow arm elbow to avoid string contact
- The anchor point should be under the chin (preferred) or at the side of the mouth.
- The arrow nock must never be near the eye at full draw.

Shooting Form

- Verify that the dominant eye matches the assigned equipment
- Stand straight up and down, no leaning
- Feet straddle the shooting line with toe tips on a line to the target (square stance)
- Head is straight up and down, no head tilting
- Consistently nock arrows below the nock locator, index feather correctly oriented
- Draw hand has three fingers on the string, under the arrow—no split finger grips
- Raise the bow with the arrow parallel to the ground and without drawing.
- Draw the string back to the face
- Anchor point puts the draw hand and bow string on the face, no air gaps
- String is released without pulling the draw hand away from the face
- The bow arm remains in place until the arrow hits the target

arrows to the ground quiver.

All class bows should be clearly numbered or marked so that archers can easily identify their own bow for that session. All bows are issued with a reminder to the archer to remember their bow number. Archers are told to put their bow on the bow rack and leave it there until told to pick it up by an instructor.

We have a list of topics that a first time archer should learn in their first class (*see left*). A quick scan reveals a lot of information, especially when considered in the context of a 1-2 hour class session.

A lot of the learning in archery classes comes through physical movement and repetition, not just reciting rules. Use movement reinforced by verbal descriptions and guidance to get people started. Find positive ways to say things and avoid using a lot of "no's."

Every subsequent archery lesson builds on the information from the previous lesson but no lesson is more important then the first one. Charlie Hull, one of Pasadena Roving Archers' most experienced instructors, has said that archers will learn more about archery in their first session than they will at any other time in their archery career. Consequently, first lessons are not a place to put your junior staff. The Safety and Orientation class should be taught by experienced archery instructors who understand the importance of getting archers off to a strong start.

This is a lot of information and skills to be learned in a one to two hour class session. How much learning should you expect? For adults and older teens, you should expect 100% compliance with all the safety rules. With shooting form, the range of accomplishment seems to be from 30-90%. Many people have poor kinesthetic sense and are unable to place themselves into the directed shooting form. Others have great fear of the string and the bow, causing defensive maneuvers and postures that are contrary to success. For others, a simple lack of strength is a key problem. Using ultra light weight archery equipment can help archers learn the shooting form while they build strength. Building strength takes time and won't happen in the first lesson.

At the end of the instruction period an archery game can be a fun closer. At PRA we have a balloon round with a prize in the balloon for each archer who breaks a balloon from a distance of 10 yards. The balloon round is very popular (*see photo above*).

Close out the session by describing the instruction options for first time archers who want to return to the range for further instruction. Let them know the days and times for subsequent classes and practices. We issue a "Completion of the Safety Class" identification card that must be shown when registering for more advance classes. There are people who want to skip the first step. Insist that every participant in your program has to take the safety class, and understands and follows the range rules during every end.

Put the equipment away after examining it for any damage or lost parts. The most likely repairs on bows are to strings needed to be replaced, string servings needed to be redone, and stick-on arrow rests needed to be replaced. Arrow repair is ongoing (and going and going . . .). At PRA we use Easton *Jazz* arrows with feather fletching and issue arrows in sets of four. We find that 10-30% of the arrow sets in use will need some repair of one or more arrows in the set after each shooting session.

The most common damage to arrows is to the nocks (having been struck by other arrows) and fletching (again mostly from arrows being struck by other arrows while in the target). Less commonly needed repairs are: missing glued-in points that have come out of the arrow shaft and bent arrows caused by arrows hitting hard surfaces such as rocks and concrete.

We standardized on two sizes of arrows: 1916 and 1716 to simplify replacement and repairs. All arrows are made up full length as longer arrows are safer than short ones. Arrow maintenance is a regular, weekly task for an ongoing program. The organization should keep the necessary tools, materials and supplies in stock to make repairs on a timely basis. Keeping the equipment in top condition is essential to running a safe and successful instruction program.

Returning Archers

There is a period of time needed between the initial exposure to archery in the First Timer Class and the commitment of a student to more structured study and training. There is a huge attrition of interest in the sport over time. People try archery out, have a fun time, sometimes do it again and then move on to other interests.

Commercial businesses with an objective of maximizing income, may want to sign first timers up for a series of classes right away after a First Timer class. There is an argument that you should "hook 'em" while the iron is hot (to mix a metaphor). Exercise gyms use early "membership" sales to boost their business with the expectation that the majority of new members will not actually use the membership benefits and facilities very much. Such a business model can be very profitable but requires a constant influx of new members to keep the money flowing.

Archery really doesn't fall into this model. Archery is a skill that develops over time and with training. Becoming a successful archer is not just a matter of fitness; it is the result of progressive training.

A better business and educational model might be a marshal arts school. In marshal arts, fitness and skills are developed in stages with awards and recognition to mark progress and motivate participants. In a martial arts model, students buy participation in monthly, semi-annually, and yearly blocks of time. The commitment of pre-payment acts as a motivator to keep students coming to classes and participating in programs. Martial arts schools have found that there is a boundary on the amount of time a student will commit to the sport. In most disciplines, the earning of the "Black Belt" is the goal of the program, a task that takes three to five years to achieve. Once the Black Belt is earned, there's not much more for the martial arts student to do other than to teach. Martial arts schools have found that after the initial attrition, most students quit after five years or so.

Archers have more opportunities to compete and achieve in their sport and there's no reason for a successful archer to quit for lack of challenges and potential achievements over time. For a commercial business, the martial arts business model may be one to explore. It should also be noted that there are a number of business support services available for membership-based commercial schools that take care of all the billing and payment tracking. There may be an advantage to having a third party collect for your monthly payments as it separates you from the untidy task of collections.

For recreational and club-based programs, the early attrition in interest in the sport can be daunting (see **Appendix L** *Archery, a Numbers Game*). Our experience, backed by industry figures on camp and recreational programs, suggests that about 3% of people who try an introductory archery class will stay with the sport long enough

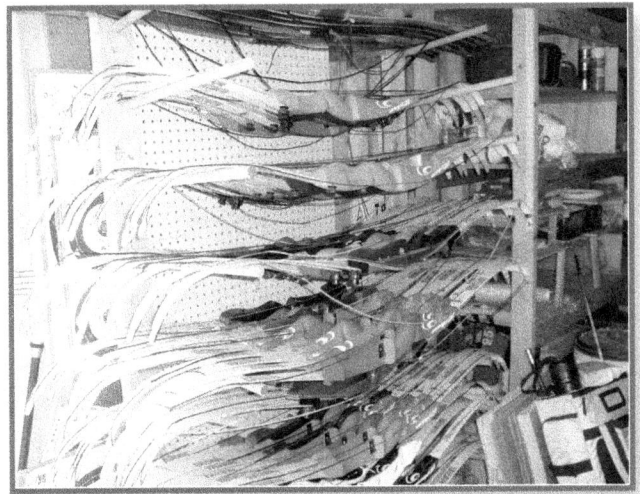
Bows are stored un-strung in horizontal racks.

to buy equipment and join an archery club. The number of archers who try a First Timer class and come back for a second class is less than 30%. For many people, archery is something the want to try and, having done so, they move on to other activities.

Those of us who have been in the sport for a while know that archery can become addictive and it's these "archery addicts" that clubs need to identify and nurture in the sport. Piling on too much structure and organized classes in the front end of an archer's learning experience may be off putting to those who have not yet been bitten by the bug.

At PRA we provide "Returning Archer" classes for people who have completed the First Timer class and want to keep shooting. A small donation is requested and the club provides all the archery equipment. Participants have an opportunity for supervised shooting and some instruction in a group setting. The goal is to have participants get experience shooting, socialize with other students and club members, and test their willingness to commit to training in the sport. While we want archers to have a fun time shooting, we deliberately create some reasonable barriers to entry into more advanced classes in order to make the most efficient use of class time and instructor resources. Getting potential archers into a class too early will only result in large drop out rates and frustrations for the remaining students and the instructor.

Archery classes are effective only if both the instructor and the student commit to a sequential series of classes with a curriculum that builds skills and fitness, based on achievements in previous sessions. It is securing the commitment of the student that makes for a successful program. In a recreation-based program, the commitment must come from the internal desire of the archer to learn and improve. Unlike a job, where commitment is secured by a pay check, or compulsory schooling, where commitment is secured by social requirements, recreational archers must be personally motivated enough to pursue archery training out of a love of the sport.

There are few significant career opportunities for competitive archers. There is no pro tour for recurve archers. A few top compound archers can make a living on the competitive 3-D circuit but there are no glamour teams, television exposure, and popular press coverage of archery events. Unlike high visibility team sports, there are no professional leagues with sponsorships and promotional money for archers. Even with all the publicity, there are few who try big league team sports that actually make a career of their game. But the allure of the professional contract keeps a lot of young athletes in sports and sports training.

Archers have to make a commitment to themselves and the sport in order to participate in the necessary training and practice needed to be successful.

A Range of Archery Disciplines

There are many disciplines within the sport of archery that may appeal to potential archers. According to the ATA survey of archery participants, less than half of adult archers describe themselves as hunters. Depending on your location in the country, though, hunting may completely dominate the sport. In more urban areas, where hunting is less accessible, target archery may be more prevalent in the market.

In compound target archery, the equipment categories are: Freestyle/Unlimited, Barebow, and Bowhunter including some variations. In recurve target archery there are: Olympic Recurve archers and Barebow archers. Additionally, in traditional archery there are: traditional longbow and traditional recurve archers. Archers will gravitate toward the discipline of archery that appeals to them the most.

Thanks in part to recent motion pictures, there is tremendous interest in traditional archery in our area. Nearly half of all new archers who stay with the sport in our program choose traditional longbows and traditional (one piece) recurve bows as their weapon of choice. Bowhunting also remains a strong influence in archery equipment selection. Target compound archery is not growing at our range. Young Junior Olympic Archery Development (JOAD) archers are attracted to Olympic Recurve archery. Keep tab on the trends in archery interest in your area and be prepared to make adjustments in your instruction program to accommodate market conditions.

At PRA we have created a series of classes that are aimed at building skills progressively leading to success in any of the archery disciplines that appeal to our archer-students.

Starting in the early 2000's PRA Coach Mike Burnham developed what he called the Basic Archery Instruction Program (BAIP) class. This was a six meeting program in archery shooting form for target recurve archers that was intended to introduce archers to the more disciplined aspects of the sport, help them become more familiar with the equipment, and introduce them to the competition rules and procedures in target and field archery. Mike and I worked together to structure the class meetings and to prepare support materials and handouts for the students.

In early 2005 we heard a presentation from Don Rabska on the then new Biomechanically Efficient Shooting Technique (BEST) method and we were immediately convinced that this was a better way to teach archery to new students. (BEST is now called the National Training System (NTS).) I completely re-wrote the BAIP curriculum to reflect the BEST/NTS approach and the revised BAIP class was very successful for us.

We did find that making a six meeting commitment was difficult for many students with busy lives. Adding a seventh meeting to visit an archery pro shop and purchase equipment made the student's time commitment even more challenging. We found that of the many people who took a First Timer class, only about 3-5% signed up for the BAIP class and completed the program. I further developed the idea of a sequential class in archery instruction to be used in recreational and outreach programs (see **Appendix B** *Eight Meeting Archery Program Instructor Syllabus*).

We also found that there was much more interest in traditional archery than in Olympic Recurve archery among the participants in our program. We decided to re-structure the classes to offer courses with shorter time commitments and to offer specialty classes in the disciplines that our students wanted to pursue.

Archery Fundamentals

Our class sequence now starts with Archery Fundamentals (see **Appendix C** *Four Meeting Archery Fundamentals Class Syllabus*). In looking at all of the disciplines and the National Training System (NTS) for Olympic Recurve archers we saw that there are common areas in the shot process and training that apply to all styles of archery. The Archery Fundamentals class focuses on establishing the necessary archery skills to be successful in whatever category of archery the athlete chooses to participate. Archers continue to use club owned equipment during the Archery Fundamentals class.

Based on the NTS steps of shooting, the four meeting Archery Fundamentals class emphasizes a solid stance, good skeletal alignment, a solid bow arm, a fixed anchor point, holding with back tension, and a smooth release. Offered in a four meeting format, this shorter time span and more limited scope has had greater appeal to our student population. We get a higher level of participation in the Archery Fundamentals class than we did in the longer BAIP program and we are able to offer the class more frequently, more easily fitting in with the student's schedules.

Archery Fundamentals is a required class to be completed before archers may enroll in any of the archery specialty classes.

Coach Obaka with Archery Fundamentals graduates.

Specialty Classes

The next step in the instruction program is specialty classes. Archers who have completed Archery Fundamentals may choose from any one or more of the specialty classes that focus on techniques specific to the chosen discipline. The instructor staff has been trained in the NTS approach and applies the appropriate elements of NTS, adjusted to the unique technique of the specialty archery discipline.

Olympic Recurve Class The Olympic Recurve Class is a four meeting program and is straight NTS (*see **Appendix D** Olympic Recurve Class Syllabus*). Mimetics (miming) and low load training aids are used. Strength exercises are introduced to build muscle capacity. The emphasis is on achieving correct shooting form and timing. Archers do stretching and warm up exercises, do form work, and shoot at a blank bale at close range. In later meetings some distance shooting at 20 yards with a target is included in the day's activities. Closing activities include Specific Physical Training (SPT) exercises and warm down stretching. Only low draw weight equipment is used in the recurve class. (15-20 pounds). The use of a bow sight is introduced. The bow is fitted with a stabilizer.

The use of a split-finger draw hand position with a finger tab and finger spacer is now introduced. The anchor point is kept under the jaw line with a solid contact of the jaw bone to the bones of the first finger. There should be no air gaps between the draw hand and the jaw line. The finger sling is introduced.

At the conclusion of the Olympic Recurve Class, archers are expected to purchase their own archery equipment. It is very helpful if the coach/instructor accompanies the archer to the pro shop for the first purchase of equipment. A pro shop can be an overwhelming experience for a neophyte archer. Having a familiar face to offer guidance can be reassuring. We strongly recommend that archers purchase their gear from a local pro shop in a face to face transaction. We discourage beginning archers from buying gear on the internet, sight unseen. Beginners have very little idea of what is appropriate for their needs and skill level. Buying on line can only lead to wasted money and disappointment. It is also important to support the local pro shop as a business by bringing customers to them. Pro shops are an essential resource to the sport. As instructors and coaches we need to do our best to see that local pro shops remain successful.

Archers who complete the Olympic Recurve Class and who now own their own equipment are in a position to develop their form and build strength. Young archers may choose to enter the JOAD program with coaching, practice, and tournaments guided by the youth program coach. Adults can join the adult advanced competitive shooting class with personal coaching and tournament practice.

Traditional Archery Traditional archery using longbows and traditional one piece recurve bows has become very popular in recent years. Many people are attracted to the simplicity of the equipment and the reduced expectations of hyper accuracy associated with more technical shooting styles. Archers are making their own bows, arrows, and accessories. Craftsmanship abounds in finely wrought, hand-made goods.

The Traditional Archery Class focuses on instinctive shooting techniques without the aid of sighting devices or the use of the arrow as a reference point (*see **Appendix F** Traditional Archery Class Syllabus*). A smooth, solid continuous motion of the bow up to the shooting position and anchor is taught with a concentration on the target throughout the shot sequence. Instructors include some of the biomechanics of the NTS into the traditional instinctive snap shot. Aiming using devices or marks is not emphasized.

Longbows and traditional recurve bows tend to

Traditional archery is taught by experienced longbow archers.

come in higher draw weights. It takes time for archers to develop the muscle strength necessary to handle this equipment properly. Finding the lowest draw weight equipment possible for beginning archers is essential. Commercial longbow manufacturers seldom make bows in draw weights of less than 30 pounds at 28 inches of draw. Finding a local bowyer who will make longbows of 20-25 pounds of draw weight can be a big asset to a traditional archer program. Excessive draw weight will crush a beginning archer's shooting form, making improvements nearly impossible.

Once instinctive archery is mastered and sufficient physical strength is developed, archers may choose to study any of a number of aiming systems including point on target, gap shooting, and string walking.

Our principal longbow instructor is a world record holder and is very open minded about integrating new techniques to longbow shooting if he can see an opportunity for performance improvement.

Barebow Shooting We at Pasadena Roving Archers are fortunate to have a world record holding Barebow archer as a member of our volunteer teaching staff. Barebow shooting is something of a hybrid between traditional longbow shooting and Olympic Recurve techniques. The bows are more technically advanced with metal risers and interchangeable limbs. The risers especially built for barebow shooting tend to be more massive than target recurve bow risers. Provisions are made for adding extra weight to the lower half of the riser for additional inertia and stabilization.

String walking is the preferred aiming technique for Barebow shooting on our range. Using the point of the arrow as a visual reference, the fingers of the draw hand are placed below the arrow by precisely measured amounts to accommodate a range of shooting distances. One or two on-face anchor points are employed to accommodate the ranges of distances usually encountered in a field round competition.

A custom built finger tab with stitched measurement marks in the tab leather allow the archer to accurately place their draw hand a measured amount below the arrow for the given shooting distance. The archer must memorize the thread counts and hand position combinations as no "written memoranda" are permitted in WA/FITA/USAA Barebow competition. The same is not true for IFAA/NFAA Barebow tournaments. Again, the simplicity of the equipment with the addition of increased arrow accuracy with Barebow shooting is appealing to many archers.

Compound Bow Archery Compound bows are very popular among hunters and target archers. Manufacturers are making smaller and smaller bows, with higher arrow speeds to suit the needs of bowhunters. It is not surprising that with 75% of archery participants using compound bows, archery companies put a lot of effort and research into developing new and attractive products for the compound marketplace.

Target compound bows are less aggressively researched and developed as the market for target equipment is assumed to be smaller than the hunting market. Crossover technologies travel from the hunting to the target side.

Teaching compound bow techniques to beginning archers can be a challenge. Unlike recurve bows and longbows, compound bows need to be precisely fitted to the archer. The archer should have a stable and firm shooting form before beginning compound bow training. At PRA we use progressive archery classes and practice sessions to ready archers for more advanced techniques (*see* **Appendix E** *Compound Archery Class Syllabus*). All participants in the compound class need to have completed the Safety and Orientation Class as well as the Archery Fundamentals Class before enrolling in the compound bow archery class.

Providing club equipment for a compound bow class is also a challenge. Compound bows need to be fitted to the archer's draw length. Adjustments to the bow's draw length must be simple to accomplish at the range. We have found that the Browning *Midas* series of bows have a wide draw length range and that the adjustment can be made in the field, without using a bow press. The *Midas* bow allows draw lengths of up to 28 inches. The *Midas* bow has a low mass, making it easier for beginners to handle. Sights and stabilizers are set up in bowhunter style with a pin sight and short vibration dampening stabilizer. For draw lengths over 28 inches we use a combination of instructor and club member bows to fill in. Much of the time allotted to the first class meeting is spent in fitting the equipment to the archer. The draw weight of the bow needs to be set at a very low poundage until the archer has built up sufficient strength to handle heavier gear.

Universal draw length bows (specifically the Matthews *Genesis*) are used in the National Archery in the Schools Program (NASP). As the cams in these bows create a no let-off, they are unlike ordinary compound bows. The axle-to-axle length of the *Genesis* bow is too short to make it a truly effective finger bow and the lack of a set draw length makes using a release aid difficult and certainly not precise. We have chosen not to use the *Genesis* bow in our instruction program although some members of the club have purchased them for personal use. (I use a *Genesis* bow for demonstration and for trick shooting at short range on television appearances.)

In shooting a compound bow, the archer trades off lower holding draw weight for higher equipment mass weight when compared to a recurve bow. Archers transitioning to the compound bow

Coach Mike teaching a compound bow archery class.

will need to build strength in their deltoid muscle on the bow side (top of the upper arm) to hold up the increased load. Some compound archers bend their bow arm and drop the bow arm elbow to increase their lifting power at the expense of a shorter draw length and a less stable shooting posture. The use of a bent bow arm is not recommended and should be corrected as the archer develops strength in the deltoid muscles. While adjustments in the NTS shooting form need to be made to accommodate the loading of the compound bow, the basic geometry of the NTS shooting form at holding can and should be maintained for stability and consistency.

Learning to use a release aid is another skill that needs to be mastered in compound shooting. Two factors are critical with this archery tool. The first is to make a solid anchor contact with the face to secure the position of the nock end of the arrow with respect to the aiming eye. The second skill is to learn to trigger the release using back tension and not pulling on the trigger and/or "punching the trigger" of the release aid. A solid foundation in back tension holding from recurve shooting will speed the transition process from finger shooting to release aid shooting. The use of a string bow is also a valuable tool for teaching release aid technique.

With the reduced holding weight at full draw, compound shooters typically hold the bow at full draw for a longer time than other archers before loosing the arrow. With a long hold, there is a tendency for archers to become distracted and lose concentration on the target. Practicing breathing techniques and meditation can reduce the tendency to over aim during holding.

As with the recurve bow, over bowing with excessive draw weight is a problem when transitioning to a compound bow. We keep the club bows at low draw weights and encourage students to purchase bows set up with low draw weights when getting their own equipment. It is easy to spot over bowed archers as they struggle to get over the peak in their draw-force curve. Instructors and coaches should make a real effort to keep draw weights low until their archers have developed sufficient strength to handle heavier gear. It is the exceptional target archer who needs a draw weight of over 50 pounds to "make target distance."

Because the compound bow needs to be so precisely fitted to the archer, compound students should be encouraged to purchase their own gear as soon as their shooting form has stabilized. Again, the instructor should accompany the student to the pro shop as an important part of the transition process. It is easy to become distracted with all the choices hanging on the wall. There's also a tendency for pro shops to sell what the shop wants to sell rather than what's best for the archer. Guidance from a qualified instructor or coach can be valuable when making that first big purchase. Discourage your students from purchasing major gear on-line. Until an archer really knows what they are doing and has access to a safe bow press, getting an in person bow set-up with a professional bow mechanic is critical.

Group Classes and Parties

Everybody loves archery and none more so than parents and social group organizers. Appointment-based group archery classes can be a big part of an archery instruction program. Scouts, church groups, schools, meet-up groups, community recreation programs, birthday parties, and corporate team building can all be sources of group class bookings.

The content of a group class session are the same as for a First Timer class. The instructor-to-student ratio should be consistent with the ratios used for other classes. For adults and older teens, one instructor for every eight participants works fine. For groups with younger archers, you will need to increase the number of instructors to provide proper supervision and guidance. You can decide what minimum age you will take for a group class.

Group classes will need a place to meet and set up refreshments while at the range. For an indoor range or a range with a clubhouse, having a "Party Room" can be a big asset for booking group classes. If you don't have food service at your facility, consider setting up a relationship with a local eatery to provide food, snacks, and birthday cakes (when needed). If you can simplify the task of running the party for the parents, they will be happy to pay the fee. Think of a bowling alley or miniature golf course as models for youth group class operations.

It is necessary to assign a single person as scheduler to book group lessons. Do not split the scheduling task between multiple staff members. All bookings need to come through a single person to insure accuracy and minimize conflicts and confusion.

Inquiries for group classes will come in by phone and by email from your web site. The group lesson scheduler will need to keep a calendar of available time slots, class bookings, deposits received and instructors assigned to teach the classes. When an inquiry comes in, check for a vacancy on their requested date and offer at least two alternative dates. Log the name, phone number, description of the group, expected number of attendees, approximate age of the attendees and the date that the booking was made. Insist that a deposit, credited against the final bill be paid in advance to reserve the date. Confirm the receipt of the deposit and the date with the group organizer by email as soon as the deposit comes in. Some groups such as scout councils may want to arrange booking and payments on an "account" basis. Accepting such accounts is up to you.

Pricing should be based on your costs and the

Group classes for families, parties, social groups and scouts are very popular at the range.

market conditions. Look at businesses with comparable services such as bowling alleys, miniature golf courses, theme parks, swimming clubs, ropes courses, batting cages and other businesses that provide group activities. Usually an archery event will be very competitive on a cost basis and we all know that archery is a fun family activity. You may choose to have several levels of pricing to accommodate non-profit groups, families, and corporate clients.

Contact the group organizing leader a week before the booking date to confirm their attendance. Indicate to the group leader a time at least one half hour before class is scheduled to begin for all attendees to arrive to fill out paperwork and be fitted for equipment. Latecomers are very distracting to the class. Include the address of the site, a phone number at the site and complete directions to the site in your package to the group leader for distribution to the attendees in advance. If the attendees are expected to be minors (scouts, birthday parties) send a PDF copy of your waiver and release form to the group organizer for distribution to the parents of the attendees. That way the forms can be printed out and signed by the parents in advance of the event and the forms can be brought to the range by the group organizer.

You may receive requests for off-site archery group classes. Such classes require that you have an entire archery range worth of gear, targets, backstops and support equipment that can be easily transported to the client's site. Off-site classes should be billed at a much higher rate, usually on a minimum charge for a half day session. You will need to factor in the cost of transportation of your staff and gear to the site, the set up, operations and clean up after the event. You will need to check with your municipality on the legality of setting up an archery range in a public area. Most cities ban archery in public parks, where people like to hold birthday parties. Archery activities held outdoors on private property may also be subject to restriction. Indoor archery in a private facility is much less restricted by local governance but there are additional risks for property damage when shooting indoors. If you are thinking of taking off-site group class bookings, it's a good idea to visit the site first to see if a range can be safely constructed. Make sure you and the group organizer are fully up to date on local regulations and conditions at the location before accepting the booking.

On the day of the group class, run a First Timer class as usual. Use only your own archery equipment for the class. Some attendees may want to use their personal gear but tell them to leave it at home and use your equipment. Using your own equipment simplifies the teaching process and gives the instructors more control over the group activities. Close out the session with a game and then make a small pitch for your archery classes, activities and tournaments aimed at attendees who may want to continue with their archery studies. Thank everyone. Collect the balance of the fees due from the group organizer. After the event, you can follow up with the group organizer with a thank you note.

Group classes are a terrific way to build awareness of your business or club and to attract new participants to the sport. Group classes can also be profitable and provide additional income for your instructor staff. Running a successful group class operation will increase the public's awareness of your business or club and can lead to increased business for your other activities.

Private Lessons (First Timers)

Some people don't like group lessons. Whether it's a matter of schedule conflicts, the desire to avoid lines of people or wanting to set themselves apart, requests for private, first timer lessons will come in. Private lessons are booked just as group lessons are booked, again by a single scheduler. A deposit is required to secure the first session. If subsequent sessions are desired, you can choose a pay as you go or package deal, paid in advance program.

Private, first timer lessons may be for families, busy individuals, birthdays or anniversaries, and special occasions. The class content is exactly the same as a group first timer class with the addition of more personal attention and more ends of shooting during the class session. In many cases, a private lesson will be a one time affair but private lessons can be a source of participants in your more general programs.

Private lessons are an additional source of income for your business or club and for your instructor staff.

The Recreational Archer

Archery is best when it is a social activity. The vast majority of recreational archers just want to shoot and hang out with friends. Only a small percentage of archers want to train and compete seriously in archery tournaments.

That being said, a recent ATA survey of archers indicated that, nationwide, 72 percent of archers shoot in their own back yard, on private land, or at "a friend's place." Only 16 percent shoot at a private club or facility (such as a pro shop). Attracting people to your location to shoot is an important part of growing your business or club membership.

Most of the people shooting in their backyards live in more rural, less densely populated areas where there is enough space to safely set up a range. For clubs and businesses located in urban areas, there will be a greater need for public access shooting ranges.

Instruction programs are a way to attract archers and potential archers to the sport and to your organization. Clubs and business have traditionally offered tournament competitions to attract archers. Based on industry figures, these traditional archery competition events are not enough.

We have found at Pasadena Roving Archers that there are a growing number of archers who just want to socialize with friends and shoot a few arrows. They don't want to be taught anything and they don't want to compete in formal tournaments. They just want to shoot arrows with friends.

A blind archer receives individual instruction.

For the business owner or club officers, creating opportunities for recreational shooters to gather is a tremendous opportunity for growth. If you could get only 20% of the backyard shooters to come to your range you could double the number of participants in your program. At PRA, our "Returning Archer" classes serve the function of providing a social as well as an instructional experience for the public. Classes are informally organized during these sessions. Instructors take small groups out on the range (we are a field archery club) for practice. Some club members bring crafts to share or food they have prepared. Our instructors have theme days for the staff (second Saturday is Kilt Day, third Saturday is Hawaiian Shirt Day; some staff even had *Star Trek* shirt day).

As our range is located in a public park (according the ATA survey, only 2% of archers shoot in public parks) there are informal gatherings of archers throughout the week. There is a longbow contingent that gathers most weekday evenings to shoot and tell stories. Families come to the range for picnics and to take their shots.

For business and club organizers, the challenge is to keep this informal social environment while maintaining safety and attracting more participants to the facility. Look to create activities that are more social and not as competitive. Pot luck lunches and dinners can work. Crafts workshops, both archery crafts and general crafts can be an attraction. Gymkhanas and novelty shoots are popular and attract archers as well as non archers.

All archers are potential customers for a business and members for a club. Find activities that appeal to the full range of your shooting public. Be open to the suggestions and activities of your audience. Often the customers or club members will initiate activities that you can profit from with the right support. The challenge is to maintain enough order and control over the shooting to provide a safe environment for all.

Competitive Training

Archers who have completed Archery Fundamentals and any of the specialty classes may want to test their skills in competition. Classes are only an introduction to the skills needed to compete successfully. Coaching, guided practice sessions, and numerous tournaments are needed to develop competitive level archery skills (see *Appendix G Two Hour Training/Practice Schedule*). As a program organizer you will want to create opportunities for all three types of skills grooming activities.

Advanced archery training and practice sessions should be run by qualified archery coaches with a minimum of a Level 3 certification. There's much more to developing a competitive athlete than just shooting form and archery practice. Coaches need to direct programs in nutrition, sports psychology, physical training, and goal setting as well as shooting practice.

An advanced program should include, where possible: mirrors and photography/video feedback for the athletes. Computer analysis of the shot sequence and body mechanics is relatively easy now using smart phones and tablet computers combined with motion analysis apps. Coach should schedule regular visual feedback sessions with athletes to update their progress and plan for the next set of training sessions.

Serious competitive archers need different coaching and often more coaching than do beginners.

Competitive archers need to practice frequently. Top archers train six days a week. Youth and recreational competitors should practice at least two or three times a week. Organized training sessions should be supplemented with individual archer practice sessions. In the early stages of training, an athlete needs a lot of directed feedback to insure that each action is performed correctly. As the archer's shooting form stabilizes, less supervision of shooting form is needed and more direction is provided for planning training schedules. The coach should be a resource of ideas and information to help the athlete progress. Coaches should have contact lists for pro shops, physical training facilities, yoga studios, sports psychologists and the like.

An important part of the training process is making the athlete accountable for their own training commitments. Coaches should keep reports of training sessions and review the records frequently with their athletes. Go over the records and establish a rewards and consequences program for coached athletes.

Archers at the intermediate and advanced level need to own their own equipment. The coaches should work with the athlete to purchase and maintain the most appropriate equipment that is within their budget. A coach should accompany an archer to the pro shop when making their initial purchase. Guidance from a trusted source can be a big help when assembling a rig. Your athletes will appreciate the help in the store.

Creating a Culture of Commitment

Archery practice is often a solitary activity. Keeping a focus on training and preparation can be fatiguing, testing the athlete's commitment to the sport. The most important commitment is an internal one, made from a passion for the sport and the desire to achieve success at a high level.

You need to create a culture within the organization that focuses on making a commitment to training and the support of the athlete. Take the time to get to really know your athletes and find out what drives them to train and compete. Work to match your training program to the athlete's motivation. Include a large helping of fun into training and practice sessions. Use games, team building and social events to lighten the mod while nurturing the competitive spirit.

With young archers look to see if the commitment to the sport is truly the archer's and not the parent's. Helicopter and tiger parents can create great stress in a young athlete. Parental support is essential for a young archer to success. Watch for excessive parental pressure on what should be a recreational activity.

Individual Coaching

There comes a time in a competitive athlete's career when individual coaching is needed to progress. The instructions and guidance provided in a group program will not always meet the needs of an individual athlete. Competitive coaching should only be done by a qualified and certified archery coach, Level 3 or higher. Selecting a coach is a very personal choice by an athlete. Don't force yourself on an athlete to become their coach. Coaches and athletes need to come to a mutual decision to enter into a coaching relationship.

It's also important for a coach not to poach athletes from other coaches. You may see a number of things that you might want to work on with an athlete being coached by another coach. If the coach is part of your own program, you might take a moment to discuss the athlete's progress with the other coach. You should not approach the athlete directly with contrary coaching instructions or attempt to lure them away to your services. If you are good enough, the right athletes will come to you.

Chapter 4
Youth Programs

Archery is often thought of as a classic youth summer program activity. Many of us got our start in archery at a summer camp. At camps, summer schools, and scouting events, archery is a featured event. So common is the association of archery with youth sports, that adults may have some apprehension about joining an archery class because they perceive it to be solely a kid's activity.

We archers all know that archery is a lifelong sport and "children of all ages" are welcome to learn and enjoy archery. That having been said, there are some important advantages to separating archery program participants by age to address their individual development and learning styles.

Kids

A big part of teaching archery is working with kids. Teaching sports skills to children is a different process from teaching the same skills to adults. Adults can learn by transferring information from their left brains to their right. Adults will listen to explanations, read instructional materials, and follow instructions (left brain activities) to learn a skill. Over time, the practice of a skill becomes a sub-conscious (right brain) process. Young children learn by demonstration, imitation, and practice. There is less intellectualization in their learning activities. As they grow, their learning abilities change and become more complex. By adapting the teaching style to match the learner's stage of development, the teaching process improves and the participants are more successful.

Learning Patterns by Age Group

The abilities of kids to learn and implement a physical activity changes with age. Kids under ten years old have limited body awareness. In most cases, they will only understand instructions directed at the positions of their head, hands, and feet. When working with very young children, demonstrate

First time youth archers shooting at the range.

what you want them to do and give them instructions in "head, hands, and feet" language. For example if you want them to line up with the target to their bow hand side, direct them to place their feet on either side of the shooting line and draw a line to the target on which they can place their toes. Even better is to have "foot prints" drawn on the floor for the students to step on to.

Kids Under 10 Teach bow handling, drawing and releasing to young kids by demonstrating where you want their head, hands and feet to be at each step. With very young children, a few will "get it" and the majority will not. You can maximize the experience for very young children by keeping them safe and rewarding success. Use long arm guards to protect the young shooters and always shoot at very short distances that insure that the arrow will land in the target backstop. The use of balloons and novelty targets improves the experience for young shooters. There's something about popping a balloon that puts a smile on a kid's face.

Ten- to Twelve-Year Olds Ten to twelve-year olds have increased cognitive ability but will still need more time to master their skills than older kids. Children in this age group will not be very responsive to detailed, wordy explanations. Use demonstrations and modeling to help pre-teen kids gain control of their physical abilities. Don't insist on young students perfecting more complex archery skills at this level, as long as they are not building bad habits that will have to be un-learned later.

Twelve- to Fourteen-Year Olds Twelve to fourteen-year olds will have much higher abilities to learn more sophisticated body movements. They will be more open to short descriptions and will benefit from plenty of practice. Use archery games to help keep the learning process fun. You can also use some written support materials with this age group. This is an age where self-awareness is coming to the front. Video taping can be introduced at this age as long as the review of the tapes is kept in a positive light. In a class situation, you can ask the class members to describe what things they see that the archer is doing right. Showing videos of top

Coach Brian supervises a first time archer.

international archers can help young students model competitive shooting form.

Photos and videos can also be used to demonstrate progress. Keep a photo log of each student. As they progress and improve their shooting form, take the time to show "before and after" photos to the archers. They will soon learn to recognize the achievements they have made as they learn new skills.

Older Kids Children fourteen and above have very high potentials for learning physical skills. They also can be easily distracted and bore quickly. Expect a lot from kids of this age. Keep them busy with practice and competition. Use drills and repetitive exercises to build muscle memory. Give assignments that include reading and web searches. Hold competitions often and reward archers both for achievement and improvement. Track their progress with achievement records and reward progress.

To help kids mark their progress, use a student record of achievement card. This card is a preprinted form with places for the archer's name and group. Each class session is signed off on the card by the instructor. Stickers can be used to substitute for a signature. When all the class sessions are completed by the student and signed off by the instructor, give each student a certificate of completion.

It is also important to make rewards meaningful. A major goal of youth sports is to build self esteem. The best way to build confidence is to help the kids make real advancement in their accomplishments. There is great pride in a skill well done. Find something that each student has done well at each session and praise them for it publicly.

Staffing Requirements

Staffing requirements are also governed by the age of the students. With archers under eight years old, you may need one instructor per active archer; 8-10 year olds may require one instructor for every 2-3 archers; 11-13 year olds can be managed with a 4:1 student-teacher ratio, and 14-year olds and up can be managed with 6-10:1 ratio. When working with any size group, having at least two teachers available allows one instructor to run the group while the other focuses on the needs of individual archers. It is too easy for a single instructor to become focused on one archer's issues and lose track of the activities of the rest of the group. It is also important for the safety of both students and teachers that two adults be present with the children at all times.

Communicating with Kids

Communicating with children can be helped by using a few simple guidelines. Dawn Barnes is the founder of Karate Kids, a youth martial arts school chain in Southern California that serves about 1200 kids per month in four locations. Ms. Barnes created the SAMM approach to communications with the children in her schools. SAMM stands for Speak in the affirmative, Ask questions, Motivate with praise, and Make agreements.

The first step in the SAMM approach is to Speak to children in the affirmative. Use positive statements for all instructions. Find ways to communicate without using the word no. When a child is doing something wrong, direct them to the correct activity rather than telling them to stop. There should always be a guided activity going on in the class. Use positive reinforcement to direct the students to participate with the others.

The second step is to Ask questions to engage the students in the class. Kids are always being told what to do. In time they learn to tune out adults who are directing them. The process of asking questions helps kids become part of the learning process. Asking questions of each student moves the energy around in the class and keeps the focus on the activity at hand. Ask questions that require a complete answer and not a simple yes or no. For instance, it is better to ask a student, "What are you working on today?" than "Are you having a good time today?" Using questions can also help with discipline as it can change the focus from a class disrupter to kids who are paying attention.

The third step is to Motivate with praise. This is a variation of the principle of speaking in the affirmative. Recognize each child every day for some achievement. Have the other kids in the class acknowledge the accomplishments of each archer at least once per class session. Use "points" to praise success. It's not important the points mean anything. Just giving points will be its own motivator. When a child does something right say, "That was great, Johnny, you get a point."

The fourth step is to Make an Agreement when disciplining kids. When a child misbehaves, ask them to make an agreement with you that further misbehavior will result in a consequence. By involving the child in the discipline process they learn that the choices they make have consequences. The goal is to discipline, not in a negative way, but in an informative way. Use positive consequences such as "meditation time" rather than time outs. After a few rounds of consequences, the kids will not want to make agreements with you and will start to get with the program.

Set reasonable goals for achievement with each class. Only a very small percentage of the students will have the motor and mental skills needed to achieve a high level of success as a top competitive archer. Do your best to nurture the talented students that you do identify. For the others, archery can be a lifelong recreational activity. Help the kids to have fun and remember that improved self esteem comes from success. When the kids achieve success, they will achieve more.

Programs for Kids

At Pasadena Roving Archers we divide our class offerings into two groups; sessions for archers younger than 10 years old and sessions for archers age 10 and older, including adults. Our children's program is lead by a husband and wife team of highly skilled youth coaches. It takes a special talent to work successfully with young children. Finding that talent in your staff is a critical first step in establishing an instruction program aimed at the very young.

If the staffing and equipment is available, offering additional separate classes for age 10 to 14 would be productive. This age group is able to do more than the little kids but they still need a little extra help.

We often get requests from families to take an introductory class together. If you choose to offer family intro sessions, they are best done on an individual family basis with a single instructor for the family. The practical reality is that very small children require lots of one-on-one instruction. Such personalized direction takes time and increases the wait between ends as the class proceeds. Only parents will have the patience to wait for their own children. As archery is a life long activity, family classes can get everyone involved in the sport with the potential for long term family memberships in the club. Providing family semi-private classes takes a lot of instructor resources so you will need to gauge which instructors are best for this type of program and then schedule family classes to their availability.

The next step in developing a children's program is to stock it with equipment suitable for very young archers. For the youngest and smallest archers, the common fiberglass bow, usable by left- and right-eyed archers, is a fine choice. As the kids get bigger, moving to a 48" to 52" take-down recurve bow of a very light draw weight is appropriate. We have found that aluminum arrows with feather fletching are the most durable and can be easily repaired. One caution is that it is easy to bend a 15XX and narrower shafts. 1716's, in two lengths, are a good choice for archers under 10 years old. For middle school age kids and older, the Easton *Jazz/Genesis* NASP arrows are popular and sturdy choices. In either case, feather fletching, rather than vanes will last longer.

First time archers should have their own class session, separate from more experienced kids. Because very young archers need lots of help getting started, be certain to match the staffing to the number of students to assure that there will be enough instructors to provide one-on-one direction as needed.

Returning archers offer the opportunity for a program to develop skills and motivation for young people to more fully participate in archery as a sport. Some children may need to take the First Timer class a second time to fully apply the safety skills needed to participate in a group archery program. For the children who can move on, the returning archer class(es) should have a curriculum that builds archery skills and performance while encouraging the children to have fun.

In most recreational programs, any student's participation is voluntary and so it is a challenge for the instructors to make each class experience inter-

Coach Terri helps a young archer line up her shot.

esting enough to inspire continuing attendance.

Some private programs are operated like marshal arts and dance schools. Parents sign their children up for classes, which are scheduled and billed on a per month basis with additional discounts for a yearly commitment. A "membership-based" business model makes it easier for class organizers to predict attendance and income. For participants, there is a commitment to attend classes regularly that facilitates progressive learning through organized curriculum.

Parents

Managing the parents of young children is an additional issue to address in running youth classes. For safety as well as liability issues, it is imperative that the parents of young children be present during the First Timer class. There are too many issues that may come up during a class session that could require a parent's attention. Some children are afraid of the bow and will balk at participation. There may be issues with clothing getting in the way of the string, hair may need to be tied back, snacks and water may be needed, and all trips to the rest room must be parent supervised.

Determining if parents should be present for subsequent classes is up to the instructor and the parent. On the one hand, you don't want our classes to be turned into a baby sitting service. On the other hand, children that need extra support may have to have a parent present.

"Helicopter Parents" are a recent issue of our age. Beware of the parent who has no archery experience or instructor training "helping out" by giving their child directions during the class period. The phenomenon of the hovering parent has been dealt with in other sports classes, often by providing a parent "corral" where parents may watch but not interfere with the course of instruction. Creating such an isolation area is easier in an indoor situation than at an outdoor range.

Because archery is a family activity, there is a desire to get the entire family involved in the sport, but not at the price of compromised safety or instruction.

Parents can be a source of new instructor candidates. If the parent is interested in the sport, has taken lessons and has a cooperative attitude, you can encourage them to take an instructor certification class and become part of the program. In general, you need to give parent instructor candidates at least six months of on-range experience before taking the instructor class.

Home Schooling

Home schooled students are another source of archery students. Many states include archery as a qualifying activity for physical education credit for home schoolers. Archery classes for home school students should be scheduled separately from the classes for the general public. At PRA, we hold home school classes on Thursday mornings, separate from our usual Saturday morning classes. The students are typically of elementary school age. The parents are almost always present during the class. The class content is the same as for beginning and returning archers with additional archery games to keep the children involved.

Home schooling parents may bring younger siblings to the archery range for lack of alternative child care. It is important that the archery instructor ensure that the parents fully supervise their non-participating children to avoid accidents and injuries.

The home school community is very closely knit and is not generally open to conventional marketing techniques. The primary referrals to your home school class will come by word of mouth. If you want to run a home school program, announce the schedule on your web page and on Facebook and wait for a response. Expect that the class attendance will build slowly as the word gets out about your program. You may also reach out to current club members or existing customers for a referral to home school parents they may know personally.

Summer Camps

Summer is a great time for archery, so archery and summer camps are a perennial couple. Creating summer programs can take several forms. Camps typically come in two scheduling formats, day camps and away/sleepover camps.

Day camps are usually local and involve campers being delivered to and picked up from the camp on a daily basis, returning home for evening meals and sleeping. Day camp billing periods are usually on a weekly basis and camp hours are typically school hours of 8:00 Am to 3:00 PM. Day camps themselves tend to fall into two categories, camps that do activities on a campus and camps that take campers to activities such as movies, theme parks, swimming pools, miniature golf, and the like.

Archery can fit into either of the day camp scenarios. If the "do-activities" camp facilities have enough appropriate space, an archery range can be set up and campers can do archery at the camp site. As a club or shop, you can provide equipment, expertise and in some cases archery instruction staff. More typically, the camp will hire councilors of college age who are expected to supervise all of the camper's activities during the cap session. You can provide archery Level 1 Instructor Certification classes for the camp staff. As many of the staff will only be gathering just before the start of camp, you may find yourself in a crush of certification classes in late May and early June. Some camp directors may choose to take a Level 2 class and certify their own councilors but I've found that most camp directors already have a full plate and are happy to pay for professional training for their staffs.

For the "go-to-places camps," your archery facility can be a potential destination. A key here is that your facility will need to have enough space and enough instructors to handle bus load quantities of children in a single session. A club with a field range, or a very large FITA range, may be well suited for a go-to-places camp. If your facility is small, the crowds may be too much to handle.

We get a lot of requests for an archery only day camp for our younger archery students. If you have access to the facilities during the week (At PRA, the city of Pasadena does not give us weekday access) you can set up a five-meeting, half day camp for your young archers. A full day of archery is too much for young recreational archers. Including archery games and some crafts can keep the interest of the campers while maintaining an archery theme.

When archery is an activity at a residential summer camp, it is usually only one of a range of options for the campers. If the camp schedule is structured, an archery instructor has the advantage of seeing the same kids multiple times during a week. Plan the curriculum around progressive course content from first time archer to building archery skills. The curriculum guidelines in the Basic/Level 1 and Intermediate/Level 2 Instructor Certification books from USA Archery are a good place to start when planning a camp curriculum.

For camp leaders, it is important to have suitable archery equipment available for the campers to use. Many camps try to get by with cheap fiberglass bows and arrows. Spending a little more at the onset of a program to acquire sturdy equipment will help your campers be more successful archers and will reflect well on the quality of your camp program offerings. Expect to spend some staff time on equipment maintenance during the camp and when putting away the gear at the end of the season.

Whether a camp is a day camp or residential camp, camp organizers can tie other camp activities into the archery program. During the arts and crafts period, campers can make targets that can be later taken to the archery range. Try to avoid anthropomorphic target subjects as some parents may find the content objectionable. If leather work is offered as a camp activity, campers can make their own finger tabs and arm guards to be used at camp and taken home to encourage the camper to continue with their archery practice. Pipe bows are a valuable training aid and can be made by campers at little expense using safe and simple tools. A camper who has made their own bow may be more likely to continue with the sport later.

Archery is often a part of Boy and Girl Scout camps. Unfortunately the current official Boy Scout shooting sports guide is way out of touch with current archery teaching practices. All scout leaders need to be certified in safe leadership practices. It would be helpful if the scout camp directors could also insure that all archery instructors hold a valid USA Archery instructor certification in addition to their scout credentials. In our recreational program, we spend a lot of time with young archers who have picked up bad habits at a scout camp. For archery program directors, make your best efforts to reach out to the local scout leadership in an effort to improve scout archery instruction.

The National Archery in the Schools Program

The National Archery in the Schools Program (NASP) is the 800 pound gorilla of beginning archery instruction. Originally created by the National Field Archery Association and the State of Kentucky Department of Fish and Wildlife Resources, NASP introduces school children, usually at the middle school level, to the sport of archery through a curriculum taught as part of the school's Physical Education classes. Millions of kids have participated in NASP programs.

Archery instructors in NASP are typically teachers credentialed in another academic discipline who have received training and certification in archery instruction programs. NASP is now in all states and is a very popular program with stu-

Summer Camp Archery Style!

dents. Some school districts, particularly in urban areas, do not participate in NASP under a "zero tolerance" policy for weapons on campus.

NASP has standardized the equipment for its programs using the Matthews *Genesis* bow, shot with fingers, and Easton *Genesis* arrows. The underlying theme of NASP archery instruction is to increase the number of bow hunters within the state. The *Genesis* "pseudo-compound" bow is an entry point for archers to get into true compound shooting.

For club directors and archery shop owners, NASP students are the perfect potential customers for your instruction and sales programs. Keep track of the schedule of when NASP is being offered in your local schools and be prepared to follow up with students and parents with flyers and local ads to promote your program or business. Hold an open house within a few weeks of the NASP session closing and invite local students to your shop or club. Be prepared with both Genesis and recurve equipment for students to try out. Offer discounts for memberships or equipment purchases by NASP alumni. NASP is a terrific starting off point for building your programs for young people. Don't let the opportunity go by without making an effort to reach these students.

Mobile Archery Programs

Some instructors have set up mobile archery programs, based out of a trailer or van, to serve camps and schools. There's a lot of work in loading, setting up, running a class and then packing up again to go to another location. If you are thinking of setting up a mobile archery service, check to see what your insurance costs will be before investing in a trailer or other equipment. Most venues will require an insurance certificate, naming them as additional loss payee. Your insurance company should give you a price for the issuance of such certificates. Some policies include a provision for additional loss payees and some policies will require an additional premium for each certificate issued. The insurance cost can quickly eat up any profits from a mobile service. Also check on the local ordinances for setting up an archery range, both on public and private property. In the city, there may be severe restrictions or an absolute prohibition of archery ranges. Know your local ordinances before initiating a mobile program.

Occasionally you may get a call from an event organizer who wants to have an archery activity as part of their offerings to the public. If you have a mobile rig and have cleared both the insurance and ordinance issues, these parties, gatherings and corporate events can be an additional source of income and an outreach opportunity for your club or business.

Archery Parties

Archery-themed parties are popular with both adults and kids. If you have the staff and the space, offering party events for both adults and children can be a profitable component of an archery program. Take a look at comparable party venues in your area for ideas on what to provide and what to charge for archery parties. Bowling alleys, miniature golf courses, themed restaurants, and swimming clubs all make money and serve their customer base with party services.

In addition to the archery range and archery equipment, you will need a space with tables and chairs for food service, storing of personal possessions and presents. You can choose whether to provide food for the party or simply provide the space. I had one coaching student who was building a new indoor archery shop and range, including the space for a restaurant in his plans. The restaurant was run by a third party and the restaurant provided both food and cake for birthday events.

Pricing for party events can be what the market will bear. You can be competitive with other venues but remember to factor in the value of your instructional services. While most bowling and miniature golf parties simply supply the venue and the gear, an archery party requires expert instruction and safety supervision. Run the archery portion of the event just as you would for a first time archer class. Provide a discount coupon to all attendees for future lessons or equipment purchases. Use the party as both a professional service to your customers and a marketing opportunity for future customers.

Junior Olympic Archery Development

The Junior Olympic Archery Development (JOAD) program is designed for young archers who want to train for and compete in target archery tournaments. Participating in a JOAD program is a good step up for young archers who are making progress in their archery and want to test their skills in competition. Archers may shoot with recurve and compound bow equipment.

USA Archery publishes a handbook on run-

Archery parties can be as casual or elaborate as you (or the birthday girls) want.

ning a JOAD program. If you are thinking of running a program, you should obtain a copy of the handbook (available on their web site) and read it carefully to get a picture of the scope and responsibilities involved. If you are currently running a JOAD program and haven't taken a look at the book in a long time, take the time to go over it again to be sure you are offing the best possible experience for your kids.

USA Archery is requiring, as of 2014, that all JOAD programs have a minimum of one Level 2 certified instructor on their staff. If you are serious about running a competitive program, at least one of your coaches should hold a minimum Level 3 coach certification. Coaching is different from instructing. The material in the Level 3 Coach Course, if studied and mastered thoroughly, will give a coach much of the information they need to take an athlete to the top levels of national competition.

A JOAD group should meet at least twice a week. More times per week are better. The content of a JOAD practice session should include more

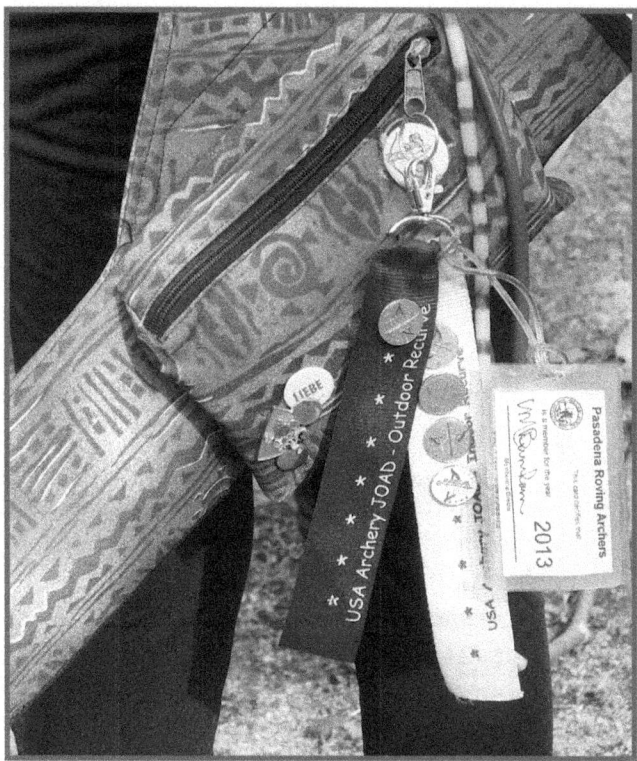

The JOAD Program has a reward system of pins earned at many levels of accomplishment.

than just shooting. Half of your available time should be devoted to strength training, aerobic training, stretching and flexibility, mental training, and sports psychology. Competition simulations should be included at least once per week. The content of a training session can be found in the appendices of this book as well as specific guidelines for teaching the NTS shooting form.

For archers shooing Olympic Recurve bows, the coaching staff should have a thorough understanding of the National Training System (NTS) and be able to provide specific feedback to archers on shooting form leading to a stable and repeatable shot. The use of mirrors and video feedback can be a terrific help in guiding competitors into the correct shooting form. The camera on a mobile device combined with analysis apps such as Coach's Eye produces a simple and effective tool for athlete feedback.

Some coaches have not adapted the National Training System as their recurve archery shooting form preference. If you choose not to teach NTS, it is probably best if you not establish a JOAD program, as JOAD is an officially sanctioned activity of USA Archery and NTS is the officially preferred recurve archery shooting style. Instead, you can train your athletes individually and have them compete as independent archers. The basic structure of the coaching and practice sessions is the same. Just the content will vary if you choose not to teach NTS.

There is really no established tradition of coaching in the compound bow discipline. USA compound archers have competed at the top level in national and international tournaments without much in the way of organized coaching. Personally, I feel that archery is archery and there are many benefits to basing a compound bow shooting style on the biomechanics of the NTS recurve system. If you teach compound bow in your JOAD program be sure you have a firm idea of how the shot should be executed and work with your athletes to develop a consistent and reliable shooting form that delivers results.

You should keep a file on each of your JOAD athletes, either in paper or electronic form with regular analysis, photographs, video, tournament scores and any other relevant information about the athlete's progress. The file should be reviewed by the coach with the athlete and the parents on a regular basis to track progress and update the athlete's goals.

Hosting and Traveling to Archery Tournaments Hosting and traveling to archery tournaments are part of the JOAD experience. Contact other JOAD groups in your area to set up friendly completions for practice and social interaction. Do the research to know where and when state, regional, and national tournaments are scheduled and plan your training periods around the dates on which you expect your athletes to compete.

When traveling, there are many opportunities for mischief, misbehavior, and abuse. Review the materials in the Safe Sport program and be alert for any dangerous situations. Remember, athletes report that 60% of abuse is committed by peers, so keep a close watch on all athlete activity. Having a clearly defined "minute by minute" schedule of the weekend's activities can go a long way to reducing idle time (*aka* "the Devil's playground").

Traveling to tournaments can be expensive. Putting together fundraising events for your JOAD

The JOAD Program has tournaments from local to national levels, introducing young archers to the world of competitive archery.

club can go a long way to defraying those costs while building team spirit. Parents are always on the hook for expenses. See if you can find ways to raise funds that don't always just tap the parents. Look for community involvement to promote your club.

When you get back from a tournament, don't hide your success under a rock. Write a press release for the local news and include a captioned photo or two. Write or adapt a PR piece for use in your club's newsletter. Post a brief report with photos on your Facebook page. Let people know that you are an active club and that your kids are having success in the sport of archery.

JOAD Camps During the summer, you may choose to have a camp for your JOAD athletes. There are a number of options that you can consider when planning a JOAD summer camp. If you decide that your camp will be for your own JOADers only, then the organizing process will be pretty simple. Athletes will stay in their own homes and the camp can be run as a day camp. You will need access to the range and training facilities during the week. For the younger JOADers, you may want to run a half-day program for five days. For the older athletes, a five-day full-day program is desirable. Plan the week around progressive training intensity and include all of the aspects of athletic training during the week. If possible, plan a field trip to a gym for strength training. Visit a yoga studio for relaxation, flexibility, and mental training. If you have access to a sports psychology program, such as at a local college, set up a mental training session during the week.

Spend lots of time at the beginning of the week on form work. While you have been working on shooting form as part of regular practice, make an extra effort to get athletes into the correct shooting form. Include shooting games that simulate tournament conditions. Practice shooting "off" to compensate for wind. Practice shooting at a quick tempo for those last second shots. Run at least two practice tournaments. If the schedule and location permit, have at least two evening sessions, one, a social pot luck dinner and the other a presentation on an archery training topic. Allow enough time for questions and for discussion among the athletes.

Try to get a Level 4 coach to come to your JOAD camp for at least a day. While the coach's content may be the same as what you have been teaching, sometimes hearing a concept from another coach will get the points across better.

Another camp option is to run a group camp for your own and other local JOAD groups. Depending on travel times, this can be a day camp or a residential camp. If you plan a residential camp you will need housing, food, travel, and sanitation facilities for all the participants. Chaperoning an overnight camp is a big job, not to be taken lightly. Be sure you have the staff to adequately run an overnight program before setting one up. While residential summer camp locations in your neighborhood will be tied up with summer camp activities, you may be able to find facilities at a boarding school or a local college campus. It takes a lot of planning to set up a residential camp. Be sure you have all the agreements in place with your venues and have all the costs well defined before pricing and advertising your camp.

USA Archery occasionally puts out a call for clubs to host a National JOAD camp. If you choose to apply for hosting a national camp, be sure to read the requirements carefully. Be certain that you have all the physical facilities, transportation and necessary resources run a national camp. Expect that the curriculum of the camp will be run by USA Archery provided coaches and that your role will be in support of the administrative side of running the camp, not so much in teaching archery itself. It's a lot of work to run a national camp but you can learn a lot about athlete training and team organization in the process.

Youth archery is the core of any archery curriculum program. Plan your youth program offerings around creating both successful athletes and successful adults.

Chapter 5
Instructor and Coach Certifications

Everyone who teaches archery to the public should hold an archery instructor or coach certification. At the time of this writing at Pasadena Roving Archers, all of our volunteer staff hold at least a Level 2 certification. The available staff roster ranges in number from 24 to 36 people at any one time. We have nearly a dozen Level 3 coaches and two Level 4 coaches. The staffing numbers change over time as new instructors earn their certifications and other instructors move on to other activities. There is no question that the success of the archery instruction program and correspondingly the growth and success of the entire club rests substantially on the shoulders of these dedicated educators.

The USA Archery/National Field Archery Association (NFAA) instructor/coach certification program and materials are based on the concept of a progressively more complete presentation of the National Training System (NTS, *aka* B.E.S.T. Method). The NTS is designed for competitive recurve archers using the principles of biomechanics to create a series of movements and postures that are structurally strong, effective, and consistently repeatable. While the overwhelming majority of archers are neither recurve archers nor tournament competitors, the fundamentals of archery, as described in the NTS system, form a solid base for learning and developing archery skills.

Another key benefit of basing an archery instruction program on the NTS system is that a student can progress from one instructor to another and receive consistent information and feedback about their archery shot. A standardized teaching approach makes running a large program simpler to organize and more effective to present. Inevitably, instructors add their own personal spins on the program content but the core of the instruction program remains remarkably consistent when everyone starts from the same fundamental premises.

I have made it a personal objective of mine to provide a complete instructor and coach training program for all of my instructor/coach students. Building on the officially supplied course curriculum, I have added elements and support materials to my classes in order to give an instructor/coach a better opportunity to be successful with their own athletes.

Level 1/Basic Instructor Certification Courses

The USA Archery Level 1 Certification course is designed primarily for summer camp councilors and other casual recreation program leaders who want to add archery to their program offerings. The assumption in the design of the course curriculum is that the Level 1instructor students have little or no experience as archers themselves. The curriculum of this training course is divided into three parts: teaching the teachers how to shoot, learning how to teach others to shoot, and basic information on equipping, running, and maintaining a simple recreational archery program. The minimum age to take the Level 1 certification is 15 years old.

While all of the instructors at Pasadena Roving Archers have a Level 2 certification or higher, I do teach Level 1 certification classes for schools, camps, and youth organizations. With rare exceptions, the majority of Level 1 candidates have had little or no archery experience. Given the very short amount of time (about 8 hours) allotted for a Level 1 class, there's a lot to do and not much time in which to do it.

When teaching a Level 1 Class, I follow the Level 1 curriculum as described in the Basic Instructor certification book quite closely, supplementing the provided materials with additional course content and practice. I have developed a complete PowerPoint presentation to support the Basic Instructor book and have used it for a number of years. I now find that with the typically younger Level 1 candidates, the PowerPoint presentation is more distracting than productive. In its stead I take a step-by-step, page-by-page approach using the written materials.

People have a large number of different learning preferences. Some people like a complete explanation and intellectual understanding of the content. Some people are visual learners. And some learn best by doing. The course leader needs to be sensitive to all learning styles and adapt the presentation of the materials to the needs of the students.

The NTS shooting system is far too complex for a first time archer/instructor to learn in a few hours. The course materials cover 10 steps of the NTS system and the students are required to know the names of the steps to pass the written exam. I have found that simplifying the NTS into a four-step shot sequence, as shown in the Level 2 book, pages 48-50, goes a long way towards helping new archer/instructors to be able to demonstrate a credible shooting style with minimal training. I spend a lot of time at the range working with the students to stabilize their shooting form and to have them verbalize the steps of shooting as they make the motions.

The core of the Level 1 Basic Instructor certification course is learning to teach archery. I have found that the best and most experienced archery teachers have developed a script of topics and an

order of presentation that works best for them. Teaching the First Timer Safety and Orientation class is fundamentally the same process for each group of students. Experienced instructors may have spent a number of years developing their own "script" even if they don't think of it as such.

The script I use (*see Appendix A*) covers the introduction to the shooting process, the safety rules, the archer's first shots and recovering arrows. Many first time instructors have a big fear of speaking in public. They struggle to organize their thoughts as they are speaking, stumble through the steps, repeat themselves, and leave out important content. For Level 1 certification course leaders, it is vitally important that each and every student in the class present the Safety and Orientation speech and demonstration aloud to the rest of the class. It is not enough to look at the paper and read silently. Each student must make the sounds pass through their lips to begin to physically, as well as mentally, be able to pronounce all the words and place them in the correct order. Working from a prepared script will greatly facilitate fluency when presenting to a class. You can save new instructors (and their first students) lots of frustration by having them memorize and use a prepared script. Over time and with experience instructors will customize the script into their own words, fully internalizing the course content.

The process of having each Basic Instructor student present the Safety and Orientation speech aloud, to the rest of the class will take a lot of time. Once learned, the entire presentation will take less than 10 minutes per student. I would budget 15 minutes per student for the first time through. If the student instructors have not yet memorized the speech, allow them to read it as they go though the presentation. Because it is difficult to hold a piece of paper and handle archery equipment at the same time, the use of a music stand or small podium for the students can simplify the presentation process. In the worst cases, another student can hold up the paper for the presenter to read.

In running a Basic Instructor certification class I can't emphasize enough the importance of having the students practice the process of teaching. Knowledge of the content is not enough. The successful teacher has a fluidity of presentation that conveys the content to the student.

Plan on spending at least two sessions on the archery range during the eight hours of the Basic Certification Class. The first session is to teach the students basic shooting form, demonstrating the 10 steps of NTS as shown in the book as well as the simplified four-step shot sequence. Work with the student instructors to see that they can establish a stable shooting form and have at least some success while shooting the bow for the first time.

The second session at the range will be to present the Safety and Orientation script, using other members of the class as students. Rotate through the class roster until every student has had an opportunity to teach and to receive instruction. If there is time, you can use examples from the skills and drills portion of the book for additional teaching content. Use peer-to-peer coaching to have students work with each other to develop their teaching and shooting skills. Use training aids such as string bows and stretch bands to provide low load practice. I often use pipe bows (see **Appendix K**), even with first time archers, as a way to develop the postures and movements of the archery shot under the lowest loads possible.

Because many of the Basic Instructor candidates are younger students in high school and college, you should expect that there will be a high turnover in staffing from year to year. Be prepared to offer the course to your staff and the staff of neighboring schools and camps at least once per year.

Level 2/Intermediate Instructor Certification Courses

The USA Archery/NFAA Level 2 Intermediate Instructor certification is aimed at archery instructors who are a lead archery instructor working with groups. As conceived during the course revision of 2005, the Level 2 Instructor is envisioned as the primary teacher of the National Training System (NTS). A minimum of a Level 2 certification is expected for instructors at Pasadena Roving Archers.

I teach the Level 2 certification class as a three day program.

Day 1 We start out by observing the program operations and teaching techniques at the Pasadena Roving Archers' regular Saturday morning instruction sessions. Instructor candidates have an opportunity to see how the class is administered, how equipment is managed and how the class sessions are divided into manageable groups for instruction. Candidates then observe the teaching techniques of our wide range of experienced staff to see how personal knowledge and teaching approaches work with student archers.

After a lunch break, we meet in the classroom and go over the entire Level 1/Basic Instructor certification class materials and programs. As Level 2 Instructors may teach Level 1 classes, it is important the instructor candidates have a thorough understanding of both the content and the approach to teaching a Level 1 class. Plus, Level 2 Instructor candidates are not required to have previously taken the Level 1 Course.

Day 2 The second morning we begin with the detailed presentation of the National Training

System (NTS) shooting technique. Most of the Level 2 instructor candidates have many years of shooting experience. Also, most of the instructor candidates are self taught, often in other disciplines than recurve target archery. For these experienced archers, there is as much to unlearn as well as to learn the intricacies of the NTS approach. I give each of the instructor candidates a string bow and a stretch band to keep for use in the class and as a model for the use of light weight training aids for teaching archery shooting form.

In teaching NTS it is important to actively involve the students with the physical activities, movements, and postures as much as possible. I have a PowerPoint show of over 180 slides covering the topic, but it is the direct physical involvement of the students in learning the steps that garners the greatest success. Start out with miming each step, then move to the use of light drawing training aids. The use of pipe bows is a very useful way to establish the relationship of the string to the body and face. Even the strongest individuals will tire quickly when using the lightest drawing archery equipment when learning the NTS techniques. Take your time to be sure that each instructor candidate fully understands the steps of the shot and can reproduce the motions and postures precisely.

The second afternoon is devoted to working on teaching techniques, communication, and guiding archery students. We work through the Drills and Skills portion of the course materials. Emphasis is made on using the process of analysis and synthesis to observe an archer's techniques, compare the observation to the ideal approach and then offer guidance to the student on how to improve their shooting form. Later in the afternoon each student gives a presentation of the Safety and Orientation speech (*see* **Appendix A**) using the other instructor candidates as student-archers for the demonstration. This process takes a lot of time but it is essential that all instructor candidates actually go through the process of speaking the words and guiding the students through their first shots at the range. Many prospective archery instructors have not had previous teaching experience and are shy about giving a public presentation. Using the class time to have them learn and practice their new teaching skills can speed their transition into active archery instructors. It is important to emphasize to the instructor candidates that the instructor class is a safe environment and they can explore their presentation skills without fear of criticism.

I also offer an optional equipment maintenance session including arrow repair and string construction. This segment is particularly well received by Boy Scout leaders who have to teach string making as part of the Archery Merit Badge.

The second day concludes with the taking of the Level 1 Final Exam.

Day 3 Although not required for the Level 2 certification I ask that all the Level 2 instructor can-

didates write out a coaching philosophy statement. The process of exploring the motivations for teaching archery helps candidates get a better grasp on what they are doing and why.

On the third morning, each of the instructor candidates reads their coaching philosophy statements aloud to the group. The variety of statements is amazing and I find that the process of reading the statements provides a terrific opportunity for conversation between the candidates about their experiences and goals for their programs.

The third morning continues with peer-to-peer coaching of the NTS techniques and practice exercises using the Drills and Skills in the Level 2 training manual plus additional elements in the After School Archery Program (ASAP) archery book. The emphasis is on mastering NTS as well as learning to communicate effectively with archery students.

The third afternoon continues with Drills and Skills presentations by the instructor-candidates. I add an additional segment on basic bow setup and preliminary tuning. While NTS makes little emphasis on tuning, instructors should have enough equipment knowledge to take a box of parts and turn them into a functioning bow system.

At various times, USA Archery has sometimes provided in the Level 2 Student Packet, a CD data disc of useful archery resource materials (see list at end of chapter). At the time of this writing, a data disc is not included in the Level 2 Packet. I have always provided a supplemental CD data disc of additional useful resource materials, course forms, data sheets and video clips to my Level 2 students. Students find these additional materials to be helpful when setting up their own classes. I also provide a number of handouts and reprints of relevant materials for reference in the class. The final exam wraps up the Level 2 Instructor Certification course.

Newly certified instructors should work with a more established instructor at first to get the hang of teaching first time students. Once new instructors have some hands-on experience with the public, they will be able to take class groups out on their own.

Level 3 Archery Coach Training Course

USA Archery makes the distinction between instructors and coaches as one of instructors teaching beginning and intermediate archers in a group context and coaches working with individual archers who have competitive aspirations.

The coach's role is much more involved with the athlete than the role of an instructor. In addition to at-the-range coaching, an archery coach needs to provide guidance and direction in equipment set up and tuning, strength and flexibility training, sports psychology, and tournament preparation, as well as information on nutrition and hydration, goal setting and accountability, and maintaining the athlete's motivation. Coaching is a complex and intensive job that requires a professional level of skills and attention to detail. It is a great responsibility to be a coach and the task should not be taken lightly.

The Level 3 NTS Archery Coach certification is the first step for archery instructors who want to increase their knowledge and skills in the sport while taking on the task of guiding competitive archers. Many archery instructors in the Pasadena Roving Archers program have earned their Level 3 certification, not so much to coach competitive archers, but to increase their knowledge and skills in working with recreational and intermediate archers.

I teach the Level 3 NTS Coach Certification Class on a three day schedule, much as I do for the Level 2 Class. The course materials, originally developed by Coach Dee Falks and updated by Coach Lee and the USA Archery senior coaching staff as well as the NFAA, are well organized in a progressive sequence of 10 topic areas with print and PowerPoint support materials for the course leader. In addition to the course syllabus topic areas, I supplement the course materials with additional topics on coaching styles, expanded sections on athlete training and sports psychology, a unit on nutrition, organizing athlete training and practice sessions and details on conducting a Level 2 archery instructor certification course.

The course packet includes a string bow and stretch band. It also includes a thumb drive memory stick with the support materials for the course curriculum in digital file format. I provide an additional CD data disc with expanded coach recourses materials, handouts, course schedules and athlete worksheets.

Day 1 I start out with a general introduction to coaching and how being a coach differs from being an instructor. A coach works with individual athletes to maximize their performance for competition. In archery, a major factor in the success of the coaching relationship is the commitment of the athlete to the sport and to training. In archery, there are no multimillion dollar professional contracts dangling in front of prospective champions. An archer needs to have the desire to compete at the top level without the expectation of financial rewards for their hard efforts.

A coach needs to discuss frankly with an athlete and the athlete's parents (if a minor) the commitment of time and money as well as the athletic talent and dedication needed to be a top competitor. One may get by with part-time training at the recreational and local level, but a top national competitor requires the resources necessary to train full time. Not many people can make such a commitment. It takes the support of all the members of an athlete's close circle to reach a national championship level of performance.

The Level 3 coach course includes an exercise in writing a personal coaching philosophy. As with the Level 2 class, the process of exploring the motivations and objectives of coaching archery is an important exercise in self exploration. I also have found that the content of each individual's coaching philosophy document can form the basis of marketing and promotional materials that a coach my use to describe their coaching services to potential athletes and their families. I emphasize that the coaching philosophy statement is a dynamic document and should be reviewed and updated from time to time.

I also include a segment on effective coaching styles, developed from materials provided by the US Olympic Committee. Going beyond the Level 3 class materials, we explore a wide range of coaching techniques, priorities, and means of evaluating coaching performance.

Sports psychology is next. The goal of sports psychology is to bring the athlete to a state of optimal "performance arousal" at the time when it is needed. For archers a major concern is quelling anxiety and reducing one's heart rate during competition. There are a wide range of techniques and procedures that an athlete can do to adjust their emotional state. The key is to practice the psychological techniques along with the physical and technical aspects of shooting. The goal is to train the mind to respond to the emotional cues that govern mental energy.

The Level 2 final exam is given on the evening of the first night, to refresh the memories of the students and to have them become familiar with the testing procedure.

Homework for night 1 is to write a coaching philosophy. Coaches who have previously taken my Level 2 class have a head start on the writing process as they have already produced a coaching philosophy for that class. Whether new or updated, the writing of a coaching philosophy provides a time for introspection and reassessment of the coach's goals and motivation to teach.

Day 2 The first thing I do is have the coaches read their coaching philosophy to the group. A lively discussion ensues and there is much to learn from each other as ideas a re presented a discussed. This can be a very rewarding portion of the class program.

Then it's time to study and practice the National Training System (NTS) in depth. I have a range of PowerPoint presentations on the topic. In the most recent iteration of the official course materials, the course-supplied PowerPoint has been shorted to fewer than 30 slides. Level 3 course leaders are expected to fully understand and be able to demonstrate all the steps of NTS with clarity and precision. I find that as I introduce each step in the shot process, it is necessary for the entire class to actively practice the motion or pose. Working first in a large group and then pairing candidates off for peer coaching, it takes lots of time for people to understand, let alone execute the maneuvers.

While coaches relatively new to the sport must learn the NTS system from scratch, it is the more experienced archers, particularly those who come from a traditional archery perspective, that have the most difficulty in learning NTS. For these veteran archers there is the double burden of un-learning decades old habits while trying to learn and implement a new and highly technical shooting style. Take lots of time and give lots of positive feedback to the coach-candidates as they practice the NTS steps.

After lunch, there are more NTS exercises and lots of peer coaching. As the course leader, I move from Peer coaching team to team, fine tuning both the candidate's own shooting form technique and explaining various methods for coaching NTS Recurve techniques to archers. Training aids including string bows, stretch bands and pipe bows are key tools at this stage. Towards the end of the practice session, we step outside for some actual shooting time at the range. Shooting time is always appreciated by the coach-candidates but the

And, if all goes well, you will have a lot of smiling faces in the group photo at the end.

emphasis here is on applying the techniques of NTS to the execution of an actual shot. It is remarkable how even the relatively low draw weight of a 15 pound bow can be exhausting for archers learning NTS. It is very easy for experienced archers to quickly and unconsciously slip back into old shooting habits. The use of photographs and videos can be a big help at this stage to give candidates an awareness of what they are actually doing on the range.

Use the NTS check list included in the Level 3 materials as part of the peer coaching training. Have one archer demonstrate the shot sequence while the student coach observes and logs the performance on the checklist form. The form provides a structure for coaches regarding the things to look for and provides athletes with a list of the steps that they are doing well as well as those steps that will require further work. This process models the type of analysis and communication that a coach will need to use with their own athletes when they get home.

Later, on the second afternoon the class time is taken up with the topic of athlete training. The term "training," in an athletic context, refers to strength and conditioning activities aimed at making the athlete more fit for their sport. There is an impression that archers are not athletes. As our sport is both highly technical and precise, the physical aspect of actually executing the same archery shot hundreds of times in a day is not really obvious. However, if you look at the top recurve archery competitors and aspirants, their athleticism is clearly obvious.

The core of the discipline of athletic training is based on the work of Tudor Bompa in the late 40's and early 50's. It was Bompa who codified the principle of periodization in athletic training. In short, the idea is that the training schedule is divided into periods of time to load the body to fatigue and then provide time to recover. In the cycles of loading and recovery, the body builds an adaptation to the load that result in increases in strength and performance.

The point for archery coaches is to plan the training schedules of their athletes to address the needs of strength and flexibility while also building sport specific technical proficiency. In practice, the training schedule for advanced archers works out to be about 50% shooting and technical skills and 50% strength, endurance, and mental training. It is the balance built into these training regimens that produces the best results.

The second day is closed out with a study of goal setting. Peter Drucker, the management guru, said that if you can quantify a value, you can improve it. The process of identifying and setting goals is critical to improving athlete performance. The coach and the athlete need to work together to identify where the athlete is in their training, where they want to go and what steps are necessary to get there. The "SMARTER" goals process, described in the Level 3 curriculum is an organized approach to goal setting. There are templates and worksheets included that a coach may duplicate and adapt for each of heir athletes. Writing things down makes them more concrete. It is much easier for a coach to point to a written goal than to continually re-explain verbally what is expected.

Homework for the second night is to work with the goals forms to produce a set of goals, either for a hypothetical athlete, an actual athlete, or for the coaches themselves. The morning discussion of these topics is lively but more technical than with the philosophy discussion. Here is an opportunity to reinforce the need for keeping records of your athlete's performances and review them regularly to gauge progress and set new goals.

Day 3 After reviewing the goals homework, the third day begins with a discussion of tournament preparation. Examples are given of the roles of the coach and the archer as well as general guidelines for getting through a competitive day or weekend. The emphasis here is on being prepared, making lists, understanding the rules, knowing the schedule, and reducing stress through preparation.

After a break, the next segment of the class is on equipment selection and set up. There is not much emphasis on equipment and tuning in the first three levels of USA Archery certification. The reasoning is that until an archer can establish a stable shooting form, equipment tuning is irrelevant if not impossible. Archers at the beginning of their training need to have equipment that is suitable for their skills and appropriate for the task at hand. At the least, and instructor should be able to take a box of bow parts and turn it into a safe and reliable shooting system.

The Level 3 Coach program introduces basic recurve bow tuning to the mix as a coach is expected to train competitive archers where arrow scores during tournaments become important. Initial bow set up, arrow choice using a spine chart, fletching and point options, plunger position, and initial plunger tension are all covered. I add information from the *Easton Bow Tuning Guide* and the *Recurve Archer's Handbook* from Balbardie Archers. After establishing bare shaft performance, an emphasis in the course materials is on using Walk Back Tuning to make congruent the line of sight and the path of the arrow flight. Equipment tuning is only a small segment of the course content and is by no means comprehensive. Some of the coach-candidates have extensive experience in archery equipment and add a lot to the conversation in this topic.

After lunch, the topic is running a training session. The emphasis here is on planning each day's activities, setting goals for each archer, keeping records and following up from previous sessions. Too many coaches simply gather their archers together and have them shoot. There's much more to be done to become a successful competitor than just flinging arrows.

The training session segment is followed by additional peer coaching in NTS technique, using the NTS checklist as a structure for evaluating shooting form. The basic shooting form process consists of a series of steps. First, the coach needs to have a very clear idea of all the steps in the "ideal" shot sequence. With this ideal image in mind, the coach observes the athlete, noting what parts of the shot sequence match the ideal, what parts of the sequence do not match the ideal and need to be adjusted and what parts of the sequence will have to be adapted from the ideal to accommodate the athlete's physical abilities, flexibility, and body type.

When observing an archer shooting, a coach may see a number of things in his shooting form that need work. As an archer can only work on one adjustment at a time, the coach will need to prioritize the issues to be addressed. In choosing what issues to address now and what issues can wait until later, the coach should focus on the issues that have the greatest impact on arrow flight and those issues that, if not addressed, will create bad habits that will be difficult to un-learn later.

Having prioritized the shooting form issues, the coach then gives direction to the archer to address the most important issue and then monitors and adjusts the performance of the athlete until the desired result is achieved. This analysis, synthesis, adjustment, and monitoring process is ongoing and crucial to a coach's effectiveness. It takes practice to learn these skills. Using guided peer coaching with the course leader providing feedback and guidance is an important part of the transition from instructor to coach.

Although not part of the "official" curriculum, I provide a block on sports nutrition and hydration. This material, packaged in a way that can be replicated by the coach for his/her athletes, is based on simple nutritional guidelines. With the obesity epidemic in this country, teaching good nutrition to athletes is an important life skill as well as a competitive necessity.

Another supplemental course content area that I include in my class is guidelines for teaching Level 2 certification classes. In this segment I describe the basic course content, teaching techniques, and how to handle the paperwork with USA Archery. I also go over the resources that the instructor and the venue will have to provide to produce a successful course. There is also a general discussion of pricing policies for teaching Level 1 and 2 classes with guidelines for gauging local market conditions.

The class closes on the third day with a general course review and the taking of the final examination. Upon conclusion of the exam, I ask that the participants fill out the course evaluation form. This form is anonymous and provides valuable feedback to the course leader on the success of the program.

Day 4/After Paperwork is verified as being complete and the new coaches are sent on their way. If the group chooses to stay in contact, an email list is circulated. As a policy, I don't distribute the email list to the class group in my correspondence to them. Emails are either addressed individually to the coaches or the BCC feature is used for a group mailing. If the new coaches choose to share their contact information with the others, that is their business.

After the class is over, all of the paperwork needs to be compiled and packaged for shipment to USA Archery. In addition to the course application form, I include a copy of their USA Archery/NFAA membership card and a copy of their most recent instructor certification. I make a copy of all the course evaluation forms and then pack the original forms with the papers to be sent in. The background checks and SafeSport verifications are handled directly by USA Archery and are not included in the paper packet. I package all the materials in a USPS Priority Mail envelope and ship it off to USA Archery within two days of completing the class.

Level 4 Coach Certification Courses

Level 4 Coach Certification classes are only offered by USA Archery and on a limited basis. Typically USA Archery will run 1-3 Level 4 certification classes per year, usually held at one of the Olympic Training Centers. The Level 4 class is a six day, residential program with a grueling 12-hour work day. The course is usually taught by Level 5 coaches. Sometime portions of the course are taught by Coach Lee. Level 4 coaches assist with the workshop portions of the class.

Additional experts in athletic training and technology may make guest presentations. The course content covers much of what is included in the Level 3 course but in more detail. Participants are expected to have a thorough knowledge of NTS and be able to present all of the steps in a teaching like situation. While most Level 4 coach-candidates pass the written portion of the Level 4 class, only a small percentage of the students are able to pass the NTS practical exam on the first try. Many candidates will have to arrange a retest of the practical portion of the class at a later date.

Level 4 certification is certainly not needed in order to run a recreational and beginning competitive program. Coaches who want to work with elite athletes striving for top national ranking may want to consider becoming certified as a Level 4 coach. General program manages and instructors will probably find the time and expense of Level 4 certification is unnecessary to suit their programs.

If you do choose to pursue a Level 4 certification, be certain that you have all the steps of the NTS system well in hand before attending the class. Seek out a Level 4 coach in your area to tutor you on the NTS technique. While you can expect that there will be changes and adjustments to the NTS steps as shown in the class (remember that NTS may stand for "never the same") you will have a slim chance of passing the practical exam if you haven't mastered the NTS technique before starting the class.

The "Range Pass"
In many volunteer-based programs, there are parents and others who want to help out but are not ready to take on the commitment of becoming certified archery instructors. As part of the U.S. Olympic Committee program to increase the safety in sports, USA Archery has initiated a number of steps to support the safety program. The SafeSport on-line training and test, covered separately in this book, are part of that effort as is the requirement that all Level 2 instructors and above pass a background check. The holding of a valid Level 2 and above certification is evidence that the individual

Supplemental Level 2 CD Disc Contents

❖ ❖ ❖

2 Hour Training Schedule
3 Hour Training Schedule
Making a String Bow
Archery practice record sheets
Archery Resource list
Archery bibliography
BEST Method Training Curriculum
BEST Checklist (Excel File)
Archery Fundamentals Instructor's guide
Archery Fundamentals Student Weekly Handout
Easton Arrow Chart
Shot cycle Grid (Excel File)
Restringing the Genesis Bow (Power Point file)
A General Introduction to Archery for the Public (Power Point file)
Basic Level 1 Certification (Power Point file)
BEST Method (NTS) (Power Point file)
Equipment Selection and Preparation (Power Point file)
Compound Bow Adaptations of NTS (Power Point file)
In Search of an Effective Coaching Style (Power Point file)
Principles of Coaching Level 2 Class Version (Power Point file)
Video Clips of Park, S.H.
Video Clips of Tim Cuddihy
Video Clips of Slow Motion Arrow Action

Supplemental Level 3 CD Disc Contents

All the contents of the Level 2 Supplemental CD Disc, plus…

Resource Materials

Archery Tournament Confidence Routines
Archery Physical Training Template (Excel File)
Photos of Various Archery Stances and Postures
Archery Coaching Resource Bibliography
Competitive Fueling Nutrition guide
Don't Choke, Buckling Under Pressure
Goals Creation Worksheet
List of Internet Archery Resources
The LA 84 Foundation Coaching Manual
Meals and Snacking Guide
Nine Basic Principles of Training
NTS Checklist
Nutrition Periodization Worksheet Calculator (Excel File)
Nutrition tips for Archers
OTC Strength Training for Archers
Physical Training Outline Template (Excel File)
Preventing Shoulder Injury
Shooting Schedule Guidelines
Training Design Plan (Excel File)
Bow Tuning Tips
Daily Sports Diary
Easton Tuning Guide (PDF File)
Archery Training and Nutrition
The Recurve Archer's Reference Guide (PDF File)

Power Point Presentations

Being a Coach
Intro to Coaching and Coaching Challenges
Coaching Philosophy

Mental Aspects of Archery and Sports Psychology

Mental Skills Notes
Mental Toughness Training for Archery
Archery Shot Execution
Training Cycles and Periodization
SMARTER Goals
Preparing for Competition
Coaching Session Sample Outline
In Search of an Effective Coaching Style

Other Resources

An Archer's Perception of the Coach Profile
Conducting an Intermediate Instructor Course

Chapter 6
SafeSport Certification

In archery, as in any competitive sport, safety is always the number one issue. Archery has a particularly strong reputation as being a safe sporting activity for both participants and spectators. There are, however, general concerns in the sports community about athlete safety away from the tournament field. Athletes may be subject to various forms of abuse at practices, during coaching sessions, while traveling, and on overnight stays.

Statistics for sports of all types indicate that 6-13% of competitive athletes, or 1 out of 8, experience some form of sexual abuse or assault. And 57% of athletes report some form of sexual harassment. Athletes are sexually harassed more by peers than by adults. And 22% of elite athletes report having had sexual relations with coaches. That's one in five, a startling number.

As a coach or program leader, you need to be vigilant for the signs of harassment, bullying and abusive behavior towards your athletes. You need to be ready to take the appropriate action to protect the athlete as well as yourself. Ignoring or excusing hazing, bullying, and other forms of abuse may make you just as culpable as the perpetrator.

According to Mary Emmons, USA Archery Outreach Director, "SafeSport, founded by the United State Olympic Committee (USOC), serves to address misconduct in sport by providing information, training and resources to parents, clubs, coaches and athletes to help members of the sport community to recognize, reduce, and respond to misconduct in sport.

"There are three key components of SafeSport:
1. Recognize: Learn about the different types of misconduct in sport.
2. Reduce: Develop a strategy to ensure athlete well being.
3. Respond: Know how to take action before there's a problem."

SafeSport, an on-line training program, will become a requirement for USA Archery Instructor and Coach certifications and renewals starting in 2014. The estimated time to take the course is 90 minutes, in your own home or office. The course is free and there is a printable certificate issued upon completion of the course. A record is kept by USA Archery to verify completion when an instructor or coach certification comes due.

The SafeSport training program consists of 16 on-line video lessons. The lesson segments range from four to eight minutes in length and include specific information about what constitutes misconduct in sports, both for youth and coaches.

Coaches are given information about what is appropriate behavior for themselves and their staff. Also included are strategies for identifying potentially abusive actions by other leaders, parents or athlete peers.

Action steps, subject to state laws, are then detailed in the course about the process of reporting suspected abuse, to whom to report, and what to report. It is made clear that reporting may be a legal responsibility and that in many states the reporting can be anonymous. The risks of amateur investigations into allegations of abuse by coaches and administrators prior to reporting are also discussed with appropriate recommendations.

The program lessons are supplemented by PDF file transcripts of each lesson segment. These transcripts can be downloaded by the course taker, stored, and/or printed out as needed. Guideline handouts in PDF format are also included for reference and to share with others in your organization.

Taking the course is straightforward. The user logs onto the SafeSport web site, selects a user name and password and then begins the lessons. The lessons are arranged in topic blocks and each lesson is viewed, supplemented by the PDF written transcript. There are three intermediate tests covering the previous block of topics. Tests are in multiple choice format and are automatically scored. A passing score on each test is required to move on to the next block of topics.

A final exam, also in multiple choice format, poses situational problems that require an understanding of the complete program content in order to correctly answer the questions.

A note on the operation of the web site itself. Each lesson must be viewed in its entirety front to back. The web site keeps track of the lessons completed and only logs a lesson done if the video plays all the way to the end. You can stop after any lesson and leave the site to come back later. When you come back you will log in with your user name and password and continue. I found out that I had to play a couple of the lessons over again after returning from a break because the site had not correctly recorded the completion of the previous lesson. This is a minor inconvenience but something to note if the site seems to lock up on you.

As program leaders and coaches it is our responsibility to see that every athlete participant is safe and secure in their person. We must carefully guide our own actions as coaches and be vigilant for signs of misconduct in others, both adults and peer athletes. The SafeSport program is an important effort by the USOC and USA Archery to see that all athletes are treated safely and fairly.

For more information on the SafeSport program from USA Archery, you can follow this link: http://www.teamusa.org/USA-Archery/Features/2013/June/11/USA-Archery-Introduces-SafeSport

To sign up for the SafeSport program and take the training visit the SafeSport home page at http://training.safesport.org/

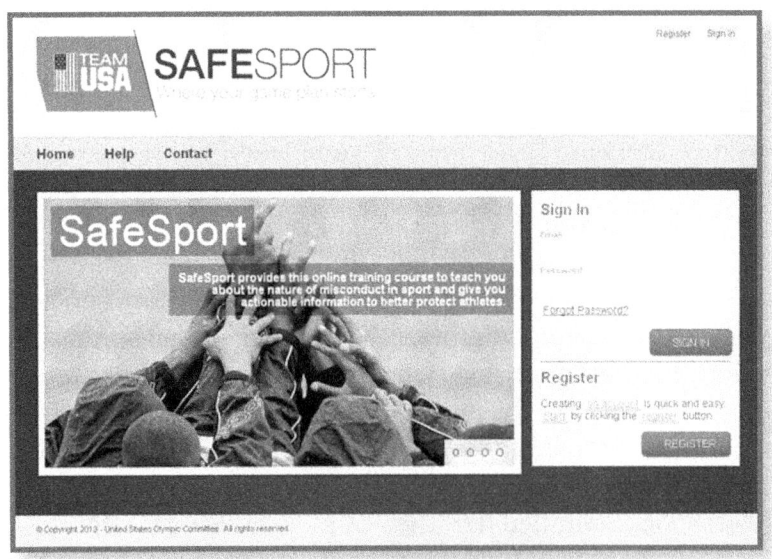

The SafeSport login page is the gateway to the SafeSport training program.

Chapter 7
Tournament Programs

Archery tournaments are the life blood of an archery club, be they Field Archery, 3-D Archery, or Target Archery clubs. Archery classes may introduce the public to the sport but tournament competition is a reward for all the hard work of learning to shoot. For those interested in hunting, field and 3-D archery tournaments are tune-up opportunities before heading out for game. Running tournaments takes time, organization, and a lot of volunteers to produce a successful event.

Weekly Tournaments

Pasadena Roving Archers (PRA) is sited at a field archery range so most of our tournament activities are centered on NFAA Field/Hunter/Animal rounds, 3-D archery, and short range target archery. We hold a 28-target Field Round qualifier tournament on the first and third Sundays of the month. A 28-target Hunter Round qualifier is offered on the second and fourth Sundays. If there is a fifth Sunday in a month we hold an Animal Round. We hold an "outdoor/indoor" 300 round shot at 20 yards on the second and fourth Sundays. A 14-target 3-D round is shot on the third Sunday of the month. We hold an American 900 round on the first and third Sundays of the month.

On the fifth Sunday of the month we host a United Bowman round, 14 ends of 6 arrows per end, shot at a distance of 80 yards using a 122cm target face.

Because the NFAA Field/Hunter/Animal rounds are run under NFAA rules, the validated scores may be used by archers to determine an NFAA handicap.

The mechanics of running the weekly tournaments are pretty simple. Registration and score cards are printed in bulk and stored on-site. A Sunday morning cashier handles participant registration, collects the fees and the completed score cards at the end of the day's shooting.

The biggest ongoing task is cutting cardboard and pasting the paper targets to ensure that there are enough targets in stock for a weekend's shoot. NFAA Field and Hunter targets come in four sizes, A, B, C, and D. A laminated target summary card is kept on-site with a grid listing each target, the distances for field, hunter, and animal rounds and the required target sizes for each target. Club volunteers walk the range pulling a cart with the targets stacked in the order of use and they pin the target faces to the fixed backstop bales. The cart is then left at the end of the 28-target range and the targets are picked up in order at the end of the day. B and C targets seem to get the most abuse and have to be replaced more often than the larger (A) and smaller (D) targets.

For the "Outdoor/Indoor" 300 Round, 40 cm, 10 ring targets are primarily used. We have some "3 Spot Vegas" targets for compound shooters. Young archers shoot at 60 cm and 80 cm targets as appropriate. The 300 round has proved to be very popular with our members as its simplified format makes for an easy transition from our Saturday morning archery classes. Many archers also prefer the shorter time required to shoot the 300 round.

A 900 round, either Metric or American (Imperial) is a simple way to move target archers on to shooting at longer distances: 30 arrows are shot in ends of 6 arrows each at the distances of 60, 50 and 40 meters or yards at a standard 122 cm target face. (This round is the only time that you will be able to shoot a 122 cm target at 40 meters/yards.) Typically the 60 and 50 distances are shot before lunch. After a break, the 40 distance is shot for a grand total of 90 arrows. PRA is now offering a 900 round on the first and third Sundays of the month.

PRA maintains a herd of 42 3-D target animals for its invitational tournaments. We offer an abbreviated 14-target 3-D round on the third Sunday of the month. Even with the reduced number of targets, there's a fair amount of work needed to get the animals out from storage, place them on the range and then repack them at the end of the day. The 3-D Round is particularly popular with our members who shoot traditional archery.

This is a very active competition schedule. Participants in our weekly tournaments are primarily club members and local guest archers. The tournament fees are low and discounted even lower for club members. Trophies or awards are not given out for the weekly tournaments.

Club members who shoot a minimum number of Field/Hunter, 300, and 3-D rounds per year are eligible for annual club trophies. One of our club members compiles the weekly scores for the Field/Hunter rounds and another member keeps the scores for the 300 rounds. Classes are divided among shooting style, age and gender. The annual awards are presented at the annual banquet and are very popular with the membership. In many cases the winners are not always the top shooters but rather show dedication to the sport by participating every week. Persistence counts in earning these annual awards.

A casual and very popular novelty tournament in the Fall is having a Turkey Shoot, in whch the prizes are . . . turkeys!

Transitioning Archers from Archery Classes to Archery Tournaments

With so many people coming into the sport of archery, there is an ongoing need to transition student archers from the comfort of a class situation to the more challenging business of competition. At PRA our instructor and coaching staff members are constantly coming up with ideas and programs to get Saturday students to become Sunday competitors. For the Field/Hunter course, we offer a "Rookie Round" option where beginning competitors shoot from the black cub stakes for the first year, enabling them to become familiar with the course and the rules of the game while keeping the shooting distances short.

Other instructors take students out on the range during Saturday classes to introduce them to the range and the targets used in Field/Hunter competitions. Three- and four-target mock competitions are held so that students can get a feel for the game and for the scoring schemes.

Because there is a social component to archery, it is often easier to get a group of students who know and like each other to try a Sunday competition. The 300 Round is a good tool for bridging students into competition. A 900 Round will get them to shoot longer distances. Mentors are needed in the early stages of shooting a Field/Hunter Round to explain the rules, etiquette, and scoring to new competitors.

Novelty Tournaments

Novelty tournaments are a fun way to get everyone involved in the sport of archery. Tournaments can be themed around holidays, special events, and fun ideas. At PRA we hold an invitational "21 or Bust" tournament every year where competitors shoot at specially designed target faces labeled with the values of playing cards. (Using regular cards doesn't work because the face value of the card is too hard to see at the shooting distance.) Archers attempt to shoot a score of up to 21 using a total of no more than three arrows without going over the 21 limit and busting. Compound shooters really like this one.

We have held themed tournaments around movie titles including *The Hunger Games* and *Brave*. In some cases, we have set these tournaments up as fund raisers for a local charity. In others we have worked with the movie studio to provide themed prizes for the competitors.

A recent May the 4th provided an opportunity for a *Star Wars* themed tournament. One of our talented club members produced properly sized targets with *Star Wars* themed images on them. The round was shot and scored as a regular field round.

At the end of October we hold a Halloween shoot with targets, often 3-D, made by the club members and placed on the range. No scoring here—just having some fun.

In November we hold a "Turkey Shoot" for the Saturday morning class participants. "C" size field targets are shot at a distance of 20 yards. We have categories for adults, children, advanced competitors with sights and traditional archers. Three ends are shot. In case of a tie, a one arrow shoot off determines the winner. Prizes are a frozen turkey for first, a whole chicken for second and a pound of bacon for third. There are lots of smiling faces at the end of this event.

Use your imagination and see what fun tournament ideas you can come up with for your club.

Leagues

Taking a page from the sport of bowling and a number of other team sports, you may want to set up a seasonal league program to encourage club members to participate in tournament activities. A successful league program requires a number of organizational elements.

A great deal of work goes into hosting a tournament. Here 3-D animal targets are being inventoried.

A league play program should be set out on a seasonal basis, typically 3-4 months per season. Teams are formed for the season, regularly scheduled competitions are held and awards are given at the end of the period. Forming teams adds a social component to tournament competition that is often lacking in more formal events. You can set up some rules for team formation that permit everyone, at all levels of skill to participate and that reduce the likely hood of cliques dominating the action. Additional social components of league play can include potluck meals, novelty tournaments, and competitions with teams from other leagues.

League tournaments are usually held on a weeknight. Having an indoor venue for league play is particularly helpful during the winter season. Plan on a once a week schedule for league play. If you have enough participants, you may set up a second league night. Be sure to include categories for all ages of participants. Promote signups for leagues well in advance of the season starting dated. Hold warm-up and try-out dates to get archers interested.

A great deal of record keeping is needed to run a successful league. Fortunately there are software programs that provide all of the structure, record keeping, standings, and scoring needed to successfully run a league program. In planning your league, be sure to identify a person who will run the software and keep all of the league records. Leagues can be a fun way to keep archers interested in tournament competition.

Invitational Tournaments

While weekly club tournaments are relatively simple to run, larger invitational tournaments take a lot of planning and work to be successful. There are scores of tasks required to promote, produce, and follow up on a major tournament. The tournament chair's primary task is to organize and staff all of the required steps in the tournament operations process. While PRA is a field archery club and the processes of running a large tournament are oriented towards that discipline, many of the steps are similar for running a target archery event. (My thanks to David A. Watts, a former PRA member, for codifying many of the required tasks in their order of need.)

Tournament attendees are given final indstructions before starting.

One of the first steps in planning a major invitational tournament is to pick the date. Most state archery associations plan their tournament calendar at least a year in advance. Check the calendars of regional and national tournament organizers to avoid scheduling conflicts. Once you have picked a date, be sure to get the date into the state association's calendar so that other event planners can schedule around you. Picking the right date is critical to maximize public participation.

Below is a listing of tasks in their rough sequence to the tournament date. Many tournament chairs create a spreadsheet to maintain a record of the tasks to be completed and the people responsible for the task. Included in the spreadsheet or kept as a separate file, are all of the financial records of expenses and income which are used to track the progress of the tournament preparations and to form the basis for a final report by the tournament chair to the club's board after the conclusion of the event.

Four Months Before the Tournament

Four months before the event, the tournament chair needs to identify and recruit the necessary staff to run the tasks. Some of the key roles include the *Event Range Master*, responsible for the condition of the range and the preparation of all the necessary targets. The Range Master may also be responsible for range clean up, the condition of the target backstops and stands (if needed) and the positioning and painting of the range shooting distance markers. When working on an established fixed range, many of these tasks may be taken care of in regular range maintenance. If the range layout is to be custom made for this event, there's a lot of work needed to prepare the site for the tournament.

Registration Event registration and score keeping and reporting represent a big task on tournament day that requires substantial pre-event preparation to run successfully. A *Registration Supervisor* will be needed to ensure that registration documents are printed and available, volunteers recruited to handle registration and range fees on the day of the event, direct the technical scrutiny and classification of equipment, prepare the scoreboard with the names of the participants, properly assign competitors to their competitive classes, receive the score cards as they are completed, sort and record the scoring results, post the results on the public scoreboard and produce a table of the final score results for publication. Registration and scorekeeping requires a dedicated and detail-oriented person to successfully complete the tournament's tasks.

Serving Food If you are planning on selling food, a *Food Concession Supervisor* needs to be named. There are a number of potential sources for food during your event. Preparing food on-site by members of the club is a simple way to go. You'll need cooks, food preparation, BBQ's, drinks, and a cashier. You may want to sell food tickets at registration so that you can keep the cash management all in one place.

Another food alternative is to have outside vendors prepare and sell food. This approach can work with larger events, reducing the workload for the club and providing more food choice variety for the attendees. With the popularity of food trucks, you may be able to invite a few of them to come to your event. Another choice is to sell food tickets on site and use an off site vendor to prepare food packages to be picked up and ferried to the range by one or more club members. Using outside food vendors reduces the work load for club members at the cost of reduced event revenue. Make your choices based on the resources available to you, both in the form club volunteers and sources of food vendors.

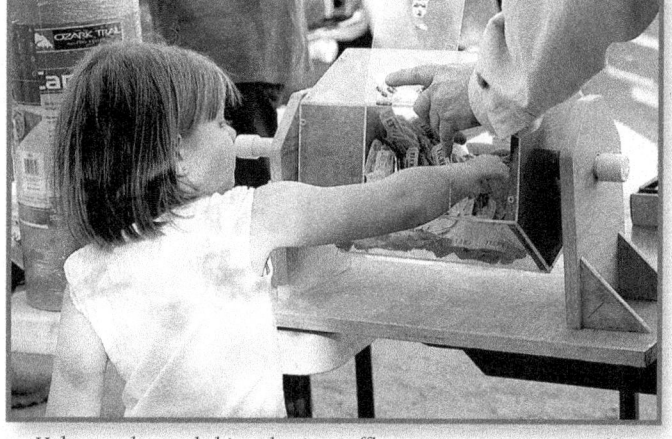
Help may be needed in selecting raffle prize winners impartially.

In either case you should have coffee and doughnuts available in the morning and cold drinks available during the day. If the range is spread out, such as a field or 3-D range, you should have cool drink stations set out along the course. Packaged snacks such as chips and candy can be available throughout the day.

The food concession supervisor is in charge of all food and drink service during the event. Be sure to have plenty of food and drink available for the club volunteers. There's lots of advance planning needed for food service with the bulk of the work to be done on the day before and the day of the event. If you choose to prepare your own food on site, you will need an estimate of the food quantities needed. Experience from previous events is your best guide here. If this is the first time for your club, ask around to other clubs in your area about their food budgets. If you have the resources, food concessions can generate as much income for the club as tournament fees.

Publicity A *Publicity Chair* needs to be named early in the process. The publicity committee will need to produce advertising and public relations copy, design and print flyers, design print ads, post notices on the club's web site, post notices on the club's newsletter, post notices on social media including Facebook, take and edit photographs and produce end of event press releases, reports and media posts. The Publicity Chair does not have to personally be able to do all of these tasks but he/she needs to be able to identify club members who have the skills and motivation to get all of these tasks completed and on time. Publicity is a big job and requires a person with good people, writing, and editing skills.

Vendors A *Vendor Relations Chair* will be needed if you plan on setting up an area at the range for commercial and craft vendor booths with products for sale or demonstration. The event committee will need to establish the policies for on-site vendors. You will need to determine how you will vet vendors for appropriateness, professionalism, and quality of goods. Will you charge a fee to vendors, either as a fixed amount or a percentage of sales? Will you invite major manufacturers and local retailers to exhibit?

A vendor and trade area can be very popular with attendees. Event organizers need to carefully weigh the potential for revenue against the possibility of limiting the number of participants. Exhibiting can be costly for a manufacturer with travel, staffing and equipment costs. It's probably best not to look to the vendor area as a source of significant income for the club. Working closely with local pro shops can go a long way towards building a mutually supportive relationship for both the retailers and the club members. Choose a Vendor Relations Chair who has some business experience as well as good people and outreach skills.

Raffles Raffles can be a substantial source of income if you expect a large turnout for your event. For a raffle to be profitable, most, if not all, of your goods and services need to be donated, rather than purchased by the club. A *Raffle Chair* will need to be named early and begin right away to solicit donations from manufacturers, retailers, service business and club members. A successful raffle needs a few high-ticket, headliner items plus a larger number of modestly valued goods to attract participants.

Raffles can be operated in several ways. Players can purchase tickets that are then drawn for items selected by the raffle chair. You can put small boxes or cans in front of specific items and participants can deposit their tickets for the items they want to win. You can run a silent auction, popular at fund raising events, where items are displayed and participants write in their bid for the item on a paper in front of each item. You may also choose to put all of the winning tickets for small items back into the pool for the showcase item. Running the raffle after the shoot has been completed and while the scores are being tallied and posted is a great way to occupy the participants during the lull in action. Be sure to get photos and the names of the winners.

Everybody likes winning raffle prizes, especially the really nice ones!

Raffles are profitable with donated goods but are barely a break even if you purchase the prizes. Raffles take an enormous amount of pre-event work and require a very dedicated Raffle Chair with the time to gather the needed donations. Raffles are best if you expect over 100 attendees so the pool of participants is large enough to disperse the prizes among a wider group of winners. You'll hear a lot of groans in the audience if one person wins more than twice. When running a large event, the raffle can produce as much as one third of your total event income. One California club, who runs an event attracting 1200 attendees, raises over $16,000 in raffle fees alone.

Start your campaign for raffle prizes early. Contact all the local archery and sporting goods-related retailers in your area for contributions. It can be more challenging to contact equipment manufacturers regarding donations. Many of the larger companies are inundated by donation requests. Some companies choose to not donate as a matter of policy. Others may offer promotional or clearance goods. Some companies don't donate but they have a discount purchase policy for non-profits that will allow you to buy their products for use in the raffle.

One of the best ways to make contact with manufacturers is through their sales representatives that call on the local archery pro shops. Work with your contacts at the shops to set up meetings with sales reps to discuss your event. If you plan on a vendor area, invite the manufacturer to set up a booth and offer a donation in kind for the raffle.

Solicit donations by snail mail, not email. Identify the company and, if you can, identify a specific person to address your request letter to. Include in your request all the necessary information about who your organization is, full contact and shipping information and be specific if you are a 501(c)(3) public charity.

Respond to any reply promptly. If an email address is included in the reply, you can shift to email communications. Should you receive a donation, acknowledge it promptly with a thank you note and a donation receipt.

Be sure to promote your business donors in all your print ads, with signs at the raffle table and with any banners you may display for the event. At the conclusion of the event, send a follow up note to the donor and include pictures of your promotional materials that include their logo. Also send a photo of the winner of the donated merchandise with their prize to the manufacturer. Remember that you will be calling again on the same people for donations next year. Good follow up will help you to build relationships that can be beneficial to both parties over a long period of time.

Parking Parking can be an issue when staging a large event. Few venues have a paved parking area large enough to park the cars for all of the participants. Expect that you will have cars totaling 60-75% of the number of attendees. If you are parking on dirt, be sure there is adequate drainage if rain is expected. Cars mired in the mud are no fun. If, as it is in California, you have tall dry grass in the parking area, be sure to mow it down within a week before the event to avoid fires started from the hot undercarriages of cars. Use athletic field chalk to mark parking lines and have a staff of safety vested volunteers to help guide attendees to their parking spaces.

Having a food service is both a courtesy and a source of income.

Parking control is a very intense activity at the start of the event and needs to have a *Parking Chair* who can prepare the parking area in advance and mobilize a staff for a short time.

If you plan on offering a clout shoot at your event, you will need a chair to organize the target(s) register the participants, score the event and award the prizes. Clouts can be a lot of fun and can produce additional revenue for the club.

Three Months Before the Tournament

Inventory the targets you have on hand and make a purchase list of targets that you will need to buy. For 3-D targets, some may need to be repaired and repainted. Some will need to be sold or thrown away. Some will be in good enough shape to use. The 3-D targets should be in good condition with all the parts attached and not all shot up. Participants will want to see a clean target presentation as a sign of the quality of your tournament offering. Shoddy 3-D targets will create a bad name and reputation for your event.

Paper targets need to be fresh for each day's shoot and for any elimination rounds that may occur. Be sure you have enough target faces on hand for each event planned.

The target backstops need to be in top shape too. If you are using straw bales, be sure to replace any soft bales and have the bales tightly bound and secured to a backing structure. If you are using foam backstops, check to see that the centers are tight and secure to prevent pass-throughs. Be sure that target backstop stands are in good repair and that you have adequate stakes and backstays to secure the stands to the field.

The pubic relations effort starts three to four months out from the event as virtually all publications have deadlines well in advance of their publication date. A print ad needs to be designed, formatted to fit a full page, half page and quarter page. The graphic design of the ad should be clean and attract the eye. The ad copy should include all the key facts about the event including the date, time location, map to the location if needed, the type of tournament, shooting classes, food?, raffle?, clout shoot?, camping?, web site link and contact info to reach the event organizers. Be sure that the advertising copy exactly matches the terms and shooting categories of the event registration cards. You don't want a dispute over classification on the day of the event.

Once you have your ad composed and formatted as a PDF file, verify that you have the deadline dates for your target publications. Send in the ad well in advance, send in the payment for the ad and follow up with the advertising director at the publication to be sure that you have all of the materials to the publisher complete, on time and fully paid for. For most archery tournaments, the state archery association monthly newsletter will be your primary publication for placing ads. If you have a strong archery community within your locality, you may want to place an ad in the local newspaper. Post event, be sure to follow up your communications by sending a press release, results table, and photos to the publication. You might get some coverage if it's a "slow news day."

Your full page ad design is also the design of your event flyer. Flyers should be distributed widely throughout the local archery community. Print flyers and personally hand deliver them to the archery pro shops. Ask that the flyer be posted on their bulletin board and be available on the counter for customers. This is a good time to reinforce the club's relationship with the pro shop by inviting the shop to participate in the raffle, exhibit in your vendor area, and invite off duty store staff to participate in the shoot. Offer to include the store's logo in your future flyers and advertising in exchange for promotion of your event and/or the donation of a keynote piece of gear for the raffle. Promoting the local retailer costs you nothing and can pay off in good will, increased event attendance, and more sales for the store.

The flyer should be placed prominently on your web site. You should also include the flyer as a page in your monthly newsletter. Send PDF files of your flyer to nearby archery clubs for posting on their bulletin board and for inclusion in their newsletters. Be sure to reciprocate with publicity for the other club's events when they come up.

If you have run this event in the past, inventory the number of trophies that you have on hand. You'll then need to order trophies as needed to fill the expected number of class winners. In designing and engraving trophies, it's best to not include the year of the event on the plaque. Same with the shooting categories. That way you have the maximum flexibility in adapting the previous year's trophies to this year's event. Trophies are expensive. Make the most of your trophy budget by not putting yourself in a corner with dated plaques.

Submit your engraving request to the trophy shop in printed form, all capital letters and double spaced so that the shop has a place for notes. Check each trophy when they are picked up to be certain that all of the plaques/trophies are correctly labeled and spelled. (As a terrible speller, I'm particularly sensitive to this issue.) Verify that you have the correct number of trophies for each category and finish place.

Within your archery community, you'll find that there are a number of archers who seem to win or place highly in their category at each event. These people often have shelves and garages full of old trophies from previous competitions. We have some competitors at our invitational tournaments who simply choose not to take another trophy home, even though they have won. We have found, especially at traditional tournaments, that competitors appreciate hand crafted awards rather that the typical faux-gilded trophy. If you have crafty club members, look to see if you can make the winner's awards by hand. The shooters will appreciate it and the award is more likely to be displayed in the winner's home.

Ten Weeks Before the Tournament

Ten weeks before the tournament, buy, make, or replenish targets. Archery materials are often backordered so give yourself plenty of lead time on any archery-specific supplies that you feel you may need.

If you are planning to cook food for the participants, make up a menu and create a shopping list, based on the number of expected attendees. As you create your menu, consider a range of tastes and diets including vegetarian and gluten free options. Plan how you will purchase, store, and actually prepare the meals. Do you have enough cooler space? Is the grill big enough or do you need several grills? Will you need food equipment rentals? What about trash collection and removal from the site after the event? Do your best to plan for every possibility.

You'll need a whole team to handle registration.

Purchase the raffle tickets. Make or buy a raffle ticket tumbler to mix up the tickets at the event. If you are doing a user's choice raffle, gather and prepare enough containers for raffle tickets for the main prizes. Follow up on donation request letters and contacts. If raffle goods have already arrived, catalog and organize them for easy transport and display at the event.

You need to design and print tournament registration cards and tournament score cards. The registration cards should include the full name and contact information for the archer, boxes to be checked for the age, gender and bow class to be shot, a complete waiver and release form and a signature line. Color coding these can help when sorting completed score cards. If a meal ticket is an option for your event, place a check box for it on the registration card. Also provide a space for listing and tallying all of the fees and charges for the tournament registration. Include provision for all of your pricing options (adult, youth, senior, family, Mulligans, hits, food, etc.).

In preparing the design for the registration cards, be sure that all of the archer classifications for age, gender and shooting class are consistent with your published materials. Put your best proofreader on the task of verifying the consistency of all published information before sending art off to press.

For tournaments where a large turnout is expected, pre-registration may be the best way to go, especially if you expect that the event will sell out. The simplest way to handle pre-registration is with a registration form, in PDF format, available on your web site and on Facebook. Participants can download the form, print it, fill out the form, and mail it with their check or credit card information to the event organizers. Fully automated on line registration takes a lot of web site programming savvy and may be too much for a volunteer club to take on. Mailed in pre-registration forms will need to be verified, sorted, payments recorded and the data will need to be entered into the event's scoring spread sheet. You may also want to make starting target assignments at this time.

Many tournaments either require a current membership in a state/national organization or offer a discount to organization members. Have a line on the registration card for the verification of organization membership. (We have found at our tournaments that some competitors will attempt to skirt the membership requirements by presenting an expired membership card with their thumb or finger covering the expiration date. Registrars should be made aware in advance of this deceptive practice and be prepared to request to see the entire membership card. Club officers should be close by to assist the registrars in the event of any conflicts on this issue.)

During the progress of the tournament, the score keepers will enter the registration data into a computer, if used for scoring, as well as posting the competitors names in the appropriate class on the scoreboard, awaiting the submission of scores at the end of the competition.

Scorecards Scorecards will also need to be designed and printed. Plan on using double scoring with two score cards per archer. The design of the scorecards should comply with the rules for the archery game being played. For official tournaments, use the template from the sanctioning organization. For novelty and one-off tournaments, design a score card that is easy to read, contains space for the archer's information and class, and signature lines for the archer

Tournament attendees expect there will be a scoreboard so they can see how they, and their friends, stacked up.

and scorers. For target archery competitions, the score card can be printed on plain paper stock as the scorecard will be held in place at the target on a clipboard. For field/hunter and 3-D tournaments, print the scorecards on card stock so that the scorecard will be sturdy enough to be written on in the field, with or without a clipboard.

Now is the time to contact the club members for volunteer positions for the event. The most likely members to volunteer are those who have previously worked on tournaments. Be sure to court these volunteers but be cautious about just handing out jobs to people that you know within the club.

Working on tournaments is a great way for new members to get to know the club's leaders and other club members. Be sure to put out a call to all of the membership and respond promptly to any volunteer inquiry. Start a contact sheet/roster and connect volunteers with the tasks that they will be expected to perform.

Scorecards have to be collected, verified, and then logged to be posted on the scoreboard (at the end of the event).

Some volunteers may have special skills or interests that will make them want to join a specific task or committee. Others may have scheduling issues and not be able to attend the event but may be available for pre or post event tasks. The Tournament Chair should act as a facilitator to connect the membership with the committee chairs and tasks that need to be done. The key here is to communicate clearly and often with the volunteer crew. People who volunteer want to work and are happy to take on assigned tasks. Keeping everybody up to date on the progress of the event is an essential part of a leader's role.

If you are running a target archery competition, contact USA Archery to identify and schedule one or more official judges to be present for your event. If you don't already have one, arrange for the rental or purchase of a shot timer with displays as needed. Assign an experienced volunteer and a backup volunteer to run the shot timer for you during the event.

Eight Weeks Before the Tournament

All of your preparations should be coming together. Now it is time to start promoting your event. Mail the flyers to your promotion list. Mail your donation request letters. Send your press release to the local press. Create and post posters for your event to be set up at the range during your regular week programs.

Six to Four Weeks Before the Tournament

Survey the range condition and make any necessary repairs. Schedule work days with the club membership to fix bales, clean up shooting lanes, paint range markers and do general range clean up.

If you haven't already done so, buy the target faces and paste them up if needed. If you are running a 3-D shoot, be sure you have enough reinforcing rod stakes in stock to secure the animals. Purchase extra sledge hammers if needed for setting up the targets.

In addition to the permanent range distance markers, you may want to put up "unmarked distance" markers for some equipment classes. Purchase wood stakes at a home improvement store and paint them a distinctive color for staking out on the range. The actual placement of the stakes won't happen until the day before the shoot but you need to have the materials well in hand in advance.

Follow up on your press releases with the local media. Invite reporters and photographers to come out to the range to cover the event. Post your progress on your Facebook page and on other social media. Verify that the information on your web site is current and accurate about the details of the event.

Raffle prizes should begin to come in now. Sort and organize the raffle prizes. If you have one or two key raffle prizes, take a photo of them and publicize that they will be given away at the event.

You will need a scoreboard to post the tournament scores on the day of the event. At PRA we had a sign shop print out a large grid and laminate it onto a ½" thick piece of Gator board. An additional "dry marker" lamination was placed over the printed grid so that classes, names and scores could be written on the board. A second lamination was bonded to the back of the board to reduce the tendency of the Gator board to warp and an extruded plastic frame surrounds the scoreboard. So far, we have had more than 10 years of use of this scoreboard and it's still going strong. It is stored indoors and off site, only coming outside on a tournament day.

Prepare a volunteer schedule, often easily done as a spreadsheet, connecting the tasks to be done with the staff available to do the job. Once you have a preliminary schedule organized, share the schedule with the volunteers to confirm that they are available to do the tasks they are assigned.

Three Weeks Before the Tournament

Buy and pick up the trophies. Verify that all of the spelling on the plaques/trophies is correct and that you have the correct number of trophies in each category. There's still time for minor fixes at this point. If you are making the awards in house, verify that the volunteers have completed the tasks and that you have inventoried the results.

If the quantity and/or quality of the donated raffle prizes have not met expectations, you will need to purchase supplemental prizes to fill the raffle table. Keep within your budget but be sure that the prizes will be appealing to the participants.

Handling Rentals You will need to order any rental items needed for the event. Portable toilets are often needed. Portable toilets are intended to serve 10 people for a 5 day work week. You can adjust the number of portable toilets based on that estimate. In some cases, portable toilets are placed to reduce the inconvenience to participants who might otherwise have to walk a long distance to reach permanent facilities. Most rental houses charge a minimum monthly fee for portable toilets, no matter how short the actual time of use. Have the toilets delivered to the range on the Friday before the tournament. Have padlocks ready when the toilets arrive and lock the doors until the morning of the event. Vandals can damage unlocked toilets causing additional charges and potential inconvenience to your participants.

And, of course, winners need to presented with their awards.

Other rentals can include pop-up canopies, tables, chairs, BBQ grills, food preparation equipment, generators, and a host of other necessities. Have one or more of your staff volunteers pick up the rental items from the rental yards, rather than having the goods delivered. That way you know that you are getting what you ordered and that it will be available at the time that it is needed.

We prepare a number of tabletop posters to be used at registration. One is a price sheet that lists all of the tournament fees and pricing options. As we are an NFAA club and the NFAA has a number of different equipment classifications that can be confusing to participants, we have several laminated posters with a listing of all the NFAA classes and pictures of the appropriate equipment for each class. We've found that spelling the classes out with pictures goes a long way towards speeding up the tournament registration process.

Stationary Supplies Put together the stationary supplies needed for registration and score keeping. You will need "golf pencils" for score cards, pens for filling out registration cards, dry markers for filling out the scoreboard and the target assignment board. If you are running a target archery tournament, be sure you have enough clip boards for score keeping at each target backstop. You should have some simple battery powered calculators on hand to total range fees and for tracking cash.

Handling Cash If you don't have a cash register, having a properly fitted cash box goes a long way towards organizing and tracking cash payments. Cash boxes or cash drawer liners may be purchased inexpensively at an office supply store. Also purchase one or more cash pouches for keeping the cash after the event and on the way to the bank. If you serve food and have a raffle, you will have three cash streams that you will want to track. Keep the receipts from each of the cash flow lines separate for security and for post event bookkeeping.

Be sure to have enough cash on hand for making change on the day of the event. Unless your tournament fees come in increments of $20.00, your cashier will be needing lots of change during registration. For a big event having $300-400 in change available is not too much.

Processing Credit Cards There are lots of advantages to accepting credit card payments at your tournament for the price of setting up some technical infrastructure. If your range has a permanent club house with electrical power and telephone service, setting up a credit card station is relatively easy technically. Credit card processing terminals are expensive and you shouldn't make an investment in a terminal unless you have reason to use it in addition to tournament registration. If you have cell phone service at the range, there are simplified credit card readers and processing services that work with a smart phone that can simplify the set up process and reduce the cost of taking cards. Do not use a club member's cell phone for your credit card operations. Set up a club-owned smart phone for credit card service.

Acquiring Photos This is a good time to identify a person to be the *Official Photographer* for the event. You will need photos for your web page, Facebook page and for general publicity. If you hold an annual banquet, photos from the tournaments are a popular subject for a background slide show. While most photos are now taken on cell phones and personal devices, identify someone who is familiar with using a dedicated camera as your photographer. You will have more flexibility with using the files after the event if they are shot on a dedicated digital camera.

One to Two Weeks Before the Tournament

This is the time to verify that all of your plans are in order and that all of the preparatory tasks are complete. Contact your volunteers and remind them of the times and locations of their service. Organize a work day just before the tournament to fully clean and prep the range. Pick up any printed supplies and trophies that are still outstanding. Go to the bank and pick up the needed change cash. Follow up with any of the local media who you have invited to cover the event.

If you are using target stands and foam targets, pick them up and arrange for them to be stored or set up at the tournament site. Verify that you have enough stands, target butts, flags, rope, stakes, target number markers and any other needed supplies.

One Day Before the Tournament

Things are going to be very busy for the next two days. All of your preparations will now have to be executed in order to produce a successful event.

Targets The targets need to be set up and ready. 3-D targets take a lot of work to transport from storage, place on the range, stake into the ground and verify the shooting positions. If you have moving 3-D targets, the mechanisms need to be tested and confirmed as working.

Field, Hunter and Animal round tournaments simply require the placement of new target faces on the target backstops (with backups stored behind the butts if appropriate).

Rentals Rental items need to be picked up and brought to the site. In placing both rental and in-house furniture and fixtures, think of traffic flow for the competitor. Arrange the placement of signage, bow racks, tables, seating, and portable toilets so that participants can move smoothly from one step of registration to another with a place for everything and all the necessary supplies at hand. Bow racks are particularly important to place just before the registration tables. A bow rack should be placed by the restroom facilities. You may need to move the bow racks from registration to the lunch area and then to the raffle and awards area during the progress of the tournament.

Pop-up shelters are a common way to provide shade and weather protection during an event. Shelters will be needed for the registration staff at the beginning of the event. Again, the shelters may need to be moved to protect the food service staff, raffle coordinator and scoring staff. Be sure to securely tie down, stake, or weight the legs of these portable shelters. A wind gust can blow them away

NFAA Shooting Styles

If You Shoot ...	and you are an ...	Adult	Young Adult/Youth/Cub/PeeWee
bow + sight + stabilizer	release	FS	FS
bow + sight + stabilizer	tab	FSL	FSL
bow + sight + short stabilizer	release	BHFS	FS
bow + sight + short stabilizer	tab	BHFSL	FSL
bow + short stabilizer	tab	BH	BB
bow + stabilizer	tab	BB	BB
recurve bow	tab	Trad-RC	BB
longbow	tab	Trad-LB	BB
recurve bow + sight + stabilizer	tab	FSL-R/LB	FSL-R/LB

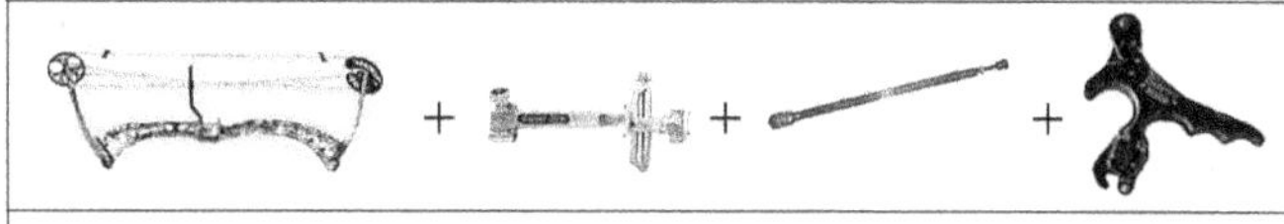

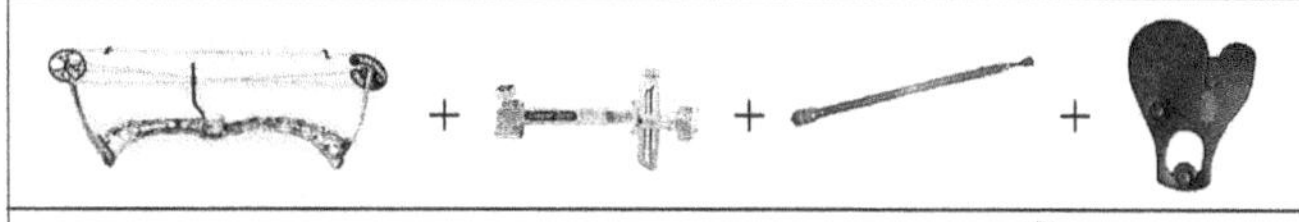

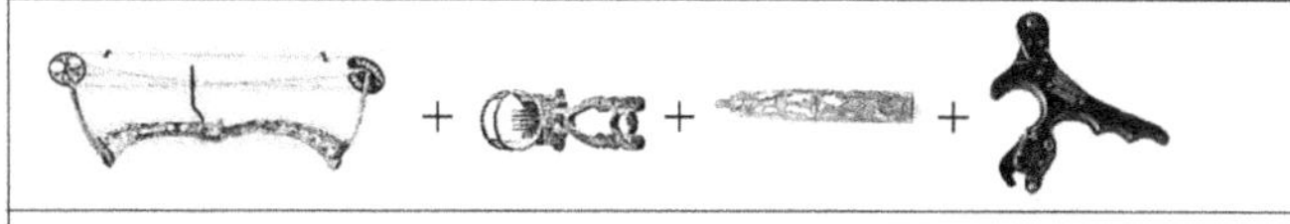

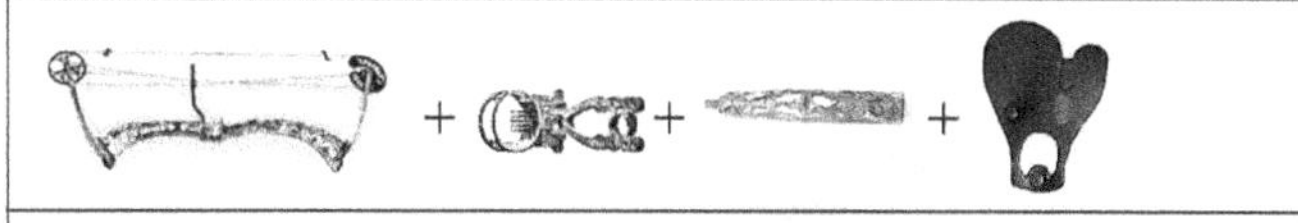

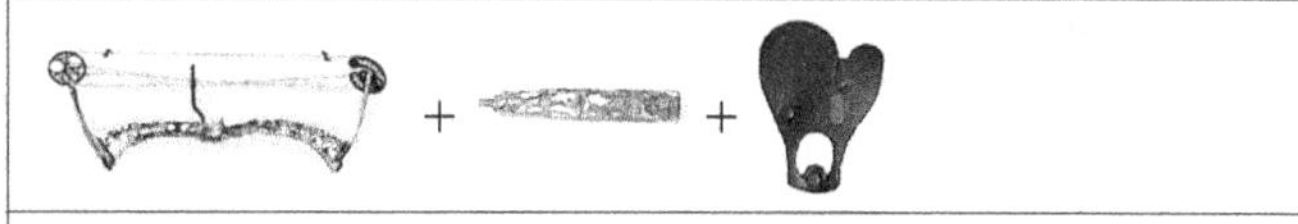

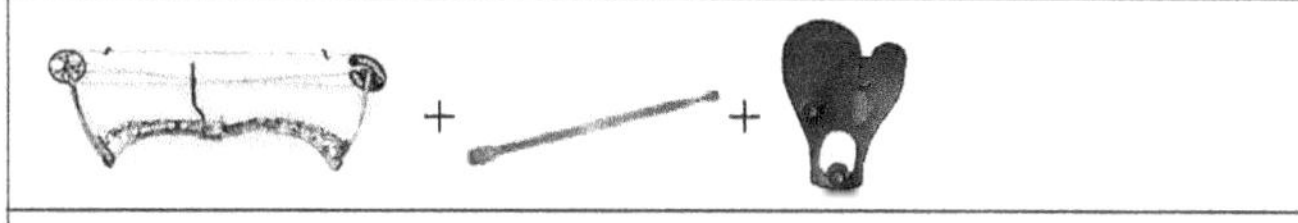

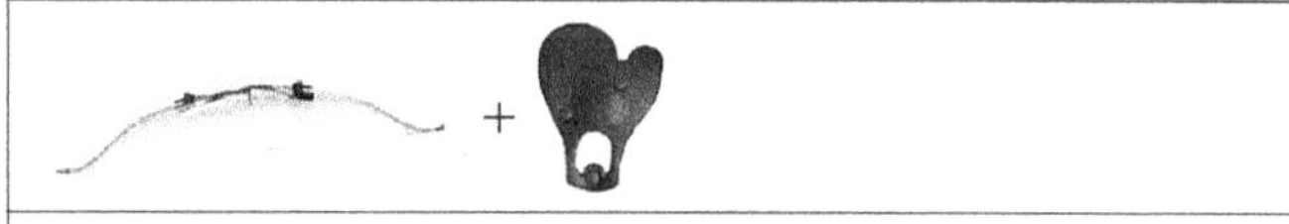

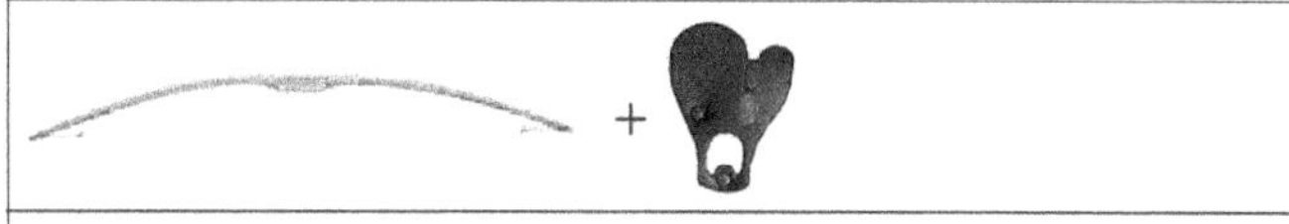

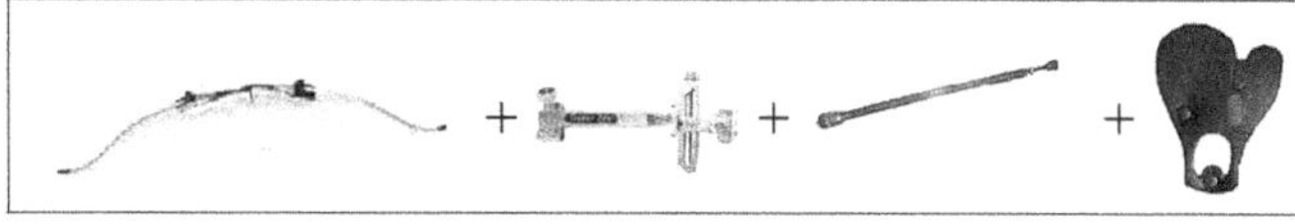

Key
FS = freestyle
FSL = freestyle limited
BH = bowhunter
BHFSL = bowhunter freestyle limited
BHFS = bowhunter freestyle
BB = barebow
Trad-RC = traditional recurve
Trad-LB = traditional longbow
FSL-R/L = freestyle limited–recurve longbow (basically FITA Freestyle)

Note—In the Junior Division—Young Adult (*15-17 years old*), Youth (*12-14 years old*), Cub (*under 12 years old*)—there are only four styles recognized—FS, FSL, BB, and FSL-R/LB.

A poster showing all of the allowed shooting styles can be really helpful especially because the styles allowed youths are limited and, in the NFAA, not the same as for the adults.

Teaching Archery

or over in an instant. You don't want your participants to be hit by flying debris.

Directions If you are running a Field/Hunter or a 3-D round that requires the participants to move from one target to another, be sure to have adequate signage directing shooters from target to target. One way to do that is to use athletic field marking chalk to place directional arrows on the ground for archers to follow.

Unless you have a paved and striped parking lot, the participant parking area needs to be staked and striped with athletic field chalk to mark parking lines. Be sure that signage and directional arrows clearly direct competitors to the registration area from the parking lot. If you are using off-site parking, be sure to mark and place signs for competitors to know where the shuttle service will stop for archers traveling both to and from their cars.

Food If you are cooking on site, you will need to purchase the food and store it safely. If electricity and refrigeration are not available at the range, you will need coolers for food storage. Consider using dry ice for frozen goods. Water ice will work fine for refrigerated foods. Purchase all of the needed paper goods including cups, plates, plastic ware and napkins. Pick up a couple of boxes of large trash bags for event clean up. Be sure to stock condiments and seasonings for the meals.

If you are using an on-site food service, such as a hot food truck, check with the caterer to verify that they are scheduled for the event and confirm the time that they will arrive at your range. Be sure that you have adequate vehicular access to the food service area for the food trucks or caterers. Food service personnel should be able to come and go freely should supplies be needed.

Be sure there is enough seating and tables for your participants during food service. Archers should not be expected to stand around with a paper plate in their hands while eating. If picnic tables are not available at your site, rental tables and chairs will be needed. Rental equipment can be placed the day before. Disposable plastic tablecloths should be available for covering the food service and eating tables on the day of the event. Be sure to have plenty of masking tape on hand to tape the tablecloths in place.

Some people won't pick up their raffle prizes until they are on their way to the parking lot, so somebody will need to be standing by.

We keep paper goods in plastic tubs to protect them from dirt and from the weather. Be certain you have enough supplies on hand to serve all of your participants. Paper goods are not perishable. Extra plates, cups, and plastic ware can be stored and used later.

Being Heard If you expect to have a large turnout, you may need a public address system for making announcements and for providing background music during lulls in the competition. For target tournaments, music can help as the archers are scoring their ends as well as for background during the lunch break. For field and 3-D tournaments, music is less important as the action is continuous. Having a sound system to provide pre-event announcements, run the raffle, and award the trophies will make it easier for all the participants to hear the presentations.

You may choose to install a small stage or a three tier podium for use during the awards ceremony. For larger events, it is now common to install a printed background behind the presentation stage for the awards photographs. A local sign shop can print a large fabric banner with your event logo on it for inclusion in the awards photos. If you hire a professional photographer for your event, the photographer may add some supplemental flash lighting to the awards stand to improve the quality of the awards photographs.

Trash Trash management is an important planning consideration. Trash receptacles need to be placed conveniently around the site. If this is a relatively small event (under 100 participants) you may want to do the trash work yourself with volunteer staff. For a larger event, you might consider contracting with a trash service that can provide disposable trash receptacles on your site and remove all of the trash after the event. Waste management is not cheap but it is an essential part of running a successful event.

With a lot of the pre-event preparations completed and materials and equipment in place, you will want to be sure that the site is secure overnight. Arrange for one or more volunteers to camp overnight at the range and regularly patrol the site. Vandals and thieves will be tempted by unfamiliar and potentially valuable stuff. Protect your investment of time and money so that there will be no surprises on tournament day.

Day of the Tournament

Plan for an early start and a long day. Volunteer staff should arrive at least an hour and a half before the archers. Have hot coffee and doughnuts ready from moment one. Caffeine and fuel are needed to get the day started. If you are planning on a breakfast service for the participants, the food area needs to be prepped and the griddle fired up. Cold drinks and snacks will need to be placed. Paper goods (with paper weights to keep things from flying off in the wind) should be set out.

Walkie-Talkies Hand held two way radios can be a big help in staff communications. While most of us have cell phones, a radio is quicker to use and is not subject to the vagaries of cell phone service.

Parking The parking supervision staff should be stationed as needed at the parking entrance and along the parking lanes to guide participants to their parking spaces. If a shuttle service is used to ferry participants to registration, the shuttle vehicle should be on site, fueled up and ready to go. Parking staff should direct the participants to the shuttle or to the range entrance. Radios can be a big help here, especially if the entrance to the parking is a long distance from the road. Arrangements need to be made for overflow parking and the staff will need to cut off entrance to the on-sit parking when the lot is full. Parking supervision is a hectic job for the first hour or so and then things settle down once the participants and their cars are in place.

Venders Venders should load in as early as possible. Have at least one volunteer to act as Vendor Liaison to guide venders to their booth space and to provide any needed communications and support with the tournament chair. Venders should be open for business when the competitors arrive. Include in your agreement with the vendors that they are to stay open during the entire event.

Registration and Check-in Registration and archer check-in will be a first priority for morning setup. If you use pre-registration, registrars will need to have the registration forms/packets arranged alphabetically by name. You may want to divide the pre-registration materials among several stations, sorted alphabetically, to speed the registration process.

Tournament packets with the score cards, a range map, day's schedule, score card pencils and any promotional items from the club or the event sponsors are issued from the registration table. Walk up registration will require that the participant fill out a registration form before coming up to the registrar. Be sure to have tables, registration forms, and pencils available for walk-up participants. Because of the frequent confusion about the various categories of NFAA bow classifications, it is helpful to have a poster or flyer with the classifications posted that include a photograph of each class of gear. With a poster, registrants and volunteer staff can easily categorize an archer's equipment and place them into the correct competitive category (*see graphic*).

Cash and checks, collected during registration should be sorted, counted, and placed in envelopes. For cash, if you are not using a cash register, the amount should be counted by two people and the total written on the outside of the storage envelope into which the cash is placed. The envelope is then sealed and the cashiers sign the outside of the envelope attesting to the amount of money therein. Checks are packaged separately. All of the funds are then transferred to the Club or Event Treasurer for deposit. Electronic transactions are tabulated separately for the final accounting for the event.

Getting in Place For field and 3-D tournaments, a shotgun start is the most efficient way to get everyone on the range and shooting as soon as possible. Registrants should progress from entry registration to the target assignment table where starting targets will be assigned. Families and other groups often like to shoot together so having some flexibility in setting up the target assignments goes a long way toward running a successful event. Keep the number of archers starting on a single target to a limit of four people. Creating shooting groups that are of uneven size will slow the progress of shooting for the others. Also think of the shooting style of the archers when assigning targets. Traditional archers tend to shoot more quickly than compound bow archers. Put the traditional archers on the first targets and the free style archers on the last targets to improve the flow of the tournament during the day.

Use a dry erase white board with a grid and the target numbers marked on it. Use a dry erase marker to fill in the starting grid as you go. Be sure to write on to the score card of each participant, their starting target number for reference. Once the grid is complete, you can post it for participants to see.

Equipment Inspections If your event requires a technical equipment inspection, direct registrants to an inspection table/area. Use a stamp on the score card or sticker to certify that the equipment complies with the event rules. Archers should be given an opportunity to adjust, repair, or replace non-compliant gear before the event starts.

Practice A practice area should be set aside for archers to warm up and a "Sight In" target needs to be set up for archers to finalize their sight settings. Event rules should prohibit the archers from practicing on the actual tournament course.

Final Checks Paper targets that were not put up the day before will need to be placed on the target butts. For target tournaments, a shot timer, signaling device and any necessary flags will need to be in place. The tournament director should walk the range to be sure that all of the preparations are complete.

The Raffle The raffle area should be set up with prizes on display at the same time as the event registration. Participants will be standing around drinking coffee and will wander over to the raffle area to scope out the prizes. Many raffle veterans like to space out their raffle purchases during the day so that their numbers are more evenly dispersed throughout the pool. The raffle table should be staffed during the entire event to serve any participant who wants to play.

Raffle sales can be increased by offering "package deals" for the purchase of tickets. One scheme that works is to price individual tickets at $1.00 ea, 6 tickets for $5.00, 13 tickets for $12.00 and 30 tickets for $20.00. Be creative with your pricing to encourage more players. If you are offering a pricy grand prize, decide in advance if all tickets are eligible or only those tickets that were not previously drawn qualify. If you are going to allow players to choose which items they want to compete for, have containers in front of the key items so they can vote with their ticket stubs. General raffle tickets should be placed in a tumbler for selection later in the event.

Getting Started For field and 3-D competitions, send the archers out to their staring targets about 15 minutes before the scheduled start time. Start your event on time. Use an air horn to signal to all the archers on the range that the tournament has begun.

Things quiet down while the archers are on the range. Staff members assigned as Range Captains should walk the range regularly to see that the event is running smoothly. Water and snack stations should be checked and re-stocked as needed.

Meanwhile the score keeping team will need to transfer the information from the registration cards to the scoreboard. Use dry erase markers to fill out the information. If the score cards come in over a period of time, keep the scoreboard turned away so that competitors can not see the scores at they are posted. There's no need to tempt a competitor to "refine" their score to place higher than a score they saw posted. This helps to keep the game fair.

If score keeping is being done electronically, all of the participant's names have to be entered into the scoring grid in the appropriate shooting category. Electronic scoring can be easier to tabulate but displaying an electronic screen outdoors can be difficult. Conventional projectors are too dim to be seen in sunlight and LED screens need to be shaded to be seen if at all under the sun. Expect that you will need some type of written scoreboard to post the top scores at the event. One California club uses a large format printer to print out any shooting division whose scores are complete for posting. Keeping the scores electronically will make it much easier to post the tournament results on line and to provide tables for publishing in your club newsletter.

The trophies should be set out on a table and organized by category and placement. All of the archers should be able to see the trophies in advance as an incentive to do their best.

Throughout the Day By mid day, the archers will be ready for lunch. In a target tournament, where everyone is shooting together and under time control, taking a lunch break is fairly easy. For a field/3-D tournament, archers will have to stop at the food service area along the way. Stopping for food will slow down your event and can cause backups for archers shooting through. Keep the food service area clean and wipe or replace the tablecloths as needed. Empty any trash receptacles that have filled. Do your best to keep the range and especially the food service area clean and free of litter.

Managing Scores and Awards At the conclusion of shooting in the afternoon, the score cards will need to be signed and turned in to the score keepers. Have enough battery powered calculators on hand for archers to use to total their scores. In some tournament rules, archers are only responsible for the arrow value. In other archery events, the archer is responsible for both the arrow value and the math. Scorekeepers will need to check the math on all top scoring cards.

The scores will need to be transferred onto the scoring grid, whether mechanical or electronic. The scores will need to be ranked for first, second, third etc. If you have a large number of participants in a single category, you may choose to "flight" the competitors into more than one group per class. You may also subdivide a popular category into "Pro," "A," "B," and if necessary "C" flights.

If you have a low turnout in a particular category you may want to employ a minimum participant rule for awarding trophies. For example for a category with three or fewer participants, only first place is awarded; five participants in a category is the threshold for awarding both first and second place trophies, seven or more competitors are needed in a category to award trophies through third place. If you choose such a minimum threshold trophy program, be sure to post the awards rules in all of your promotional materials, on you web site and on all of the registration cards. That way everybody knows what to expect at awards time.

While the competitors are waiting for the scores to be tallied up, this is the time to run your raffle. Offer some last minute time for ticket purchases and then begin pulling tickets. Ask for a volunteer form the audience, usually a child, to actually pull the tickets for you and then read the numbers. The raffle will then pass the time while the score tallies are completed.

When presenting the trophies, keep the presentations moving along quickly. Have one person make the announcement and another person handle the trophies. Take the time to be sure you have a photo of the presentation of each award given. For a large tournament, you will want a photographer's assistant to track the photo frame numbers to the names of the awardees for later photo captions. If you use a hand written scoreboard, be sure to take a photo (or more) of the scoreboard as a record of the final results. The photo can then be used as a data source to produce a results table for publication if necessary.

Food sales receipts and proceeds from the raffle are counted, sealed in an envelope and signed. The funds are then transferred to the Treasurer for deposit into the bank and for the final accounting for the event.

Same day clean up should include putting away all of the targets and temporary facilities, cleaning up all the trash and removing any rental items. You can put out a call to the competitors to help with putting things away and you may be surprised at how many people are willing to help. In a large organization, you may schedule club volunteers specifically for clean up. Because a tournament day is a log one, volunteers who helped with setup should not also be expected to stay for clean up. Recruit a fresh set of volunteers for end of tournament work.

After the Tournament In the weeks after the tournament there are a number of tasks that need to be completed.

All rental equipment and portable toilets need to be returned or picked up on the next day. Rental gear should not sit around in the weather. Portable target backstops and stands should be stored properly. 3-D animals should be stored safely. Any food preparation equipment needs to be put away.

Right away, all of the financial reports need to be

completed. A cash flow spreadsheet should plot all of the income and expenses. If there are any post event bills that need to be paid, checks should be issued and accounted for. The treasurer and the tournament chair should organize the materials into a report to be given at the next board meeting. A post event review should be prepared by the Tournament Chair noting both success and problems with an eye to toward improving the process for the next event. A roster of volunteers should be prepared for appropriate recognition of their efforts.

The photographs and results tables need to be sorted and organized for publication. The publicity chair should write up a press release that describes the event, notes any special events, recognizes the winners and provides information about organizing group. Photos should be processed, cropped and captioned for publication.

An event report may be published on your web site. Be sure to include lots of pictures. A shorter version of the report with even more pictures can be posted on your Facebook page. Send a copy of your press release along with the results table and a number of photos to the state archery association for publication in their newsletter. If you have had any contact with the local media, send a copy of all of your press materials to them for publication or broadcast.

Take a moment and look at who participated in your event. Analysis of who came may help you identify weal spots in your advertising for your next event. For example, if few kids came, make a greater effort to include pitches for youths to come.

Take a moment to thank yourself and the volunteer staff for a job well done. Archery competitions take a lot of work to run successfully. Recruiting, supporting and recognizing your volunteer staff will go a long way to insure the ongoing success of your tournament programs.

Chapter 8
Fundraising and Grants

An archery club is not a business. While it should be run in a professional manner, an archery club depends on volunteer labor and is not structured to be a profit making organization. Nevertheless an archery club needs money to fund its operations, facilities, and programs.

When a club is just starting out, the founding club members often fund the club's initial operations personally. Such personal funding is not without its limits and at some time the club will need to raise or earn enough money to sustain its existence. The primary source of funding for a club is its dues. Dues amounts should be calculated based on projected overhead costs. Dues should be enough to sustain the core of the organization without being so high as to scare away potential members. You can establish various tiers of memberships and dues amounts based on such social factors as age, family v. individual, student, junior, working and non-working or whatever distinctions that the board chooses to make.

The second source of income for a club is through payments to the club for services and events to the public. Such services may include archery instruction, both basic and advanced, archery tournaments for club members and the community and archery outreach activities away from the home base range such as schools and camps. With an all volunteer staff, the rates for these services can be kept low while producing income for the club for future program expansion.

A third source of income can come from larger fundraising tournaments (*see Chapter 7*). Large tournaments, intended to attract archers on a regional level, take a lot of work. Clubs should be cautious when first starting out to offer regional tournaments. Start small and then grow your event over time as your skill, capacity, and reputation increase.

Another tournament option is to offer an event with proceeds going towards a charitable cause. You can start with a local charity. You may want to coordinate your fundraiser tournament with a national charitable organization for greater visibility. Another option is to hold an event to benefit another group or individual in archery such as a community member who needs funds for medical expenses or and archery club that lost equipment or facilities during a disaster. Producing fundraising events for the community can raise your profile and build your image as a club.

You can also organize your club members to participate in community fundraising events for other causes. Community run/walk events, bike rides, clean ups, park building, and a host of other opportunities are available every year. Look for chances to put the club into the mix and raise the visibility of your organization while doing some good. PRA regularly participates in the "Spark of Love" toy drive during the holidays which is a good chance to help the community and raise our profile.

There may be a number of benefits to becoming a 501(c)(3) non-profit charitable organization (*see*

Chapter 12) If you have legal non-profit status, you can engage in fundraising for a cause and issue receipts to the donors that may provide evidence of a charitable donation for income tax purposes. Having 501(c)(3) status is an important stepping stone in expanding your program offerings. With a non-profit designation, you can seek out grant funding for operations and capital improvements.

Using Grants to Fund Archery Programs

Archery education, training, outreach, and range development projects are expensive. Finding the means to pay for the equipment, staffing, and operations of archery programs is a constant challenge for organizers. One method that can be successfully used to raise money is grant funding.

Grants are donated monies provided by funding organizations for specific purposes. Grants are not loans. The money granted, if used as required by the grant, does not have to be repaid. This "free" money, however, is not without cost. Grantees (organizations receiving the grant money) are required to plan programs, submit grant proposals, respond to inquiries, keep scrupulous records of finances and program participants, and produce written reports to the grantor (the organization giving the grant money) on finances, program goals, and accomplishments. The reward for all this administrative work is the financial means to initiate or expand an archery program to reach new participants and to create new program offerings.

Grant Funding Organizations

Grants are offered by charitable and governmental organizations. Charitable foundations often have a mission or agenda to support specific types of programs. Many large companies have foundations supporting community activities. For archery directors, foundations with charters to support youth sports, parks and recreation, outdoor activities, wildlife management, disadvantaged youths, general education, and public and private schools are all potential sources of funding. Web and library searches can identify potential sources for private grant funding. One starting place is *A Grantseeker's Guide to the Internet* (www.mindspring.com/~ajgrant/guide.htm) which has a host of advice and links.

Government agencies are another source of grant money. Local and State Parks and Recreation Departments are the first place to look for unassigned funds that may be appropriate for archery organizations. Local and State Park and Recreation Departments as well as Wildlife Management Departments (Departments of Natural Resources, Fish and Wildlife Departments, etc.) have educational missions that may be served by an archery program. School districts and local colleges may also have funds for athletics that can be directed to archery. An example of federal government funding is Pittman-Robertson funds. Enacted in 1937, the Pittman-Robertson Act placed an excise tax on archery and firearm equipment. The monies collected are to be used for wildlife management. Under the Act, one half of the available funds may be used for hunter education and shooting range construction. If a program includes hunter education, archery range construction and expansion, it may fit the criteria for Pittman-Robertson money.

The Archery Trade Association's *ArrowSport* program has set a goal of increasing the number of archery ranges available for shooters. Check with ArrowSport (below, www.archerytrade.org) to see if your proposed project may qualify for federal funding.

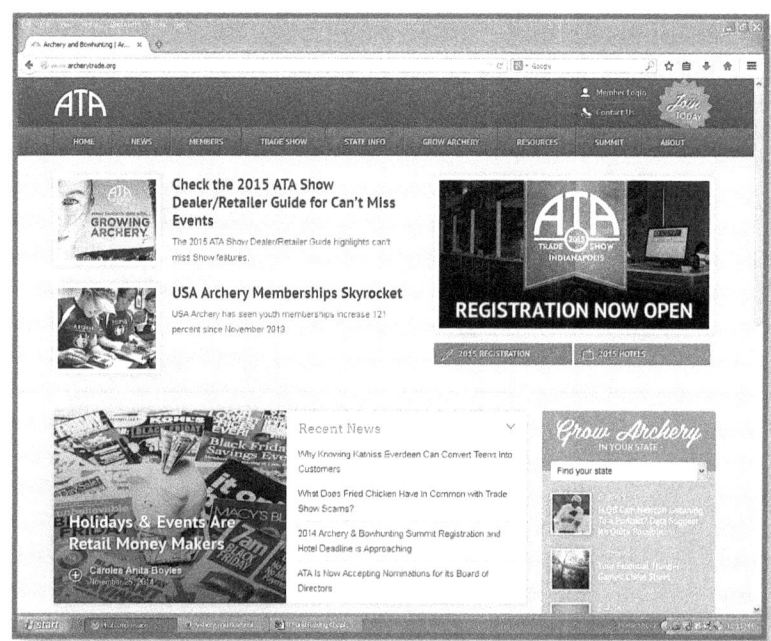

A major funder of archery programs in recent years is the Easton Sports Development Foundation (ESDF). Easton has helped to fund major facilities as well as local school and archery club programs. Check at Easton Foundation web site for details, terms, and requirements for their archery grant program (right and www.esdf.org/apply-for-grant/).

Local, state, and federal government programs can also be a source of grant funds for capital improvements in parks and on public land. Archery ranges proposed for, or located in, a public park can seek funds for range installation, upgrades, and maintenance.

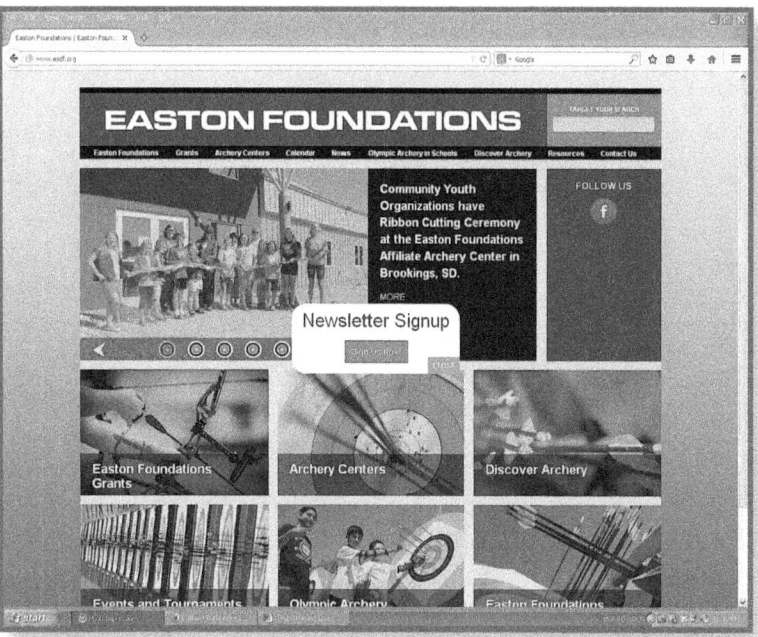

When looking for opportunities for funding, expand the search beyond the direct needs of a range. Improvements in parking, disabled access, signage, paths, restrooms, and landscaping are all grant fundable and add to the value of an archery program.

Who is Eligible for Grant Funding?

Grants may be given to individuals, community groups, non-profit organizations, and government agencies. Grant giving organizations usually have a mission to serve social or public charitable interests. The most likely recipients of grants, therefore, are non-profit organizations and public service government agencies. Individuals may have a tougher time proving that their activities match a foundation's agenda. Archery clubs may wish to establish themselves, or a parallel group, as a non-profit corporation. By establishing non-profit tax status, groups can solicit funds that are tax deductible to the donor. There are numerous web and print based guides on establishing a non-profit corporation in your state. Structure the non-profit organization to parallel the existing club governance to simplify operations. Organizers will need to open a separate bank account, book keeping, and tax filing for the nonprofit corporation. Because the laws in each state are different, it's best to consult with tax and legal professionals to get a non-profit organization set up properly.

Individuals who are running archery educational programs may also be eligible for grant funding. Look for foundations and agencies that are giving grants in the archery program's area of interest. It may take more research to find the right one, but the results will be well worth it. As the research develops, look for ways to adapt the program to fit the needs of the granting organization. Educational programs for youth, minorities and the disabled are all services that can enhance an archery program. The right grant will expand a program's offerings and increase the public good at the same time.

Schools, Parks and Recreation Departments, and Wildlife Management Agencies are suitable sources of grant money. There probably will be someone within a government agency who is responsible for identifying and submitting grant proposals. Locate that person and determine what opportunities they are pursuing. Describe the program's needs and ask if there are funding opportunities available.

It's important to be creative. Keep an open mind and maximize the communications with the program's partners. Teamwork can accomplish more than working separately.

Defining the Program Goals and Objectives

Grants are given to accomplish specific goals. It is the responsibility of the grantee to define the objectives and scope of the grant-funded project. It is important to be specific and factual in defining a program. Strategically, grant funded projects

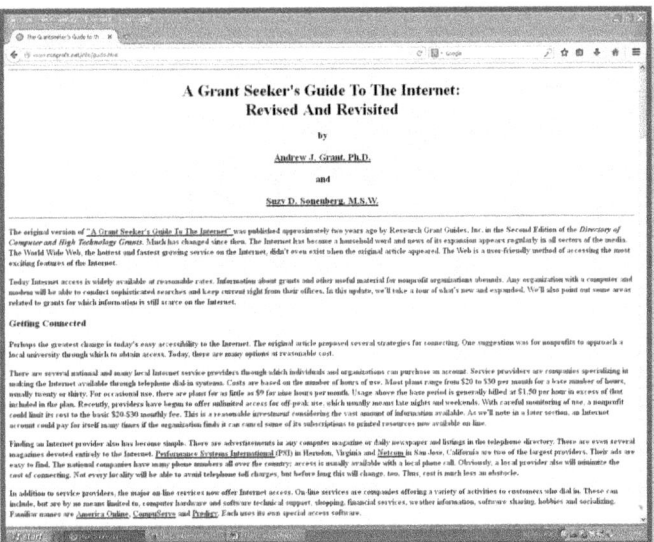

should be aimed at improving or expanding existing activities. Because grants have many uncertainties, including the time and amount of funding, it's not a good idea to use grant money for everyday operating expenses.

Think of grants as an "add to" rather than a "primary" revenue source. Start by specifying the overall goal or mission statement of the program. For example, "This instruction program will teach basic archery skills to middle school students in the Tri-County area."

The next step is to define the specific tasks to be accomplished and the resources necessary to make them happen. Be precise at this stage. For example, list the location of the project, the principal people involved and their qualifications, the equipment required, other organizations providing services, the marketing plan, and plans for participant tracking and program evaluation. Each item should support the mission statement of the project. Develop a schedule of actions required. List dates, number of hours, staffing needs, publication deadlines, marketing distribution, administrative time, construction, installation and/or maintenance time. Be sure to factor in staff training, bookkeeping, participant tracking, and report creation.

Take all of these elements and create a budget for each item. Use a spreadsheet program to track and calculate the budget. Be very specific with each budget item. For example, don't just list "New bows, $1000.00," rather state, "10 ACME Deadeye bows, 66", 23# @ $99.99 ea. = $999.90 plus tax." Whenever possible, have a specific vendor in mind for each budget item and get an estimate for the items that will be needed. Be sure to include taxes, and shipping and handling charges that may add to the cost.

Budgets with lots of line items are easier to read if they are divided into subcategories that are individually subtotaled before being merged into a grand total (*see below*). Another advantage is that the grant giving organization may agree to fund just a part of your request and it is easier for them to do so if they can see the part of your request they can grant.

A properly designed budget will also serve as a financial roadmap for administrating the project. By tracking actual costs against projected costs, problems can be corrected sooner. The budget will be a key part of the grant application. The grantor will use the budget to evaluate the program's progress and disburse funds. Put a lot of effort into getting the budget right before writing grant applications.

Creating Your Grant Application

Each grant giving organization will have its own procedure for grant applications. Start out by contacting the grantor by mail or through the web. Request instructions on how to make the applica-

```
                    Pasadena Roving Archers
              Amateur Athletic Foundation of Los Angeles
                    Remaining Grant Budget Summary
                            9/14/04

Personnel
Level 1 Training  5 X $150.00/ Person              $  750.00
Level 2 Training 12 X $150.00/ Person                 1800.00

Equipment

Arm Guards                                         $  159.00
Fletching Jigs (6 X $150 EA)                          900.00
Bow Press                                             350.00
Bow Sights (30 @ $ 17.00 EA)                          628.09
Feather Stripper                                       10.00
Feather Trimmer                                        90.00
Feathers                                              200.00
Fletching Supplies                                    500.00
String Jig                                            100.00
Shooting Gloves (12 X $ 8.00 EA)                       96.00

General and Administrative

Outreach Materials and Travel Archery Program      $ 4058.02
```

tion. Many grantors start out by asking the potential applicant for a one-page letter describing the program. This brief overview typically includes the name and background of the requesting organization, a brief description of the proposed program, a listing of the target audience, and a broad scope indication of the scale of financing required. Because the grant application and approval process is long and work intensive, grantors use introductory letters to screen potential applicants. This first level look allows the grantor to determine if the proposed project falls within the scope of their interests. An early screening based on a simple letter can save everyone a lot of work later on.

If the grantor has an interest in your project, the next step is to complete a grant application. The grantor will provide specific instructions for the information it requires, the form in which it is to be presented, and the supporting documents needed. Here is where the effort in defining the goals and objectives for the program pays off. If the preparation is done well, most of the effort in filling out the submission will merely be in configuring the existing information to comply with the required grant application format.

Neatness counts when preparing a grant proposal. Grantors look at many applications. Try to make their job easier by following their forms and printing out all materials in clear type. Use quality paper, but don't go overboard with fancy colored papers and cumbersome folios. In the rare case that a grant application contains extensive information, the application may be bound or presented in a three-ring binder.

Grant applications often have deadlines. Be sure to comply with all of the required forms and dates. It may be helpful to use an express service or delivery receipt mail to confirm that the application package has arrived on time.

Preparing a grant application may be tedious, but it's not rocket science. It requires a detail-oriented person who can follow directions. Find someone in the organization that is eager to contribute time but may not be available to do range maintenance or other tasks. Grant proposal writing can be done at home, during the evening, or on weekends. This is an opportunity to get more people involved with the project.

Grant Approval and Funding

It's important to remember that grant giving organizations are in the business of donating money. Most foundations have a mandate to fund a specific number of dollars per year. Your application is important to them, but it is one of many. Be patient when waiting for a response to your submission.

Often the grantor has a board of directors which reviews and approves applications only a few times a year.

Expect to be notified of the application's status in a letter. If the proposal is denied, don't be discouraged. Read the letter carefully. They may even suggest a better time or way for you to get your project funded. If you have questions, contact the grantor's administrative staff. They are often helpful in helping you to create a more successful application later.

If your application is accepted, you will receive an acceptance letter and a grant contract. The grant contract is a document, prepared by the grantor, that spells out the terms of the grant project. In the contract, much of the language and descriptions that were used in the application will be employed to define the organization's responsibility in the grant. There will also be a budget, based on the grant application, modified or edited by the grantor's board.

Don't be surprised if the board approves only a portion of a project. They may have limited funds or other projects that have a higher priority. Be prepared to be flexible with the program to adapt to the resources provided. With proper planning, a project can be subdivided into independent "chunks" that can be operated separately. The grantor may require additional training for the project's staff. In some cases, the grantors themselves will offer the training sessions. In other cases, staff will be required to seek out and complete specified training programs. Classes in coaching techniques and/or safety procedures and first aid or instructor certifications may be required.

The grant contract will be signed by the principals of the organization and the grantor.

Making Progress Reports

It might be expected that upon signing the contract, the grantor issues a check, wishes you well and asks the recipient to let them know how things turn out. The reality is usually not that simple. The grant contract is an authorization for monies up to a specific amount and defined by specific budget categories. In the contract the grantee is required to produce reports, usually quarterly, on the goals, accomplishments, and expenses for the period. Upon approval of the report, the grantor will issue a check.

It is important to keep careful records of all grant related activities and expenses. Set up a separate bank account and bookkeeping file for grant monies. Keep all the receipts. The grantor will require that the organization submit copies of the receipts with the reports. In addition, many grant projects are subject to audit.

In reporting expenses, each item must fall into a budget category. When reporting, list the contract budget amount, the amount previously reported, the net amount available, and the amount requested. If the bookkeeping setup is based on the contract budget categories, reporting should be a simple matter. Reported expenses need to be stated to the penny and include shipping and taxes where appropriate. Every expense requires a receipt.

Keep track of all work hours by the project staff, both paid and volunteer hours. Also, record any special training or advancement by staff members. Many grants require demographic information about program participants. To insure that the demographic profile of the participants matches the goals of the grant, the organization may be asked to collect home zip codes, age, gender, race, and ethnicity data. Emphasize to the participants that this information is being complied to insure that grant monies are being spent appropriately and that the information will not be shared with other organizations. Also respect a participant's right to refuse to provide demographic data.

When filling out a report, be prepared to write a simple paragraph on the tasks completed during the reporting period. Also, write a short paragraph on the expectations for the next reporting period. These should reflect the goals and timetables described in the contract document.

Completing a Grant Funded Project

At the completion of the grant period a final report is required. Included in that report are all of the same types of information and supporting materials provided in the quarterly reports. Expect to write several paragraphs on the accomplishments of the project during the entire grant period. Include goals that were not completed during the grant period and an explanation of why they weren't. Describe difficulties that arose on the grant project and how those difficulties may be addressed in the future. Include a description of how the grant-funded project will benefit ongoing activities of the organization.

The final report includes an accounting of all monies spent, staff hours, and participant demographics. Any unspent money has to be returned to the grantor. The report needs to be both timely and accurate. Remember that there is a person at the receiving end of all reports. The clearer and more complete the paperwork, the more favorably the project will be received. Grant funding isn't for everyone. Successful grant proposals are the result of lots of planning and paperwork.

Finding a person or persons within an organization who have the drive and interest to pursue grants can be very rewarding. If 100 hours of your administrative work yields a $20,000 grant, that work is worth $200 per hour to the organization. Grant money can open new areas of program and facility development that would be unattainable otherwise. If there's a project that needs to be done and a lack of money is standing in the way, see if a grant can make that vision possible.

Chapter 9
Building Archery Participation and Club Membership

Maintaining a range and providing competitive opportunities requires a strong and active membership. While hunting forms the basis of many field archery club's membership, Pasadena, California is in the middle of a large urban area. Some of the Pasadena Roving Archers' members do hunt, even though they have to travel long distances to find legal game. Rather than depend on member interest in hunting, the club has found that its program of free archery instruction has formed the basis for expanding the local archery community, providing both club membership growth and financial stability.

As part of the park use agreement between the club and the City of Pasadena, Pasadena Roving Archers (PRA) offers free introductory archery classes to the public every Saturday morning. These classes were begun in the early 1960s by Ed Ryman, Wright Huff, Morey Miller, and Ken and Lyetta Clark. The founding teachers were not certified, except in their years of experience. Their dedication, however, set a standard for future instructors.

What started out as a small group with perhaps a dozen students on a busy day, has expanded into an active, multi-faceted archery education program serving up to 80 students at a time. Student archers, traveling from over 125 zip codes in Southern California, line up every Saturday for the *Safety and Orientation Class*, our four-week sequential *Archery Fundamentals Class*, and supervised shooting on the practice range.

These free programs see hundreds of new, first time archers in thousands of student-class contacts during the year. Many of the students are exploring the sport for the first time. They come in all ages and backgrounds. The club teaches children from 5

An Archery Fundamentals class out on the range.

Teaching Archery

to 18 years old. Adults range in age from college students to retirees. A high percentage of the participants are adult women. All are motivated by the challenge of directing an arrow to a target.

The Safety and Orientation Class is given to beginners who have never shot at the PRA range before. Even if they have shot elsewhere or, as is sometimes the case, having shot many years ago, all first time archers are required to take this class. The one and a half hour Safety and Orientation Class has three goals for first timers: to learn range safety rules, to learn basic shooting form, and to have fun.

After a warm up and stretching session, beginners are divided up into groups of 8-12 archers for instruction. Safe equipment handling, shooting line rules and range whistle commands are demonstrated and practiced. Students learn to shoot from a "T" stance with an emphasis on body alignment, smooth draw, and solid anchor. Many instructors include an archery game during the class. At the conclusion of the orientation class, new archers join the more experienced group for a "Balloon Round." Archers who burst a balloon may claim a prize inside.

The more advanced Archery Fundamentals Class was originally conceived by PRA President Mike Burnham as a six week sequential class in shooting form. Archery Fundamentals is now a 4 week class that more easily fits into the busy schedules of our participants. Subsequent specialty classes are offered in Olympic recurve target archery, compound bow archery and traditional longbow archery. The syllabus and course materials were developed by me and by members of the PRA teaching staff. Based on the fundamentals of the National Training System (NTS), students are lead through a progressive program of shooting skills. Additional topics include equipment choices, maintenance, selecting arrows, a bibliography, and archery resources. Students shoot practice tournaments on both 10 ring targets at fixed distances and on field targets at varying distances and terrain. The goals of the Archery Fundamentals and the specialized classes are to develop the skills of the archers; direct them to choosing and purchasing their own equipment; increase the participation in the club's tournament offerings; and to encourage membership in Pasadena Roving Archers.

Students who have completed the Safety and Orientation Class are invited to participate in our supervised shooting program. Archers shoot at 10 and 20 yards and are guided by the instructors in improving their shooting form. The Saturday classes provide an opportunity for students to ask the instructors for guidance on selecting equipment or setting up their new bow. The Saturday morning shoots have also proved to be a popular social time, as people get to know one another and share stories.

All of the instructors are volunteers and club members. They are USA Archery certified instructors and coaches and follow the USA Archery guidelines for safety and shooting form. It is the

An Archery Fundamentals class graduates!

staff's belief that starting the student out with the correct form from the very beginning reduces the number of bad habits that have to be unlearned later. As one instructor said, "Beginning students will make more progress in their archery on the very first day than they will on any future day."

The value in this instruction program, and the opportunity for other archery clubs and archery retailers, is in the use of free instruction as a lure to draw new participants to the sport. All of our introductory programs are free and the club provides all of the recurve bow equipment at no charge. The only obstacle to joining in is just showing up. Expanding the number of people participating in archery expands the number of potential club members as well as the market for archery equipment and accessories.

For participants, this free program is a great way to try a new sport without the expense of gearing up and paying for lessons or joining a team. Parents are thrilled that there is an activity for their kids, that cost the parents nothing and in which they can play, too. By reducing the barriers to entry, people are willing to try something new.

For the club, the free archery classes have increased the goodwill of the club in the community. Our membership is growing and diversifying. We add multiple members and families every month. By offering a 300 rRound, the participation at our tournaments is up. We are adding more instructors too. Students who have completed the program are being certified to teach the next group of newcomers.

In a broader context, these free archery classes, and others like them, are bringing the fun and challenge of archery to a whole new audience. Kids, who may not have found their place in team sports, can be successful with archery. Adults are finding an activity that they can share with their children and not just sit on the sidelines. Many adults are coming to archery from other sporting disciplines including fencing, marshal arts and firearms shooting. They are enjoying the competitive challenge and the social network that archery provides.

Pasadena Roving Archers has found that about 3% to 8% of first timers stick with archery long enough to purchase equipment, join the club and shoot in tournaments. While that may not seem like a big number, it is consistent with industry figures for participants in camp and youth archery programs. The high volume of archery students PRA sees in its free archery programs translates over time into a solid base of committed archers who will benefit the sport as participants, competitors and retail consumers.

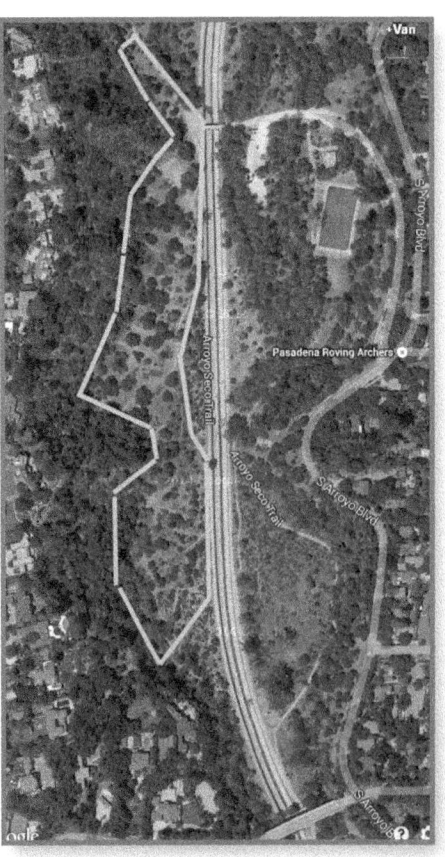

(Above) The view from the extreme end of the PRA range shown at the top of the Google Earth image (Right). The Pasadena Archery Range is located in the Lower Arroyo Seco Park in the City of Pasadena, just south of the Rose Bowl stadium.

Chapter 10
Range Location and Maintenance

Archery ranges, especially field ranges, take up a lot of space. Whether indoors or outdoors, there's a lot of real estate to deal with when setting up or running an archery range. On top of that, keeping the range facilities in top condition is an on going job.

Range Layout

Range operations start with the range layout. For most clubs, pro shops, and recreation department ranges, the layout was defined a long time ago. At the Pasadena Archery Range, operated and maintained by Pasadena Roving Archers, the original field archery range location was established, along with the club itself in 1935. The range is sited in a native oak woodland on the west side of the Arroyo Seco (Spanish for "dry gulch"), a continuous, north-south strip of natural parkland that runs from the mountains behind Pasadena to the adjoining cities to the south. The Arroyo is nearly a hundred feet deep, with a flat floor and a concrete lined open storm channel that follows the path of the river that originally cut the valley in the first place.

Occupying about 13 acres, the Pasadena archery range has 28 field target butts, a sighting-in target, and six practice butts. A temporary 3-D range is located north of the fixed targets and is only available for use 13 times a year. Classes are held on the range every Saturday morning and tournaments are held every Sunday morning. The range is un-fenced and open to the public without charge or supervision after 2:30PM on weekends and from sunrise to sunset on weekdays. Archers using the range during the week are required by the range rules to shoot only at the designated target butts, stay within the shooting lanes, and not shoot from any point behind the farthest distance marker on any shooting lane.

The City of Pasadena maintains the general property of the range area through its public works department. Under the PRA operating agreement with the city, Pasadena Roving Archers pays for and maintains all of the archery related facilities on the range including the target butts, shooting lanes, bow racks, permanent seating, and shooting distance markers.

In a natural setting with trees and shrubs on the property, sightlines need to be maintained from the shooting position to the target permitting additional visual clearance to the side of the targets for safety. Allowance needs to be made for the arcs of flying arrows so that no tree limbs obstruct those paths to the target. Periodically, the range captain needs to survey the range, noting sightline and arrow flight clearance issues for range maintenance.

Lighting For outdoor ranges used during the

day, the lighting comes from the Sun. Shooting lanes need to be aligned so that during active shooting times, the archers are aiming with the Sun behind them or to the side. Archers should not be shooting while looking into the Sun. For target archery ranges, the preferred range orientation is for the archers to shoot from south to north (in the northern hemisphere). For field archery ranges, the orientation is optimum when shooting from south to north or from east to west for morning shoots. The majority of the field archery targets at the Pasadena range are shot from east to west with a substantial hill behind the target butt positions for protection.

Some outdoor ranges offer nighttime shooting, extending the time for archers to use the range. The use of artificial lighting will add additional utility and maintenance costs to range operations. Nighttime lighting should be aimed downward to include the targets but not be aimed into the air to minimize light pollution and make the most of the lighting budget expense. Ranges looking to add night lighting may want to see if a solar or wind energy solution will be a cost effective energy source while reducing environmental impact.

Safety The range layout needs to have appropriate backstops or extended distance behind the target butts for public safety and to accommodate missed arrows. The USA Archery specification is that there be a minimum of 50 yards clear behind the target butts if the land is flat. The NFAA requirement is that the distance behind the butt be no less that half the longest distance on that particular target. For example, on a 50 yard target, the required minimum additional distance behind the butt is 25 yards. Hillsides can form a natural barrier that may shorten the needed backstop distance. Trees and other forested areas do not provide adequate backstop safety so the distances specified for flat ground should be used in the woods.

The range layout should provide for the safety of participants, spectators, and passers by. All spectators should be located safely behind a waiting line and out of the way of competitors. Passers by and those not involved in the archery action should be able to walk by the range safely and without impacting the archery operations.

This is a particular issue at the PRA range. Because the range is unfenced and the park is used for a wide range of non-archery activities, there are potential points of conflict of use on the range property. PRA has been working with the community and the city government to implement natural barriers and signage to discourage non-participants from wandering onto the archery range while the range is in use.

Placing a range in a "peninsular" location so that the range is a destination and not on a thoroughfare goes a long way to alleviating potential conflicts of land use.

Archery ranges need a lot of materials and equipment to support archery operations. Secure and convenient storage on site is essential. Common steel shipping containers are a popular storage option. Shipping containers are sturdy and weatherproof. They are also unsightly and not always of an appropriate size for storage needs. I have seen a composite storage facility made by placing two shipping containers parallel to each other with a space of 10-20 feet between the containers. A roof structure is then built over the entire space including the shipping containers producing a barn like building. Filling in the ends, adding doors, windows

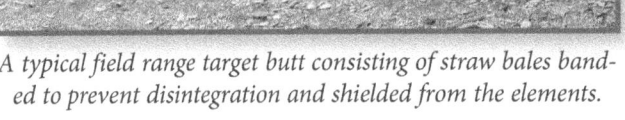

A typical field range target butt consisting of straw bales banded to prevent disintegration and shielded from the elements.

and lighting completes the structure.

At PRA we have been hit by burglars who have attacked our shipping container with battery powered cutting tools. (They even brought cutting oil to cool the blades while breaking in.) If you have a container(s) look for aftermarket security devices to attach to the container's doors to reduce the chances of theft.

Because archery range targets, butts and support materials may be bulky, finding off site storage may be required. Pick a location that is secure, nearby and easy to access during evenings and weekends when most volunteers are available to help with club duties. Be cautious of locating club storage on private property that is tied to just one club member. If that person has a change in circumstances, you may need to relocate materials on short notice. Club owned property, rented facilities and public land access through a long term operating agreement are your best bets for off site storage. At "Public Storage" type rental facilities the monthly bulls can add up quickly.

For more information about setting up an archery range, see the Archery Trade Association (ATA) Archery Park Guide: www.archerytrade.org/uploads/documents/ATA-Archery-Park-Guide-Final.pdf. This PDF file is packed with information and detailed case studies of range set up and construction.

Field Maintenance

Grounds maintenance is an ongoing task. Natural settings create the dual issues of nurturing those plants you want to grow while keeping in check those plants that are pests. On a field range, the principle plant maintenance issues are keeping the shooting lanes and walking paths clear while maintaining the character of the landscape. Generally, string trimmers take care of the weeds while pole saws and loping shears will keep branches in check.

If your site has a lawn grass field, you can expect a lot of regular turf maintenance. Watering, fertilizing, mowing, and trimming are all part of lawn care. In most cases, even for an all volunteer club, it will be best to hire a professional service to care for a turf field. You can use automated sprinklers for watering but mowing and trimming a large area is best left to the pros.

Lane/line markers have traditionally used powdered white lime, purchased at a home improvement store and applied with a hand pushed machine. Lime is a toxic material and now is often banned by local ordinance for field marking use. Ground limestone is inert and available in 50 pound bags. Look for an athletic field supplier in your area to purchase field marking powder. If you have a place to store the bags, purchasing a pallet of bags from a manufacturer will provide years of supply at very low cost per bag. Shipping costs can be an issue as the weight of the bags adds up.

General range clean up is a task well suited to volunteer club members. Start by having an adequate number of trash receptacles placed in convenient locations around the range to reduce loose trash buildup. We've found that one of the greatest sources of litter is used target faces, cans, bottles, and balloons around the target butts. In addition, the impact of the arrows striking the butts and their removal produces a cloud of shredded straw on the ground around the target. Regular raking up of the

This is the steel strapping caddy used to hold the materials and equipment for strapping bales together on the range.

litter and putting it into trash bags is an ongoing task.

Plan regularly scheduled work days for the club membership to keep things tidy. Add a social component to the work day with a potluck or snacks. Have plenty of hand tools, gloves and trash bags on hand for the work day. Be sure to have a clip board with a sign in sheet so members get credit for their work hours. At PRA, the city provides trash pickup from designated areas and bins. Be sure to have a strategy for disposing of the collected material to an off-site location.

Target Butt Maintenance

The PRA field target range uses compressed straw bale target butts. At one time, the club had its own hydraulic bale compressor. Club members took ordinary straw bales and repacked them using steel bands. The compressor was lost during the club house fire in 2002. Since then we have used commercially made archery backstop bales ordered and shipped from a supplier in Washington State. To consolidate shipping costs, we order bales in truck load quantities and currently we store surplus bales at an off site location.

We stack the bales three high and strap the bales together using steel bands and a commercial band strapping tool that tightens the bands and crimps on a band connector. The bales are further strapped to the steel posts that hold up the protective roof over the bales. We have found that some archers like to shoot at plastic bottles and other targets set up just at the edge of the bale. When these archers miss the targets, the arrows hit the tightly tensioned steel bands, cracking them and bursting the bales. There is an ongoing effort by the club to keep unsupervised archers from damaging the bales.

The bales are very heavy and the volunteer work crews who do bale maintenance need to team up in order to lift the bales into place. Old bales are broken apart, packed in plastic trash bags and taken off site. Although bale straw can be used as mulch, it takes a long time to break down and the city of Pasadena considers bale straw to be litter, not native organic material. In other areas, where it is permitted, old bales can be sold to backyard farmers as mulch.

Straw bales will deteriorate over time if the bale is not protected from the rain and Sun. Water will soak in from the top of the bale, rotting the straw inside. We provide a weatherproof shed roof over each of the bale stacks. The structure is made up of two steel pipe posts with a cantilevered top bracket that holds the roof in place over the bales. A wood and plywood roof structure, covered in heavy roofing material protects the bales. All of the steel structure is behind the bale stack and there is an additional layer of heavy rubber conveyor belt material behind the bales to catch any arrow that might get through a softened bale as well as to protect arrows from striking the steel support posts. An additional strip of conveyor belt material covers the wood fascia board at the front of the roof covering to keep ill-shot arrows from sticking in the

Folding bow racks built by PRA member Frank Cerimele. The tubing is EMT conduit and foam insulation is used to cushion the racks and protect the bows.

wood.

The open, cantilevered design of the roof shed, makes for a clean appearance, allows plenty of room around the bales for maintenance work and avoids having posts on either side of the bale that might be struck by arrows. In the mild climate of Southern California, bales last about 18-24 months before needing replacement.

Round or square format foam target butts are commonly used on target archery ranges. Plans for building portable wood stands for these backstops are readily available on-line. Once constructed the wood stand should be given a protective finish. While paint is an easy option, paint doesn't last well outdoors and will need to be repainted frequently. A better choice is exterior wood stain, a product that will last and doesn't peel.

Foam targets are not very durable outdoors so you should expect to put them away after every use. Out of the weather, on-site storage is needed to make the most of foam backstops. Be certain that you use a back stay on the backstop frame when you put the target in place. A simple rope attached to the top of the foam backstop and tied to a tent stake behind the target stand will prevent the backstop from falling forward off of the stand, damaging any arrows that are in the backstop and possibly causing injury to anyone who is near by.

One or two extra tall backstop stands can be constructed and used close to the shooting line for blank bale practice. The tall stand raises the backstop so that an archer can hold the proper posture for long distance shooting. With a standard height backstop stand, an archer needs to aim downward to prevent arrows from flying over the target at close distance.

Bow Racks

While many target archers have personal bow stands, it is often convenient for the range to provide group-use racks behind the shooting line and at the target butts for field ranges. Permanent bow racks can be made of wood or steel with cushioned hooks or rails to hold the bows.

Temporary, folding "X frame" bow racks can be inexpensively made from electrical conduit and covered with tubular foam insulation to protect the bows. "X frame" bow racks made out of wood tend

Concrete test cylinders, donated from a construction site, are buried vertically, flush with the ground and the tops are used as shooting position markers on the field range.

to fall apart over time and are not recommended. Providing bow racks for all of your participants insures safe storage of the bows and improves range safety. All archers who are not actively shooting should keep their bows on the bow rack. The Range Master can easily see if the bows are properly stored.

Shooting Stakes and Lines

Distance markers are placed on the field range to mark the shooting locations for the archers as they move through the course. Markers should be made of a permanent material and be embedded into the ground for safety and accuracy. At PRA we use concrete testing cylinders cast as part of large construction projects and normally used to test the strength of the concrete material in a project. Many more of these cylinders are cast than are actually used for testing so surplus cylinders are often available from construction sites and testing laboratories. Cast concrete pavers, available at home improvement sores may also be used for shooting markers. Wood stakes should only be used as temporary markers as they are not durable enough for permanent installation.

Here's the interior of our storage facility. You can see that space is at a premium.

is relatively simple. Doors that might open to the shooting area can be equipped with one way locks that permit safe exits but prevent passers by from entering the range accidently from the outside.

Temporary indoor ranges, located in gyms and other mixed use recreation buildings are more likely to have doors that may provide unsafe access. Signage is not enough to keep people from authorized entrance. More positive traffic control will be needed for potentially dangerous doors. In devising a security scheme, remember to take no action that might prove to be a barrier for occupants exiting the building in an emergency.

The shooting distances and colors of the markings for each of the Field, Hunter and Animal rounds are specified in the NFAA rules. Additional markers should be provided for cub and youth distances. On the PRA range, we have added Metric markings on our longest distance targets for archers who want to practice for FITA/WA tournaments. We have a circular stencil that we place over the concrete marker and use spray paint to color the concrete.

The number marking is done with white paint and number stencils with the correct distances marked in yards except for the shortest target where the distances are marked in feet. Metric distances are stenciled in yellow paint on green concrete markers. We have found these markers to be very durable and the painting will last several years before having to be refreshed.

Indoor Facilities

Indoor ranges allow year-round, all-weather shooting. While there are a handful of indoor ranges that will permit shooting out to 70 meters, the majority of facilities are set up to shoot 18 meters or 20 yards. Either way, the space needed for an indoor range makes for a lot of empty cubic feet that have to be heated, cooled, and maintained.

Securing the access to the shooting area while preventing accidental intrusion into the arrow flight path is the first issue in indoor range layout. In a permanent indoor range facility, controlling access

Backstops

Permanent indoor ranges often have a continuous arrow catching backstop along the target wall. Tightly bound layers of plastic foam are commonly used. Some ranges use surplus telephone books, stacked with their page ends toward the shooting line as a backstop material. Straw bales can be used but straw is messy and can harbor outdoor critters that may be best if left outside. Because there can be gaps between a stack of foam bales, you'll want to line the backstop wall, behind the bales with ¾ inch plywood sheeting to protect the building's interior finish surface. Target faces are attached directly to the backstop material without the need for additional target butts in front.

Some interior range operators add movable target butts in addition to the backstop wall to permit archers to shoot at various distances at the same time. Mobile butts can be especially helpful for mixed skill level class sessions.

Temporary indoor ranges usually use a Kevlar safety curtain behind portable target butts. Getting a safety curtain securely in place can be a challenge. The curtain material is heavy and needs to be supported at the top along its entire length. Some venues have stretched a steel cable from wall to wall and suspended the curtain from the cable. Cable of more than 20 feet in length will need multiple supports along the span. Attaching support brackets, poles or cables suspended from the ceiling will prevent sliding the curtain along the horizontal cable. Such a mounting system will require that the curtain be attached to the support cable with clips that will have to be done and un-done with each installation. A theatrical retractable curtain mechanism may also be used, albeit at considerable expense.

Safety curtains can be supported by pole columns with cross tubes of the type used at convention centers for creating sales booths. Pole supports need to be adequately braced with guy ropes to prevent them from tipping over. Some gymnasiums have embedded pole sockets and bracing anchors in the floor that can be used with the appropriate hardware. Sandbags can also be used to provide stability and support for a pole mounted curtain.

Safety curtains need to be placed at least five (5) feet away from any parallel wall behind the curtain to allow enough space for the curtain to deflect when struck by an arrow. The curtain should drag on the floor to prevent arrows from sliding underneath the curtain. Tubular sandbags along the base can also help to prevent undershoots.

Safety curtains work with larger diameter arrows shot from relatively low-powered bows such as student archery gear. Small diameter arrows shot by compound bows and competitive recurve bows will travel right through a typical safety curtain. Multiple layers of curtains may help to prevent shoot throughs but it is better to use a full wall backstop for higher powered equipment.

Indoor Lighting

The lighting of most indoor spaces is from the ceiling pointed straight down. Downward pointing lights do little to illuminate vertically mounted target faces. Additional lighting fixtures, mounted in the ceiling and pointed at the targets will help archers to see their targets. If you suspend lights from a bar or track, be sure to add a deflector board to protect the light fixtures from stray arrows. Check to see that there are no lights in the shooting area that shine directly into the archer's eyes. Provide deflectors or re-aim lighting that might be distracting to the archers.

Note the uniform lighting on the targets. The wall behind the targets is covered with foam material to stop stray arrows.

Indoor Shooting Lines

There are multiple ways to mark the waiting, shooting, and target lines on the floor of an indoor facility. Permanent line markings can be made with paint or ceramic tile. I've seen a beautiful indoor range with a light toned hardwood floor and lines marked with inlayed dark toned hardwood.

Temporary lines on wood surfaces can be made with painter's tape. Regular masking tape should be avoided as it degenerates quickly and can be difficult to remove. Tape should be avoided for long term use as tape wears out and can leave a sticky residue on the floor that is difficult to clean.

Interior and exterior concrete surfaces can be temporarily marked with sidewalk chalk. Chalk is easy to apply, environmentally harmless and is easy to remove.

When setting up a temporary range in a gymnasium the existing painted lines for other indoor sports may be adopted for archery use. When there are multiple lines painted on the floor, finding the correct line for archery may be confusing to archers. Adding traffic cones along the preferred line can help to avoid confusion. One enterprising program bought a long rubber walking strip and painted the lines on it. It was rolled up for storage when not in use.

Training Supports

Interior facilities allow for the inclusion of lots of

training support equipment that would otherwise be subject to damage outdoors. Planning the layout of an indoor range to permit more sophisticated archery training can be a real plus for your facility.

One of the simplest training aids is a mirror. The use of mirrors is an essential part of the training process for nearly all top archery competitors. Large, dance studio type mirrors can be installed along a wall. Mirrors can also be mounted on moving stands so that the angle of view can be adjusted by the archer or the coach. Having both fixed and movable mirrors on the range can allow for very precise feedback on posture and movement.

Glass mirrors can pose a hazard if they break. Mirrors made with a plastic substrate are available from athletic facility suppliers. Mylar mirrors can be mounted on the wall with double stick adhesive tape or they can be fitted into frames for fixed or mobile applications. Mylar mirrors are often times not perfectly flat but they do provide valuable visual feedback with the assurance of additional safety.

Video and computer imaging and feedback can be more easily implemented indoors rather than outside. First there is access to electrical power, necessary to run electronic equipment reliably for long periods of time. Second is lighting control. For video and still images to be useful, proper lighting is needed. Exterior lighting under the sun can be too contrasty, obscuring critical details in glare or shadows. Inside the lighting can be controlled yielding more useful images.

In an indoor facility you can install multiple cameras from a variety of points of view, whose images can be recorded simultaneously for a more comprehensive picture of an athlete's performance. Indoor facilities can provide a fixed location for video equipment and lighting that simplify its use by coaches and athletes.

Computer analysis of athlete performance is pretty much standard practice today in most sporting disciplines including archery. Mobile device apps and more sophisticated desktop software are all being used by coaches to analyze and improve archer's performances. Indoor setting make this process much easier as lighting control makes for

The fluorescent lights give general overall good illumination while the spots make sure the target faces are well lit. Often a fascia board is put up to protect the units from stray arrows.

clearer images and electronic screens are much easier to see indoors.

Electronic shot timers are an essential part of any target archery competition. Indoor venues allow the operator to permanently install shot timers for both tournaments and practice sessions. Tournament shot timers are also available as an app for tablets. For or practice use, some method of controlling the volume of the signal horn can be helpful.

While an archery range is not a fitness gym, having some exercise equipment available on-site may be helpful for a facility that trains competitive archers. Free weights, stretch bands, medicine balls and exercise balls can all be easily employed in a training program without taking up a lot of floor space. Adding a weight bench with lat pull down capability is probably as far as an archery facility should go in setting up a fitness area at the range.

Meeting/Conference Room

Space is always at a premium in an indoor facility. Every square foot costs money to buy/rent, heat and cool, and maintain. When laying out an indoor facility try to find enough room to set up a meeting room separate from the active shooting area. A meeting room large enough to hold 20 or so people will be invaluable in ongoing operations. Have enough tables and chairs available to set up the room for meetings, training, conferences, parties and even for use as a parent "corral."

Birthday parties and social events can be a big part of a club's/business's outreach efforts. A sepa-

Replacing the bales on a field range requires many hands from multiple work parties to do the heavy lifting required.

rate space for food and drink service can help to keep the shooting area cleaner. Parents appreciate a place where they can hold a youth birthday party with a controlled interior space. You can add to the bottom line with water, soft drink, and snack vending whether by machine or over a counter. Coordinate with a nearby pizza restaurant for take out party food.

Adding video playback and sound system capabilities to a meeting space makes it more useful for training and team meetings. Whether for athlete training or instructor certification classes, an indoor space with comfortable seating, work tables and AV support will get a lot of use.

Restrooms are a necessary part of a facility but usually are an afterthought at best. I once attended a retail consultant's presentation where he visited stores and to evaluate their effectiveness. One of the first places that he looked was at the restrooms, both for the public and for the staff. Clean and orderly facilities spoke clearly about the management's attitude towards the people it served. Restrooms don't need to be fancy but they should be clean and regularly serviced.

Indoor ranges also provide an opportunity to have a workshop for bow and arrow maintenance. For a club, running a full service pro shop is not really appropriate but having a place to do repairs and help club members with their equipment is an important component of your service. A maintenance area could be equipped to cut arrow shafts, glue points and fletch arrows, build strings and have a bow press for compound bow servicing.

Club Organization and Maintenance

Archery clubs are usually structured around volunteer labor and committee-based planning and supervision. At PRA the staffing starts with the Range Captain. The Range Captain is responsible for surveying the condition of the range(s), organizing range work parties, inventorying and ordering target faces and 3-D animals, and maintaining the target butts in shootable condition.

Periodically the Range Captain and the club President walk the range and make a list of items that need attention. The Range Captain then sends an email to the membership notifying members of a scheduled work day. In advance of work days the Range Captain secures all of the tools and materials needed to complete the tasks on the range condition list. On the day of a work day, a roster is created of the members attending so that they can get credit for their work hours against their annual work obligations to the club. The Range Captain supervises the range work and checks off the tasks as completed. Often a work day will conclude with a pot luck meal or other refreshments as a thank you to the volunteers.

The pasting of target faces onto cardboard backings is a constant range maintenance task. If you have a workshop area at the range, installing a 36 inch paper cutter can be a big help in sizing cardboard sheets. Otherwise a utility knife and a straight edge are needed to trim the cardboard to fit. Buying a big paper cutter can go a long way to speeding the target preparation task and reduce the potential for injuries from handling a sharp knife. If you use canned spray adhesive to mount the faces onto the backing, be sure to spray and paste outside to avoid breathing toxic glue fumes.

Some tasks may be beyond the range of skills or time to be completed by a volunteer crew.

Professional staff may be required for heavy projects and extensive maintenance. At PRA, the park land is owned and maintained by the City of Pasadena. The city hires professional crews to do annual weed abatement clearing for fire control on the property. The city also provides trash bin service on a weekly basis. Occasionally, the city will hire a professional crew for landscape and other park improvements. While the city maintains the park land, the club pays for, installs and maintains all archery-related facilities within the park. The city has no investment of time or materials in the range itself.

Professional Facility Maintenance

A professional facility such as an archery pro shop or a private range for hire will not have the benefit of volunteer labor. All maintenance work will need to be done by a professional staff; either part of the regular crew, independent maintenance contractors, or a combination of both.

Within a small professional business there are a number of roles that will need to be addressed. The first is general business management. The business manager sets the strategic directions of the business and then makes the operational decisions that support the goals of the business.

Range Management deals with the overall condition and operation of the range. The range manager ensures that the range is in safe operating condition, orders range supplies and materials as needed, and manages the range maintenance staff. The range manager may also serve as the scheduler for range use during the week as well as assuring that proper staffing is available to accommodate individual and group shooting sessions.

The *Range Supervisor* or *Director of Shooting* is the staff person assigned to directly supervise the activities on the archery range during use. Whether for practice, group classes, or tournament competition, a Range Supervisor should be present at all times of active shooting. The Range Supervisor should hold a USA Archery Level 2 or higher certification and may additionally hold a USA Archery judge certification. For a professional business, the Range Supervisor should additionally hold a First Aid/CPR card.

Grounds and/or building maintenance in a pro-

Fletching and refletching program arrows is a frequent task, one that requires the dedication of a few club members.

fessional facility will usually be handled by a professional independent maintenance contracting service. Grounds maintenance will not require the specialized archery knowledge needed for keeping the archery facilities in shape. The conditions of your grounds and indoor facilities reflect directly on the public's perception of the quality of your business. Keeping things fresh and well maintained will go a long way to supporting your business image.

Target maintenance should be done by someone with specific archery knowledge. The target butts and back stops need to be checked regularly for soft spots and repaired or replaced as needed. Be certain that the target butt materials are securely fastened to assure that the butt won't fall down during use.

Paper target cutting and pasting is a thankless but necessary part of regular range operations. You can foist this task off on to new employees or maybe you can talk some of your JOAD club members into having a target pasting party. Having fresh targets available as needed is essential to smooth operations.

3-D targets can get pretty beat up. There are target fixing kits that include chemicals to make foam fillers for damaged animals. Working with these materials is potentially hazardous. All work with the chemicals should be done outdoors and by qualified adults. Staff members with an artistic streak may be recruited to repaint the 3-D targets as needed. At the end of the target's useful range life, you may be able to sell the used targets to customers who want to have a target at home for practice and are not overly concerned about its condition.

In a small business and often in a medium-sized business, the business manager often takes on many of the operational tasks that would be delegated in a larger company. (I had a friend many years ago who was the president of a medium-sized electronics parts manufacturing company. His title on his business card read 'Janitor") A business owner needs to be able and willing to do any task necessary to support the business.

Combining an Archery Range with Other Sports Venues or Skills Training

Archery ranges located in public parks often share the park land with other athletic facilities and recreational uses. Park facilities are often laid out for safety and traffic flow but there is usually little synergy between venues and occupancies in a park setting. From a marketing standpoint, an archery range in a park will be seen by other park users but there is no active cross promotion between sponsoring sports.

An archery range, indoor, outdoor or both, is usually part of an archery pro shop facility. Archery ranges take up a lot of space and for a retail operation, the return on operations on a dollars-per-square-foot basis for an archery range can be hard to justify. Maximizing the service income from an archery range with public shooting, instruction, parties and tournaments can make the space more profitable. Outdoor shooting sports facilities that may include a gun firing range, trap, skeet and sporting clays shotgun ranges. An archery range can be part of a professional range complex. Combining shooting sports together can build interest across disciplines. When a firearms enthusiast tires of spending $200 per session on ammunition, the relatively low operating cost of archery may have some appeal. Crossbows also fit better into a firearms environment where range operations and safety procedures are more suited to a trigger-based weapon. Crossbows are currently the fastest growing segment of the archery business. Having a crossbow friendly range will be attractive to customers.

Another option for multiple sport facilities is athletic training centers. One archery training center in Southern California has combined archery with martial arts under one roof (in separate rooms) to maximize the efficiency of business operations and increase the variety of traffic into the business. Located in a business office park, many of the surrounding businesses in the park are learning and training centers. Math, science, reading, and general school skills training are joined by fitness and yoga studios within the business park. There is a synergy of interests among the business tenants that attracts customers to the complex and exposes each business to a wider audience.

City/Landlord Issues

It could be said that in the best of all worlds, the operator of an archery facility would own the real estate on which it is located. The advantages of ownership are numerous including: control of the land use, freedom of operating hours, and the ability to implement improvements. With land ownership there are also responsibilities including mortgage payments, taxes, and upkeep. But the freedom to make operational choices without external interference is a big positive for owning your own facility.

For most organizations and businesses, land ownership for an archery range is not a practicality. The alternative is to rent land from a private landlord or to set up an operating agreement with a local government for the use of public parkland.

At Pasadena Roving Archers, the parkland on which the range is located is owned by the City of Pasadena. Since 1935 PRA has had some form of facility operating agreement with the city for the use of the range. The operating agreement has been updated and revised from time to time as situations for the city and the club has changed over the years. Broadly stated the operating agreement specifies the land area to be used; the times and terms of use by the club and by the general public; the responsibilities for maintenance of both the land and the range facilities; and the terms for the payment by PRA for the use of the park.

Whether the range property is privately or publicly owned, it is important for the range operator to have a cooperative and productive relationship with the land owner.

Outdoor Archery Ranges on Private Land

For outdoor ranges located on private land, the relationship with the landlord starts with the lease. When negotiating a lease, be sure that all of the terms and expected responsibilities are clearly defined. Use a realtor or real estate attorney to help you with the document. Conflicts that may arise later are usually caused by a lack of specificity in the lease document. Remember that "assumption is the mother of mistake." Get things right the first time.

Define the term of the lease, and the date and times of lease payments. It is particularly important to specify maintenance tasks and responsibilities. Be sure that the neighbors know about the use of the property as an archery range. "Out of the loop" neighbors can cause real problems if arrows start flying onto their property. You will be required to provide liability insurance for your operations. If there are buildings on the property, the landlord will be responsible for basic fire insurance but you will need additional coverage for your improvements and possessions on the site.

An archery range is best when it has a secure perimeter with controlled access for club members and/or customers. Be sure you know the condition of any existing fencing and any restrictions on installing fencing on the property. Access to the range should be controlled with gates and a professional staff during business hours.

Indoor Archery Ranges in Private Buildings

An indoor archery range located on private property, whether an independent facility, club operated or as part of an archery pro shop will require a lease agreement similar to an outdoor range with additional terms for utilities, signage, access, and interior improvements. Leasehold improvements to the interior of the building have a number of options.

Some landlords will "build to suit" putting in all the interior walls and finishes. Such an agreement gives you a move-in space at the price of a higher lease. Other landlords may offer a "four wall lease" where the building space is completely empty and you will have to pay for and install all interior walls and fittings. With a four wall lease, you will have to remove all of your "improvements" at the end of the lease period, an additional expense.

I have yet to see an indoor archery range of any longevity that doesn't have arrow damage in the ceiling and walls. Be prepared to pay for such damage at the end of the lease period.

The building owner will usually hold a basic fire insurance policy to cover the building structure and improvements made by the owner. As a tenant you will need to have insurance coverage on your own contents of the building as well as a business liability policy covering your operations. Your landlord may also require a certificate of insurance naming them as additional loss payee in the case of a suit. You may want to also include an additional umbrella policy to cover extraordinary losses. Check with your insurance agent and with the building's management for insurance requirements. Insurance expense can be a very large part of operating overhead.

Your lease document should specify the assignment of maintenance responsibilities on the property for the landlord and the tenant. Be sure you have the maintenance obligations clearly defined before signing your lease commitment.

Outdoor Archery Ranges on Public Land

Setting up an outdoor archery range on public land can have several different types of use agreements. As with private property, a lease agreement can be used to establish the terms of the land use. Another type of arrangement is the operating agreement which permits the range property to be used at a specific time and for specific activities by payment of a defined fee for use. The operating agreement format may reduce the cost of use of the land when compared with a straight lease but at the price of a lack of control over the property. With an operating agreement, the cost of any improvements and buildings must be born by the operator without retaining any ownership of the improvements

Don't get so focussed on the seated members of your city council ...

themselves. Operating agreements are usually short term with options to renew.

The governing body controlling private land can be federal, state, county, and/or local. Within the governing body can be elected/appointed commissions and a professional staff that are responsible for setting the terms of an operating agreement and administrating those terms on behalf of the governing body. It is important to maintain a positive and cooperative relationship with the administrative staff. Often a simple phone call to an administrator can take care of an issue quickly when there is a good working relationship.

Maintenance responsibilities need to be clearly defined in an operating agreement. Each party needs to know what maintenance tasks are expected by the parties. At PRA, the maintenance of all archery-related equipment and supplies at the range are the responsibility of the club. The City of Pasadena is responsible for all grounds maintenance. The city specifically prohibits PRA from doing any cutting or trimming of plants, trees, and landscape elements. PRA is also prohibited from making any structural improvements or constructing of any buildings on the property without the City's permission.

The operating agreement requires that the operator provide the city with a certificate of insurance, naming the city as additional loss payee, in a specified amount of coverage. In some cases, the owners of adjacent properties may also need to be covered by the operator's insurance policy. In addition to using the USA Archery and/or NFAA club insurance policies, an operator may need to secure additional insurance or an "umbrella" policy to cover extreme contingencies. As archery is an inherently safe sport and losses incurred due to archery operations are very low, insurance costs should be reasonable. However, because archery is a shooting sport, many government officials and members of the public may perceive archery activities to be more dangerous than they truly are.

Negotiating an operating agreement with a governmental body can be a tedious and time consuming proposition. As of this writing, Pasadena Roving Archers is in its fourth year of negotiations and hearings with the City of Pasadena to secure a new operating agreement for the use of the Pasadena archery range. The park in which the range is located is a natural area in the center of a large urban population, not only of the city of Pasadena but the surrounding communities as well. There are many park users who are not archers and the archery range is not secured by a fenced perimeter. That means that non-archers may come onto the range property unfettered and at any time. Balancing the needs of the archers, the general public, natural preservation and public safety makes for a complex series of issues to be

... that you forget that often the people supporting you and the staff of the council have more to say about your range than you think.

addressed in an operating agreement.

There is a disturbing trend in public recreation administration to monetize recreational resources. Private and non-profit organizations are being charged ever increasing fees for the use of public park land while providing recreational activities to the general public. The public-private partnership espoused in contemporary recreation administration circles appears to be both an attempt to raise more civic income while putting off the responsibility and the staffing of running recreational programs onto private operators. No distinction is being made in this effort between for-profit businesses and non-profit service organizations. The trend in operating agreements is toward increasing fees to be paid to the governing body and reduced services from that body with more workload placed on the private sector.

Negotiating the terms of an operating agreement starts with "deal points," the key aspects of the terms, responsibilities, schedule of use, maintenance, and revenue issues that will be written into the final agreement document. Typically, the governing body's staff will present a list of deal points for discussion. As a facility operator, these first discussions are with the city's staff. Informal meetings may be supplemented with written proposals and comments. In these negotiations is important to recognize that the city staff are doing a job. The staff is responsible to the city council and not the operator. While a friendly atmosphere goes a long way to reaching an agreement, the staff cannot just be on the operator's side. Their responsibility lies with the city and all the park users, archers and non-archers. Also, the staff will be meeting with and gathering input from other stakeholders in the community.

The result of this negotiating process is not an agreement but a set of staff recommendations. Staff recommendations are then presented to the parks and recreation commission for their review and approval. The commission's decisions are not binding but are themselves a recommendation to the city council.

> "There is a disturbing trend in public recreation administration to monetize recreational resources. Private and non-profit organizations are being charged ever increasing fees for the use of public park land while providing recreational activities to the general public."

The staff recommendations may not fully meet the operator's goals. During the negotiating period and especially after the staff recommendations have been published, it is important for the operator to contact the commissioners and give them a full picture of the range operations. Be clear about what parts of the recommendation you support and what parts you would like to modify. The commissioners will pretty much make up their minds about the issue before any public hearing. Do your best to get them to understand your position before any vote is taken. Invite the commissioners to come to the range and observe or better yet participate in your program. A well run program will speak for itself.

At the commission meeting, public input is solicited from interested parties. Such input may be submitted in writing, to be included in the agenda packet, or verbally at the commission meeting. The commission meeting is a form of civic theater. The commissioners have already made up their minds on the issue and only open the floor to public comment because they have to and to show that they are acting openly. Most public commissions are generally dismissive of input at public meetings. They are just going through the motions. That having been said, a public presence is not without impact. Putting on a good show will support your cause and demonstrate to the commissioners that you operate in a business-like fashion (*see "Some Guidelines for Operator Participation at Public Meetings" above*).

Once you have a signed operating agreement it is essential that you fully comply with all of the terms of the agreement. Many agreements are structured in a way to give the city an out for failure of the operator to execute their part of the bargain. Keep records. Have all your paperwork in order. Make all of the required reports to the governing body on time and accurately represented. Keep your insurance current and provide certificates of insurance to the governing body in a timely manner. Make all payments in full and on time. When the agreement comes up for renewal, one of the first questions will be "Are they currently complying with the previous agreement?" Don't give your opponents an opportunity to challenge you on poor or incomplete performance.

Most commission votes are not binding into ordinance but simply a recommendation to the city council for the council's action. Preparing for a city council meeting is the same process as preparing for a commission meeting. You will need to do the same pre-meeting activities, only now directed to the council members. If your organization serves a large community as PRA's does, you will have members of your organization who are not residents of the city that controls the property. If that is the case, residents of the city should contact their council members to offer input on the issues. Be sure that each organization member identifies themselves to their council member as a constituent when offing comments.

At the council meeting observe the same guidelines as at a commission meeting. Expect that most of the council members will have already made up their mind in advance as to how they will vote. A disciplined and respectful presentation from your group will not sway opponents to your side but will reinforce the decisions made by your council supporters.

Only the council can approve deal points that can be integrated by the city attorney into a document that is legally binding and ready for signature. Governing bodies will require that their own attorneys handle the wording of any agreement. You should have your own attorney review the agreement before signing.

Indoor Archery Ranges in Public Buildings

Installing an archery range in a public building such as a school, gymnasium or recreation center usually involves the use of temporary, portable archery range equipment. Provisions have to be made to install, operate and remove the equipment on a timely basis. Because of the temporary nature of the indoor range, a place will need to be located for preferably on-site storage of the archery gear when not in use. Off-site storage will introduce additional costs renting a storage facility, moving the equipment to and from storage as well as set up time.

I worked on a program that packaged all of the equipment necessary to run an indoor archery program into a trailer. The trailer was stored off site and towed to the venue for set-up and operations. After the archery activity was concluded, the trailer was repacked and towed away. I found that there were plusses and minuses to a trailer-based program. On the plus side all the equipment was packed in a single space and the trailer could be stored without unloading. The down side was that the trailer was hard to maneuver in tight spaces and was subject to break-in or being stolen all together. In addition, it was difficult to find archery instructors who had vehicles capable of hauling a trailer. A better option would be a cargo van that was self-contained.

When installing a portable range in a room, two key safety issues need to be addressed. One is behind-the-backstop protection for the walls. The use of a Kevlar safety curtain is about the only viable portable choice. You may need to install double curtains to prevent arrow penetration. When using an arrow curtain, remember that they really can't stop high performance arrows shot from compound or competitive recurve bows. Limit the archery gear used to student grade equipment with low draw weights.

The second major safety consideration is securing the door access to the archery area to prevent anyone from entering the range in the shooting area. Signs and barriers will be required. Being able to lock the doors from inside to prevent entrance but not block an escape rout in an emergency is the best option.

Public facilities will require liability insurance paid for by the operator and naming the governing body as additional loss payee. I've found that the cost of insurance may be as much as the revenue from offering archery instruction classes. Be sure

Some Guidelines for Operator Participation at Public Meetings

Be prepared. The amount of time available for public comment will be limited, especially if there are a lot of speakers on the agenda item. I have seen the amount of time for speakers reduced to as little as two minutes per speaker. If you have a number of points to make, meet in advance with your colleagues and divide the topics among the presenters so that all the issues are covered and there are no repetitious remarks.

Public comment periods are not debates. You will not have any opportunity to respond to comments made by the commissioners or any of the public speakers. Be sure in your planning to look for any possible issue that may be raised in opposition to your view and have a rejoinder prepared in advance fully integrated into your presentation topics.

While it should go without saying, be scrupulously honest. Make sure that you only speak and write the truth. Have documented facts to back up any statement you make. Any attempt conceal, cover up, or mislead will be discovered by your opponents and used against you. There is great strength in integrity.

Write down the full text of each person's comments in advance and read each presentation aloud, timing it with a stop watch. Silent reading is much faster than reading out loud. Reading out loud will also identify awkwardness's in wording that can be smoothed out with some editing. Practice reading the script aloud as many times as you can until the words flow smoothly and the time to speak the text falls well inside the expected allotted speaking time. Many people will say that they feel more comfortable "just winging it." Unscripted remarks will run long, sound stumbling, and may leave out key points. Have the discipline to write your text in advance and, remembering that the meeting is "public theater," take the time to rehearse your lines for the best performance.

Stay calm during your presentation. No matter how strongly you feel about an issue, maintain a disciplined demeanor. Shouting, accusing and ranting will do your cause no good and will demonstrate a lack of professionalism in your operations.

Be respectful at the meeting to both the commissioners and to members of the public who are expressing contrary views. Shouting down or cat-calling another speaker reflects badly on you. Sometimes your opponents may make statements about you or your group that you know not to be true. You will not have an opportunity to directly rebut an opponent's false statements at the meeting. Proper planning will insure that your message gets out correctly. Have the discipline in your group to maintain order no matter what the circumstances.

Do your best to have a large turnout of your members and supporters at the commission meeting. Use social media and your own membership list to notify your supporters about the meeting including the date, time and specific location. If you have a club shirt or jacket, request that all attendees wear theirs to the meeting. You can print up small, very simple, signs or logos on 8.5" x 11" pieces of card stock for attendees to hold up during the meeting to show the commissioners the level of support you have for your position.

Dress in business or business casual attire. Do not wear any camouflage clothing; do not wear shorts or jeans. Remove your caps and hats while in the meeting room. Dress as if you were going to a job interview because you are being judged on your ability to operate an archery range in a safe and professional manner.

Contact the local press about the meeting and

arrange for an interview with one of your club leaders who can talk about your side of the issue. Local print is read by local people and can help encourage local awareness of your program. Many people in the public may have participated in one of your classes or tournament and have an increased interest in supporting your views. Also recognize that reporters make mistakes and may leave out important topics or alter the intent of your comments. Reporters will not generally run a story by you for review before publication.

Invite reporters from local media, including electronic as well as print publications to attend the meeting and report on the events. All reporting builds awareness of your program and can help with public support. Put links on your web page and on your Facebook page to articles about your programs and the issues before the commission as well as articles reporting on commission and council meetings.

The commission may vote to approve the staff recommendation as presented, approve the recommendation as modified by the commission, send the recommendation back to staff for further work before any vote or they may vote to reject the proposal entirely. Once the vote is taken, there are no further actions that the operator may take to influence the outcome of that meeting.

Chapter 11
Archery Equipment Choices and Maintenance

Running an archery instruction program will necessarily require the purchase and maintenance of a substantial quantity of archery equipment. In addition to the archery range gear, you will need bows, arrows, quivers, finger tabs, arm guards, bow racks, arrow racks, and target faces. In choosing archery gear, safety and durability are the key factors to consider. All of the subtleties of bow tuning are irrelevant with instructional equipment. Buying quality gear that will last is your best investment in log term success. (see **Appendix H Camp Archery Program Equipment List**).

Arrows

Start with arrows. While there are a range of arrow shaft materials available, aluminum is the safest and most durable. Wood shafts will last only a few seasons. Fiberglass shafts are too heavy. Carbon shafts are expensive and are subject to cracking during heavy use, creating a safety hazard. Carbon shaft arrows should not be used in a beginning archery instruction program.

Eason *Jazz* and *Blues* aluminum arrow shafts are the ones that we use at Pasadena Roving Archers for our instruction program. We have standardized our arrow stock on two sizes, 1916 and 1716 for ease of repair and the stocking of replacement parts. Easton 1514 shafts may be used for very short arrows for your youth program with the caution that such slim shafts bend easily.

The Easton *Genesis* shafts for the National Archery in the Schools Program (NASP) are designed for the *Genesis* universal draw length compound bow. The *Genesis* shafts are too heavy to work well with the light drawing recurve bows we use in our program. They also use Easton "G" nocks which can be easily replaced if the nock is partially broken but require more extensive repair if the nock breaks off completely leaving a loose piece of plastic rattling around inside the arrow shaft.

Occasionally club members will donate arrows to the instruction program. If the arrows are aluminum and within the length specifications that we use for instruction, we will add them to our inventory. Non-conforming arrows are collected and donated to a local charity that puts together archery setups for disadvantaged youth.

We have found that feather fletching holds up the best for class arrows. We have settled on a three-inch long, solid color feather fletching for all of our instruction program arrows. Arrow points are inexpensive "glue in" target points. We avoid screw in points for club arrows as the points easily loosen with use.

Bows

For many years we used recurve bows with wood

PVC pipe bows are inexpensive, yet effective, training aids.

risers and removable limbs in our program. They were durable and provided years of service. As the bows aged, we replaced them with similar bows using plastic, rather than wood risers. The plastic risers hold up well, are weatherproof and have a smaller grip which is easier to hold for many of our students. We did find a quality control issue with the newer bows. In the first year of use, we had limb cracking and disintegration on about 15 percent of the new bows. Replacing the limbs returned the bows to service but with an unnecessary expense.

In choosing bows for class use, pick the lightest draw weights available. For children 10-12 pound bows are fine. For adults pick 14-16 pound bows. Returning archers may be able to shoot a 20 pound bow if they can hold form.

The biggest problem with heavier draw weight bows is that student-archers are not strong enough to hold proper body alignment under those heavier loads. For many beginning archers even 15 pounds is too much draw weight. The use of ultra light PVC pipe bows (see **Appendix K** *Making and Using PVC Pipe Bows as Archery Training Aids*) may be required to help archers develop the appropriate body awareness, alignment, and strength to move up to heavier equipment. Archery instructors should monitor each archer's progress carefully and only allow archers to use heavier equipment when they are strong enough to do so.

A simple test of archery strength is the 30 second Specific Physical Training (SPT) Exercise of holding the bow at full draw with back tension, in proper alignment and without shaking for a minimum of 30 seconds. If an archer can maintain the hold, they are probably strong enough to shoot that bow's draw weight. If they can't hold the bow for 30 seconds, more strengthening is required before they move up to a heavier bow.

Be sure to put an easy to read identification number on each bow so that the archers can readily identify their assigned bow for use during the class. With all the bows looking alike, it is easy for students to become confused as to which bow is theirs unless the bows are clearly labeled with a bow number.

The bow strings supplied with many of the inexpensive training bows are often the wrong size, usually too short. We've seen a substantial variation in the finished length of these types of bows. The result is that custom bow strings are usually required to be made in the first year of a new bow's use.

The Hoyt plastic *Hunter Arrow Rest*, attached with a double stick adhesive has proved to be the most durable for class use. Student archers like the hook at the end of the rest arm as an aid for holding the arrow on the bow. As the rests wear down, they can be easily replaced in the field. They are quite inexpensive.

Accessories

Bright orange traffic cones make excellent ground quivers.

For outdoor archery, simple belt clip, tube quivers work fine. We issue four arrows per archer reflecting that four arrows are shot in a field round end. A quiver and four arrows are clipped to the archer's waist belt. For indoor archery, ground quivers may be more convenient for archery classes. Ground quivers can be made from PVC pipe and a square of plywood as illustrated in the Level 1 Instructor book. Another easy option is to use traffic cones with the tops opened up a bit to allow easy access.

When choosing arm guards for an instruction program, only use long arm guards. The arm guards should cover the bow arm from the middle of the upper arm down to the archer's wrist. We have tried a wide range of commercially made arm guards. Common issues with them are: materials failures in the straps and closures on the arm guards. We have not found a single armguard solution that is durable in an active program. Armguard repair and replacement is a common part of equipment maintenance.

All armguards should be fitted onto a beginning archer by the instruction staff. Archery equipment is unfamiliar to the public and students may be confused by how and where to place the armguard on their arm. When fitting an armguard onto a beginning archer be sure to cover the "bump" on the inside of the elbow where the string is most likely to hit the arm of a beginner. Until an archer learns how to rotate their bow arm elbow outward for string clearance, the inside bump of the elbow joint is the most likely place that the string will hit the bow arm.

About 15-20% of archers, especially female archers, will have a condition called pronation or hyperextension of the elbow joint where the elbow actually bends beyond 180 degrees, placing the arm in the way of the string. Explain to archers with this condition that they will have to learn to slightly bend their elbow as well as rotate the elbow slightly outward to avoid string contact. Be sure to fit the armguard to protect the portion of the arm and elbow that is likely to fall into the string path.

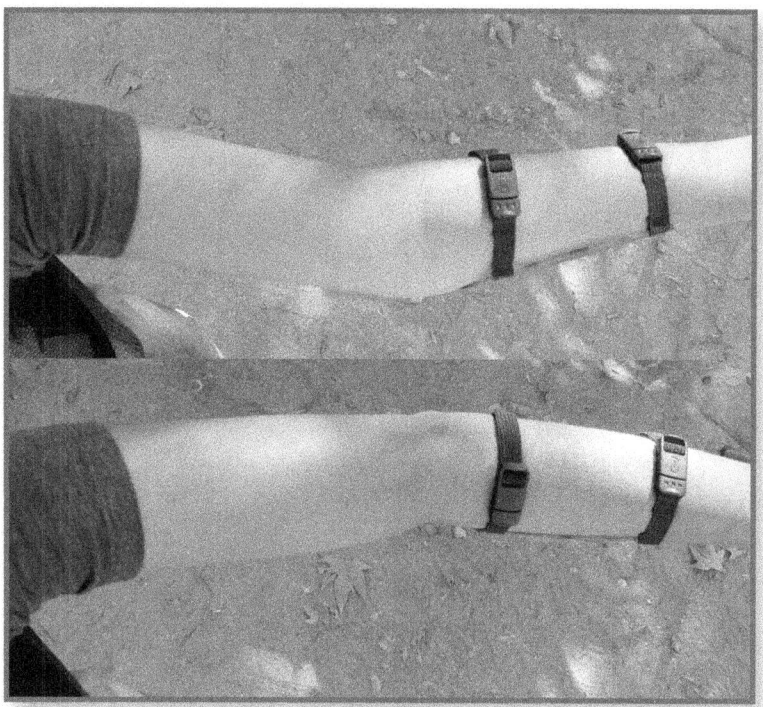

Photographed from above, a pronated bow elbow (top) has the crease pointed upward. A proper bow elbow (bottom) is rotated so the crease faces the bow.

Finger tabs for beginning archers should be small and easy to fit onto the archer's draw hand. We have a club member who makes simple finger tabs for club use, cut out of leather and tied onto the hand with a simple cord. One piece, slip-on tabs work as well. Avoid oversize tabs that may get in the way of the arrow, string or anchor on the face. We avoid using finger tabs with separators for first time archers as the separators are bulky and can be difficult to manage. Also we start out all archers with a "3 fingers under the arrow" grip on the bowstring. A split finger grip and the use of the finger separator are introduced when archers transition to using a bow sight on the bow.

Archery Fundamentals Class and Olympic Style Recurve Bows

The first class in the structured portion of the PRA instruction program is Archery Fundamentals. The equipment used in Archery Fundamentals is a "step up" Olympic Recurve Bow with a metal riser and the same type of squared off, single mounting bolt limb system as the plastic riser bows. The draw weight is 20 pounds which is okay for archers who have practiced a bit. Some archers are still not strong enough to hold form at 20 pounds, so they

Robert Storts, Instrument Maker and Master Machinist, shows off the arrow racks he made for the class equipment.

use the General Program 15 pound bows with the plastic handles. Hoyt plastic *Hunter Arrow Rests* are fitted. A Cartel carbon stabilizer and a metal bow sight are available for each bow. Again, the supplied bowstrings are often the wrong length and new, custom strings are required to achieve the correct brace height and string position on the recurve portion of the bow limb.

The stabilizers and sights are added to the bows on the last session of Archery Fundamentals as a bridge to the Introduction to Olympic Recurve Target Archery class.

Light weight training aids are also used in both the Fundamentals and Olympic Style Recurve classes. String loops, stretch bands, and PVC pipe bows are all employed to help students develop their shooting form. The "Formaster" training aid is used to learn back tension and scapular movement.

Arrows for the Fundamentals and Olympic Style Recurve Classes remain the Easton *Jazz* with feather fletching.

Traditional Archery Class

Traditional longbow and traditional (one piece) recurve bow archery is very popular in our area. Nearly 50% of all adult archers who enter our program and go on to advanced classes choose to shoot in the instinctive, traditional style. Commercial bow manufacturers do not offer light draw weight longbows. The lightest bow commonly available is 30 pounds, making the transition to traditional shooting difficult for beginning archers. To help our students make the transition and to build their strength, we use lighter draw weight takedown recurve bows to teach the beginning of traditional style archery. As their strength and skills grow, we transition them to 30 pound draw weight imported longbows.

The traditional archery class uses a wood finish, traditional-style carbon arrow with a 3½" to 4" shield- or square-cut feather fletching. Screw in field points are used on the traditional arrows. Leather back quivers are used. A leather cuff type arm guard is used along with the three finger shooting glove. Some of our class members, along with some of the traditional archery instructors have made their own longbows. The "crafting" element in traditional archery seems to have as much appeal to the archers as the shooting of the bow itself.

Compound Bow Archery Class

Picking equipment for an introductory compound bow class can be a challenge. The biggest issue is fitting the bows to the archers. Bows that require a bow press or optional specialized parts to adjust the draw length just don't fit into an introductory compound bow program.

One alternative is to use the universal draw length compound bow such as the Matthews

Genesis bow. At PRA we have chosen not to use the *Genesis* bow because the compromise in the bow design makes it nearly impossible to teach true compound bow techniques. The combination of lack of let-off and the absence of a "wall" at full draw really precludes the use of a release aid for shooting with a *Genesis* bow.

We have found the Browning *Midas* bows have a combination of low draw weight, a true compound draw force curve with let off and a wall, and the ability to adjust the draw length in the field with simple tools and without the need for a bow press, makes the *Midas* bow the right choice for us. The only limitation of the *Midas* bow is the maximum draw length of 28 inches. Archers with longer draw lengths will have to borrow a club member's bow or make the commitment to purchase their own bow in order to participate in the class.

Another option that we haven't yet tried is the Diamond *Infinite Edge* which features draw length settings adjustable between 13 and 30 inches without changing the limbs or using a bow press. The draw weight range falls between 5 and 70 pounds. A terrific option that will be on our purchasing list for future equipment acquisitions.

Carbon arrows with plastic vane fletching are used in the compound bow class. The bow sights available include hunter type pin sights and magnifying scope type sights. We have a selection of release aids including hunter wriststrap types, thumb operated hand held "T" handle, and triggerless hand held "T" handle releases. This way students get an opportunity to try a variety of different types of release aids before making a purchase of their.

Equipment Maintenance

Archery gear used in an instructional environment gets a lot of wear and tear. A maintenance program that services damaged equipment after every session is critical to keeping an inventory of tackle available and in safe operating order for each class session.

Arrows get the most abuse. Beginning archers

JoJan fletching jigs are used to maintain PRA class arrows.

often forget to correctly orient the index feather, resulting in damage to the fletching after a few ends. Once arrows are in the target, they are at risk for being struck by subsequent incoming arrows. Struck arrow damage can include broken knocks, fletching being torn off and pierced, or bent arrow shafts.

We issue arrows in sets of four arrows per set. If an arrow is damaged, the entire set is removed from service and kept together during the repair process. We keep enough arrows in stock so that students can continue with their archery practice with a replacement set, issued on the spot.

At PRA we do not have a building facility at the range so equipment slated for repair must be picked up at the range, taken off site to a shop, be repaired there and then returned to the range before the next class session. As our classes are only offered on Saturdays, a week is allowed for repair time.

Standardizing of arrow components is a key step in making repairs in a timely manner. We stock two arrow shaft diameters with suitable points and nocks available for replacement. All fletching is 3″ feathers, stocked in a range of solid colors.

At the time of this writing, there is some concern about the adhesives used for nocks and fletching. Legacy archery brands that had been in use for years seemed to have lost their grip, with feathers flying off of arrow shafts like confetti during classes. At one point the adhesive issue had become so serious that we had to repair 45 sets of arrow after a single class session because of lost fletching. Claims and counter claims about changes in glue formulas and the anodizing of arrow shafts produced no clear source of the problem.

Searching for a solution, I came on Loctite's "Go-2" glue as a reliable adhesive for applying feathers on aluminum arrow shafts. Go-2 glue does not work well for securing plastic knocks, so Duco Household Cement has proven reliable for attaching nocks to arrow shafts.

A JoJan *Multi-Fletcher* with straight clamps is used for re-fletching arrows. An abrasive disc cut off saw is used for cutting shafts to length when required. Target points are secured with hot melt glue and are easy to replace in aluminum shafts. Points in carbon shafts are secured with two part golf shaft epoxy adhesive. For shafts with inserts and screw in points, a small dab of rubber cement will help to keep the points in place while still allowing for easy removal when needed.

As noted above, bow strings are subject to wear and the best solution to replacing bow strings is to make your own. While student grade bow strings are available at relatively low cost, we've found the strings are often mislabeled as to length on the package and the actual required length is not available as a pre-made product. String making is beyond the scope of this book but you will need a sturdy string jig and the appropriate string and serving materials. We've found that a 14-strand string of *Fast Flight* material works well on the recurve bows, is durable and with the appropriately-sized center serving, fits well on the arrow nocks.

Bow limbs do crack over time. When they do there's not much you can do but buy replacement limbs. Bow risers will need to be cleaned from time to time. The Hoyt *Hunter Arrow Rests* do wear out and need to be replaced when they do. Keep a stock of both RH and LH arrow rests at the range for replacement as needed.

Occasionally the plastic reinforcement at the tip of the limb may come off. When it does, the sharp edge of the limb will quickly cut into the bow string. A replacement tip reinforcement can be made using a piece of hard wood, cut and shaped to match the contour of the limb. Another option is to salvage the limb tip reinforcements from broken limbs. Before tossing a broken limb, turn the limb with the tip downward and strike the tip sharply on a concrete surface. The bow tip reinforcement will fly off after a couple of whacks and you can set it aside for use later.

Metal quiver belt clips are very easily lost. Keep a stock of extra clips at the range for on-site replacements.

Fabric and synthetic leather arm guards have elastic straps that are constantly wearing out. The small pads of Velcro fall off and get lost. Metal and/or plastic buckles will break or fall off. Finding a club member with sewing skills and a heavy duty sewing machine is essential to keep armguards in working order. Alternatively, expect to replace 15%-20% of your armguard inventory each season.

Student grade archery equipment is relatively affordable and will give years of service if maintained properly. Clubs that want to run an instruction program will need to identify resources within the club's membership who have the skills, time, and interest to keep the archery gear in top shape.

Chapter 12
Business Operations

I have had the opportunity to be a member of, and volunteer for, a number of non-profit organizations over the years, ranging from international professional societies to local special interest groups. Whether large or small, all organizations rely on a combination of volunteer and sometimes professional resources to run their business and mission specific operations.

While an archery club is not a commercial business, a club does perform services, collects and spends money. Setting up a business structure for a club is an important part of sustaining an on-going organization.

Non-Profit Organizations

Most non-profits run on a consensus based management structure. In a 501(c)(3) non-profit corporation, the standard bylaws specify that the membership elects a board of directors who then appoint officers, either from the board or from outside the board, to run the business affairs. This is a somewhat complex and counterintuitive approach to governance. Normally one would expect that the membership would elect the officers who would serve for a term as defined in the bylaws. With a non-profit, the more complex elected board and appointed officers gives more operational control to a diverse representation of the group's membership.

As a practical matter, there are very few members of an organization who are willing to serve either as board members or as officers. Club leaders emerge through a pattern of participation with increasing responsibility by individual club members. People who show up for meetings, participate in work days, and earn their instructor certifications in order to teach regularly are the folks to look to when identifying potential club leaders.

While a monthly business meeting of the general membership is pretty standard, not much actual work gets done at general meetings. These meetings are for the giving of reports, the directing of tasks and coordinating the efforts of the membership.

The real heavy lifting in volunteer organizations is in the sub-committees that meet between general meetings and take on specific tasks. Under the direction of a committee chair (who often does most of the work themselves) committee members perform the needed tasks of sustaining a complex organizations. Kinds of committees include finance, range maintenance, membership, tournament organization, archery classes and instruction, city or landlord relations, publicity, newsletter, social media, web site, equipment acquisition and maintenance.

> "The real heavy lifting in volunteer organizations is in the sub-committees that meet between general meetings and take on specific tasks."

There's a lot to do and gathering a bunch of people among whom to divide the work helps to see that all the necessary tasks get done.

A caution is that with multiple committee members working on different tasks, there may be communications issues between groups leading to either duplicate work being done or some tasks being not done at all. Using the monthly general meeting for committee reports lets everyone of the leaders hear what is going on with the others in order to keep the club's progress moving forward.

An early step in the management process is identifying the interests of the members that you have and the people who you want to attract/join the club. In many areas, hunting may be a prime motivator for establishing an archery club, whether hunting is done on club-owned property or the club organizes hunting trips to other locations.

In urban areas, hunting may be less popular or even off putting for potential members. Pasadena Roving Archers is a recreational and competitive archery club. While some members of the club do hunt, the club does not organize or participate in any hunting activities. The vast majority of our members are target archers only. Any emphasis on hunting would be a turn off for many local families and would be a political liability with the City. We are a family-oriented organization and attract outdoor enthusiasts of all ages.

Licensing and Taxes

You will need to determine if any form of business license is required by your municipality permitting your club's operations. Social clubs are often exempt from business licenses but commercial businesses may not be so exempt. If you sell equipment, food, or supplies or offer classes for a fee, local licensing may be required. You may also be subject to equipment, inventory, and/or business personal property taxes if there is a commercial component to your activities. Check with your local government for details.

If you sell goods, your state may require you to obtain a resale license and to collect, report and pay sales tax to the state.

> "Insurance can be one of the biggest overhead expenses after rent and utilities. Both USA Archery and the National Field Archery Association (NFAA) offer liability insurance coverage"

It is important to establish your income tax status from the start. Your bank will require a tax identification number to open an account. You can incorporate as a simple business and be subject to reporting and the payment of income tax as would any other business. There is a special tax category for special interest groups whose total revenue is less than $25,000. If you fit into that category, your income will be tax free up to the $25,000 amount. Cross that threshold and you will be subject to income tax.

If you feel that your organization can qualify for a charitable tax exemption you may choose to apply for 501(c)(3) tax exempt status as a non-profit charitable corporation. The IRS will be looking for a mission statement and operational plan that contains a substantial public benefit component. At PRA, our instruction program fits that description and is the foundational basis for earning the 501(c)(3) designation.

Applying for 501(c)(3) status is a time consuming process that requires legal expertise. I have worked with groups that have tried to do the application process themselves, have used an on-line legal paperwork service and have used a local professional attorney to prepare and submit the application. Doing the task yourself is fraught with pitfalls and is not recommended.

If you use an on-line legal paperwork service, expect long delays, forms returned for incomplete information and most troubling, there's not a single person that will take your call if you have a question. Any inquiry from you is met by a bank of telephone operators who have absolutely no personal knowledge of your application. Using an on-line documents service will at least double the amount of time it takes to complete the forms and make the actual application.

The best way to go is to use a local attorney that you know to prepare and submit the forms for you. Expect to pay $2000 to $3000 for the service. If you can afford the fees, it is money well spent, insuring that the forms are filled out correctly and that you have a person who will answer your questions as you go along.

Once submitted, expect that the IRS will take 4-6 months to actually process the application and get back to you with their determination. You may find that some time into the process you will receive communications from the IRS asking for additional information or more details for your application. Do your best to respond to inquiries and requests from the IRS as quickly and accurately as possible. Delays will put your application at the bottom of the pile and only make the process take longer.

It may be done electronically but it is still paperwork!

While your application is in progress, you may be subject to both state and federal tax obligations which you should pay promptly. In some cases, some or all of the taxes you pay during the application process may be refunded to you once the non-profit application is approved by the IRS and you receive the much anticipated letter of acceptance.

As in all matters regarding taxes, you should consult with a local tax professional when making decisions and preparing any forms for submission to the IRS or to the state. The money you pay to a tax pro is small change when compared to the taxes, fees and penalties that you may face for not handling your tax obligations properly.

Insurance

Insurance can be one of the biggest overhead expenses after rent and utilities. Both USA Archery and the National Field Archery Association (NFAA) offer liability insurance coverage to member clubs for archery operations. This insurance is relatively affordable and can offer coverage to officers of the club as well as the club's general corporation.

If you rent your facility, the landlord will have general fire insurance on the building. Such insurance will not cover the contents of the building owned by you and the club. The landlord or municipality will require that you hold a valid liability policy in a specified amount ($1 million is a minimum) and that they be named additional loss payee in a certificate of insurance made out to them. Both the USA Archery and NFAA insurers can provide this certificate of insurance for you.

The USAA/NFAA insurance will not cover your property. Check with your insurance professional to see if property coverage under an Inland Marine policy makes sense financially. If the total value of the personal property is relatively low, the cost of insuring it against loss may be too high to justify the expense.

If you own your own property, your mortgage holder will require you to maintain a general fire insurance policy to cover any losses to their mortgaged interests. If you operate in a high risk area for fire, flood, wind, earthquake damage or other potential natural disasters, be sure you know what is covered and what is not covered in your insurance policy.

If you hold outreach events in the community, run the archery program at a summer or youth camp or provide any archery services outside your own operational perimeter, you may be required to provide evidence of insurance and an "additional loss payee" certificate to the organizers or owners of the off site property. Check with USA Archery/NFAA to see what additional fees may be required for the issuance of these types of certificates of insurance.

Currently certified archery instructors/coaches who are members of USA Archery are covered individually by a $1 million general liability insurance policy, but only in association with official USA Archery activities (like JOAD classes, or USAA-sanctioned tournaments, etc.). Instructors should check with the USA Archery web site for details on the instructor/coach insurance program.

Assumption is the mother of mistake and never more so than with insurance. Be certain that you have the full information on what is covered and what is not in your insurance program well in advance of any possible claim. Keep meticulous records of your operations and duplicate records off site in case of a disaster.

Your insurance company should be able to provide you with the wording for any waiver and release of liability forms that you may create for participants. Have all participants over the age of 18 sign the waiver forms in advance of participation in your programs. Have the parents or guardians of any participant under the age of 18 sign the waiver form for their children. A signed waiver form does not entirely protect you from liability lawsuits but it can be a deterrent to frivolous claims.

Volunteers, Employees and Professional Services

As a club or business grows there may come a time to transition from all-volunteer labor to having some employees. At first you may be tempted to pay instructors and other staff as independent contractors, issuing a 1099 form at the end of the year instead of a W-2. Don't succumb to this seemingly simpler route. The IRS vigorously cracks down on independent contractor claims and you could be facing formidable fees, fines, and back payments for failing to comply with the labor laws.

Becoming an employer involves a lot of paperwork and compliance issues. On the paperwork side, it is probably best to have your bank or a professional payroll service process your employees time records, calculated withholdings, make deposits into the appropriate impound account and issue the payroll checks. You will have to make quarterly payments to the IRS for withholdings and file the appropriate forms. A payroll service can make this process much easier for you at the price of a small fee for their services.

Depending on your state employment regulations you will have to maintain a current worker's compensation policy. You will also be required to post notices of employee rights in a place where employees can see them. Private companies produce composite posters for sale that include all of the required posting information for your state and are a good bargain. Expect to update the employee notice posters once per year.

From time to time you may need services from outside professionals. Accounting and tax help are commonly given to professional companies to assure complete and competent compliance with regulations. The services of an attorney may be needed for setting up a corporation, applying for non-profit status or for negotiating agreements with landlords and municipalities. Be sure you have a clear understanding of the services to be rendered and the fees to be charged.

Many professionals charge for their time, rather than by the project. Under an hourly rate agreement, every piece of paper, phone call and email is logged for time in increments of an hour that can build up quickly. Finding a five figure bill from a professional's office in your mailbox can be a sobering experience. If a professional chooses to offer their services on a *pro bono* basis, be sure to get a memo in writing should an unexpected invoice arrive.

Professional services may also be needed for grounds maintenance, building maintenance, advertising, public relations, graphic design and other specialties that can't be sourced from the volunteer club membership.

Pricing Strategies

Determining a pricing strategy for your club's events and services is as much an art as it is a science. A preliminary approach to setting pricing is to use a cost basis. Determine the actual costs for putting on an event, add a reserve for overhead expense and another reserve for retained earnings and divide the total by the expected number of attendees to arrive at a unit price. With a service type business, such as running an instruction program, the major expense is labor. In an all-volunteer organization, the labor cost is zero so the net price to the participants will be artificially low.

Another approach to pricing is market-based, rather than expense-based. In market-based pricing, you survey the prices for similar recreational offerings and then weigh the price/features of their services with your own to come to an estimated market price. For archery, comparable business might be bowling, miniature golf (big golf has its own marketing issues that are out of the scale of an archery club.), trampoline clubs, batting cages, ropes courses, skating rinks, laser tag and even the movies. The market for these services is already well established and consumers have voted with their pocketbooks as to how much they are willing to pay for a recreational experience. Your pricing will have to fit in with the market's expectations. Make the price too high and you'll have too few participants. Make the price too low and the public may mentally discount the value of your offerings. Finding the right market price takes research and a bit of trial and error.

Offering free, first timer archer lessons is a terrific way to introduce the public to the sport of archery and to your club (*see the chapter on free archery lessons for details*).

If you are a non-profit organization, don't think that you are prohibited from retaining earnings. While "profits" may not be distributed to the members, you may use earnings towards capital improvements, a building fund, endowments, the issuing of grants and scholarships and any other charitable use within the 501(c)(3) guidelines. Salaries may also be paid to employees without violating the non-profit rules. For complete information on compliance with 501(c)(3) non-profit regulations including required tax filings, see IRS Publication 4221-PC, "Compliance Guide for 501 (c)(3) Public Charities."

Once you have established the prices for your services, there are a number of different pricing strategies that you can explore to maximize your participation and income. The most obvious is for individuals to pay as they go. Having a cashier collect class, tournament, and range use fees at the gate is simple, albeit labor intensive.

Members of Pasadena Roving Archers are entitled to free Saturday morning archery classes as a benefit of their membership. As the instruction program has expanded, we find that people apply for membership, not because of their love for the sport of archery or for the camaraderie of other archers, but simply as a means of discounting their archery activities. This thinking is similar to people who join a commercial gym. The "club" component of social interaction and activities with other members is diminished in such an environment. It is up to the club leadership to promote events for dedicated archers that nurture the relationships among members and support the sport of archery.

Package deals are another form of discount pricing that can encourage repeat participation by the public. Rather than using memberships as a incentive, a package deal for a number of visits at a discounted price can be an option for people who want to reduce the cost of their archery activities. Families are particularly hard hit by individual pricing that can add up for a family of three or more. Offering a package pricing option can help to keep families involved in the sport for a longer time.

On most Saturdays, we have 20-30% more people show up for our free introductory archery classes than we have spaces and equipment available for them to participate. We issue rain check cards to the first 20 people in line that we are unable to admit that day, entitling them to come to the front of the line on the following Saturday morning. We find that about 50% of the rain check cards that we issue are claimed. The issuing of rain checks softens the disappointment of not getting into a class and serves to encourage potential archers to come back and try again.

Group Archery Classes

Archery is a popular activity for youth groups, meet-up groups, larger families, birthday parties, and corporate team building events. At the Pasadena club, our time during the week for the use of the range facilities is limited which in turn severely limits the number of group events that we can offer each week. We are restricted to two hours of range time on Saturday afternoons for group lessons. We could easily double or triple the number of group classes if we were permitted more range time by the city of Pasadena.

The process of booking group classes starts with an inquiry, usually by email, from a group leader. As with all email inquiries, you should have a bank of standard email replies that you can copy, paste and personalize in your email response. The canned email content should include the days, dates, and times that you offer group classes, the location of the classes, the number of people permitted in a single group and your pricing for group lessons. You should require that a deposit be paid to secure a given booking and that the deposit will be applied to the final cost of the event. At PRA we have a minimum price for a group class of up to five participants and then an additional cost per participant up to the class size limit of 20 people. Our deposit check requirement is the minimum price. You should have a published policy on group reservation cancellations and the return of any deposit money.

A booking is confirmed by email upon receipt of the deposit check. The scheduler should then send a confirmation email that includes the group leader's name, the date and time of the booking, the check number and the amount of the check, any special instructions for participants, and a thank you for booking the session with your organization.

You may choose to offer additional services for group classes, for example and especially birthday parties with food, cake and party favors. It's up to you as to how much work and expense you want to put into your group class offerings. You may have scout certified instructors who can provide merit badge classes and signoffs. School groups may want additional instructional components about history, physics or sports competitions. Adult meet-up groups and corporate event leaders like to include some simple competition in the group class offing. Balloon targets, shot in an elimination format, are popular with both kids and adults.

A calendar should be maintained for the group class bookings. Each group class booking entry should include the group leader's name, phone number, and email address. The name of the group, if known, should be listed. The date that the booking was made is noted along with the date and amount of the deposit check received. Additional information about the group participants including number of expected people, age range, and any additional instructions.

It's a good idea to send a reminder email to the group leader about a week before the scheduled date to reconfirm the booking and to give any additional instructions that may be needed for the participants.

On the date of the group class, the participants go through the standard individual registration procedures, sign all the forms, take an eye dominance test, and are issued their equipment. The instructional course content is exactly the same as a regular first timer class with the possible addition of a contest or tournament at the end. Count the number of attendees and collect the additional fees as agreed upon. At the end of the class, take just a few moments to explain the programs and classes that you offer and invite folks to return to the range. Issue safety and orientation class completion cards to all the participants and thank them for coming to the range.

Group classes can be a substantial portion of your instruction program's income if you have the time, staffing and range access to make the most of this opportunity. If you are running a commercial archery pro shop or archery range, providing dedicated space, seating and tables for group archery classes can increase both your marketing exposure and your bottom line. Make group archery classes a priority in your instruction program.

Membership Management

Maintaining an accurate and up to date membership roster is a demanding task. As the number of club members grows, the job of keeping the records becomes ever more complex. In an all volunteer organization, the job of membership chair needs to go to only the most dedicated of club leaders. People join the organization each month, people move out of town or drop out of the club, contact information changes, instructor/coach certification status changes, dues need to be calculated, billed, collected and recorded. There's a mountain of work needed to keep a club roster current.

The board should establish the membership categories, requirements, and dues pricing. The benefits of membership should be clearly defined and published for both the members and the public to see. You will want to set rates that cover your costs, are market compatible, and offer real value to people who choose to join. Membership pricing that is favorable to families encourages more participation in the sport from archers of all ages.

With a small organization, it may be possible to use MS *Excel* or some other spreadsheet program to log member information. Spreadsheets are relative-

Did I mention the meetings? Board meetings, subcommittee meetings, etc. There still is no better way to make sure everyone is on the same page.

ly simple to set up but are not very flexible when looking for specific information about a member or a certain group of members. Using such a system, necessitates that memberships be calendar year-based rather than yearly individualized. An annual membership term concentrates a lot of work at the end of the year to send out renewal notices to the entire membership and then additional work to process all the renewals, prepare and issue current membership cards and account for the dues collected. There is additional follow up with members who did not send in their dues on time. Reminders need to be sent to non-renewing members. At what point do you drop an individual from membership for non-payment of dues? There's a lot to do and a big workload for the membership chair.

Membership communications is tied to the membership roster. Notices to the members need to be sent to only the desired recipients and not spammed to everyone who has had contact with the club. Synchronizing the club emailing list is a tedious chore if not automated.

The same goes for club elections. Working with the Club Secretary, the Membership Chair has to be able to produce a mailing list and labels for active members who are eligible to vote. Envelopes need to be stuffed, labels and postage applied, and the package has to be delivered to the Post Office. Incoming ballots need to be verified for eligibility, counted and the results reported to the board and then to the general membership.

Club newsletters are now almost entirely distributed as a PDF file by email to the membership. The membership chair needs to be able to produce an accurate email address file for each newsletter mailing. In most mass emailings, about 1-5% of the email addresses will bounce as members change their email addresses and email services. The membership chair needs to be able to verify the correct email addresses for members whose emails have bounced and update the records to reflect the change.

At some point it will be best to shift from Excel-based recordkeeping to dedicated member management software. A quick Google search produced hundreds of software choices. There were so many choices that I found a separate company that just specializes in providing consulting services and advice on choosing which software program to purchase and implement. Many of the software programs offer free trials to get your feet wet.

An archery club doesn't have a lot of data points to manage. Still, the scope of information for membership can add up. Among the possible categories/fields are:

Family Names,
First Names
Membership type
   Individual
   Family
   Student
   Senior
   Working
   Non-working
   Honorary
   Life Member
Number of individuals (individual, family, etc.)
Annual dues
Telephone Number
Email address
Mailing address
City
State
Zip
Date joined
Work hours, if a working member
Instructor certification level
Other notes or comments

Look for membership programs that are simple to operate and update, can produce selected email lists, provide automatic membership renewals and reminders, print membership cards, and are easy to update with changes in roster information. Even the simplest of these programs will require some substantial computer skills as well as the time needed for data entry, updates, reports, and reminders. It takes a really dedicated person (or a paid employee) to run a membership management system.

If you run an ongoing tournament program or league program for members, there are a number of league management software programs that you can employ to keep the necessary records. It is probably best that a separate person be in charge of keeping tournament records and providing the lists for end of season and end of year tournament awards.

This was the banquet for PRA's 75th Anniversary celebration. We never run out of people to thank.

For clubs with working membership, a volunteer coordinator needs to log and input the work hours of club members.

Large clubs and archery pro shops and ranges may want to consider contracting with an outside firm for membership management services. Fitness clubs, yoga studios, martial arts business and the like have found that using a membership management service has a lot of advantages at a moderate cost for operations. With a membership management company, all of the tasks of keeping records, sending notices, collecting dues, especially if a contract specifies a monthly dues payment, issuing credentials and sending reminders are performed by an off-site business.

For a for-profit business, using a membership management company can save the cost of one or more employees, allow the management and staff to concentrate on what they do best, and leave the business of collections to a third party. With a third, off-site, party running the membership cash operations, the range staff is not put in the position of having to confront a member about collections and range access. Putting the issue of membership outside the walls of the business can be a big advantage. Is a membership management service desirable for a non-profit, club based organization? Only the club's board can make that yes or no decision but professionalizing membership records is a viable option for very large clubs and for profit businesses.

Banking and Money Management

The Club Treasurer is usually the person responsible for bookkeeping and the mechanics of collecting money and paying bills. Money matters can be a source of distress within an organization. Having a systematic approach to financial procedures goes a long way towards reducing administrative stress.

Fiscal organization starts with a commercial banking account in the group's name. For most banks, you will need a resolution of the board, signed by the secretary of the corporation naming the authorized signatures for the account. You will need a copy of your DBA form as filed with the city/county. The signing officers will need to go to the bank in person to sign the signature cards. You will need to decide whether one or two signatures will be required on your checks. Plan on having at least three officers authorized to sign checks so that bills can be paid promptly when one or more officers are out of town.

Bank service fees can add up. If you are a 501(c)(3) nonprofit corporation, you bank may offer reduced or waived fees for your checking account services. Be sure to ask at your bank what their policy is for non-profits and don't be shy about changing banks if you can find better terms.

Routine, monthly expenses such as utilities, telephone, and internet service can be set up with direct electronic payments to the vendors. Invoices for individual expenses should be signed by an authorizing officer and a check is then issued by the Treasurer with the required check signatures.

It may be practical to maintain a petty cash account for small expenditures but accounting for petty cash can be a headache. More often, club members will make purchases on the club's behalf and then submit copies of the receipts for reimbursement. An officer will need to approve the reimbursement and the treasurer will issue a check to the member.

Revenue can come into the club/business in a number of forms. Class and event fees are often paid to the club in cash. Handling cash is labor intensive and subject to errors. Using a cash register can be very helpful in tracking cash transactions and providing an electronic/paper record of the day's receipts. Alternatively, having two people separately count the cash, put it into a sealed envelope, and sign the envelope can provide a modest level of cash management. Many banks now add a service fee for handling cash at the teller window.

Checks are common forms of payment for membership dues, classes, and fundraising events. You should make it a practice to scan or copy each incoming check before depositing it into the bank. A copy of the check in your hands can go a long way to clarifying questions about payments to your organization.

Credit card payments are common for most retail transactions. You can set up a credit card merchant service with your bank or with an independent company. Credit card terminals are expensive to buy and require a telephone land line and AC power to operate. If you have a fixed business location, the ability to take credit cards is a must. If your operation is in the field or at the range, separated from utility service, cell phone based credit card readers and services can be a viable option. Companies such as PayPal and Square offer credit card services without the cost of purchasing a dedicated terminal. For an organization, don't use a club member's personal phone for credit card transactions. Obtain a dedicated, club-owned cell phone for your credit card accounts.

Electronic transfers of money are more and more popular with consumers. When PRA offered a Pay Pal payment option for membership dues, about 50% of our new and returning members chose to pay electronically. With more and more consumers opting out of traditional bank accounts in favor of "electronic money" you should be prepared to adjust your revenue systems to meet the consumer's needs.

Bookkeeping is the next step in the financial management process. While one can keep books successfully on paper and with programs like Excel, a dedicated bookkeeping program, such as Quicken, can make the process simpler and more accurate. Internal account income categories can include classes, sales, events, donations, fundraising, club dues and any other category that you feel will be useful for later analysis. Expense categories include rent, utilities, telephone, office, materials repairs and maintenance, professional services, insurance, and salaries and withholdings (if you are an employer)

Bookkeeping programs can generate reports as needed. A monthly cash flow report should be presented by the Treasurer to the board and the membership at the monthly meeting. End of year reports will be needed for any tax filings. Specialty reports may be requested by the board for operational analysis.

Any IRS and State tax form should be filled out by a tax professional. A 501(c)(3) non-profit charitable organization may only have to fill out a simple reporting form if their total revenue is below an IRS specified threshold.

Security and transparency are always an issue when dealing with money. Building a checks and balances system into your financial procedures will reduce the temptation for the misappropriation of funds. Requiring that all bills be approved and signed by a designated board member (usually the president) and requiring double signatures on checks are both good first steps in securing your financial activities.

I am a member of the board of a small 501(c)(3) organization (not archery related) that has established in their bylaws that a member audit committee, separate from the club treasurer, review all the club's transactions for the year and submit a document attesting to the accuracy and completeness of the official financial records. These club members a re not accountants but, given the simple nature of the club's business, they are able to verify that the money is being handled honestly.

You may also note the old saying that bookkeeping is a science and accounting is an art. For a small to medium sized club operation, bookkeeping is all that you will need to meet your fiduciary obligations to the club membership.

An archery club is usually not a business but employing sound business operational practices can help insure that the club will have a long and successful future.

Chapter 13
Commnications and Outreach

On-line media are a daily part of our lives. Email, Facebook, Twitter, web sites and streaming video assault us from all angles. Is there a place for electronic media within the archery world? Many athletes have web and Facebook pages. Sanctioning bodies, trade associations and support institutions do the same. On-line retailing is almost a requirement.

In the face of all these lines of communications, how is a club's administration to develop a strategy for using new media to build a successful local archery program?

Marketing communications starts out by identifying the audience for your message. Broadly speaking, there are two main categories of audiences: informed and un-informed. The member of an informed audience is a person who knows who you are, what you do, and has interest in learning more about your programs. Informed audiences include club members, participants in your classes, competitors in your tournaments, and customers of your business.

The uninformed audience is the general public who may have an inclination to learn about our sport and how to get involved but they have not yet made a connection with your organization. The uninformed audience is the toughest to reach efficiently for a small organization.

The first step in the communications process is to organize and compose your message. The process of determining the content of your message may be one of the most difficult aspects of developing a marketing program. The message has to be clear, simple and consistent across all media. As a marketer, you have no way of knowing how your message will reach your audience, especially when addressing the general public. People may find you on your web site, on a third party web site, on Facebook, in an article in the news paper, on TV, or on a store flyer. In whichever case, your message needs to be uniform in content.

Your web site will be visited by both informed and un-informed audiences. Un-informed audiences are looking for information about an activity in which they have interest but little or knowledge. Your web site should act as an electronic brochure to inform and motivate the general public to participate in your program offerings. For the informed audience, people who know about and like your services, the web site is a touchstone to confirm dates and times of events and programs. You will want to post the schedule (and costs) of your regular offerings along with notices about special events and tournaments as they occur.

Subject areas for marketing content can include:
- Your physical location including directions and a map
- Your mailing address
- Your phone number
- Your email address for inquiries
- A list of your programs and event offerings

- Detailed descriptions of your programs with a fee schedule
- A schedule for both regular and special events
- Other services including maintenance, repairs, and supplies available for purchase
- Contact information about custom events, parties and private instruction.
- Brief biographies of principal staff
- A history of the organization
- News about your recent activities

Once you have gathered the necessary information, put it together in a simple written text. Our experience at Pasadena Roving Archers is that people don't read carefully and even when they do read, they don't believe what they've read. Write out the copy in bullet points. Keep the wording short. Avoid long paragraphs of information.

Take the time to write your copy carefully and have it proofread by people who are not involved with your business, sport, or organization. It is easy to assume that a reader will know what you mean and by definition some of these do not. Test the copy with lay people to be sure.

Building a Web Site

Choosing a web site designer can be a daunting task. For clubs, it is tempting to find a club member who can put your site together for you. The danger here is that club members change jobs and locations with the potential to leave you high and dry with a web site that can not be easily updated because you've lost access to the person who put it together in the first place. Avoid writing custom computer code for your web site that can only be accessed and updated by a computer professional. There is plenty of web site template software available that can be built and updated by a computer savvy novice. Even if you have a hired or club professional design and implement your site, insist that the software be easily modified by members of your organization. You can and should password protect your web site development but don't dig yourself into a hole with a site that is controlled by only one person.

Even if you are not a Web Master yourself, you can specify much of what your site will look like and how to navigate on it. Some simple guidelines include:

- Pick a uniform and simple look for your page. (Your logo, home, services, products, find us and contact us should be at the top of each web page.)
- Avoid animations; they only slow down the page for visitors and they draw important attention away from other things.
- As these pages are informational, you should be able to navigate from any page to any other page within your site.
- Place menus of pages on the top or on the left hand side of your page.
- You can use links in your page copy if needed for navigation to other pages on the site or even other places on the same page.

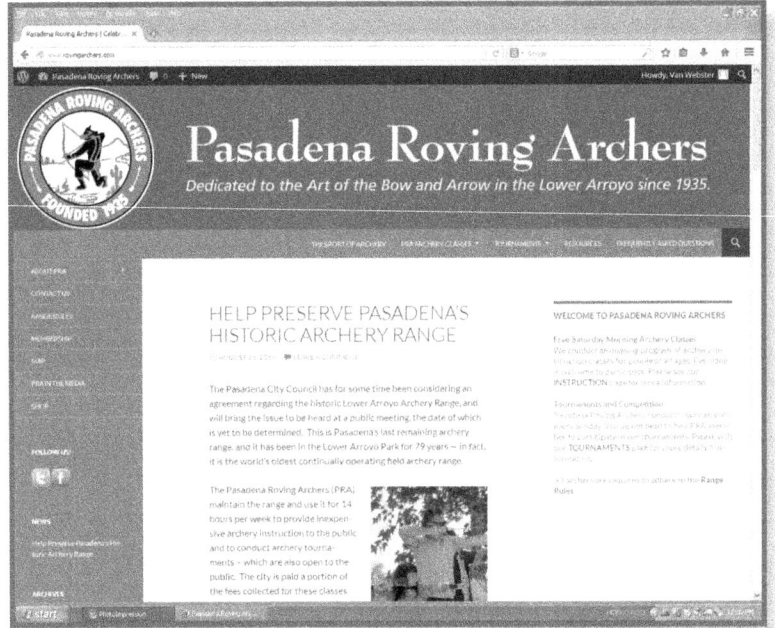

A web site is an excellent way to communicate to a wider audience . . .

- If you want to link to other sites, create a separate page for such links. It is easy to distract the visitor and have them leave your site when following external links and they might not come back.
- Include a picture to illustrate each page.
- Include a link to your Facebook page on every page on your site.
- A contact us page should include all of your contact information and an "email us" page that visitors can easily send notes to you.

- Format your page for optimal viewing on mobile devices as well as desktop screens.
- Include a photograph to illustrate each web site copy point. Photos should be clear, of high contrast, and close up enough to see detail, especially people's faces. Wide open photos of broad landscapes don't do a good job of telling your story. Make sure each photo shows people enjoying your events or services.

Once created and tested your web site is both a destination and a gateway for people to find you, learn about what you do and plan to attend your programs. A web site is never "done." You will want to revisit the content often, updating the information to your most current program offerings. Inaccurate web content is worse than no content at all! Here's where having a web site authoring program that can be updated by your own staff and not

. . . as is a Facebook page.

just a web specialist is so important. If you have to depend on one person, you are trapped if that person is not available. And if that one person is a web professional who bills you for each change, the cost of maintaining your site can skyrocket.

The down side of creating and maintaining a web site is that you have to drive traffic to the site. Advertising in print media is one technique for gaining site awareness and potential traffic. Print advertising is expensive and its effectiveness is based on a very small percentage of responses. In general, have a policy that no piece of paper you generate leaves your control without your web site address, email address, and phone number on it.

As a general rule, if you print something, always put useful content on both sides of the piece of paper. When making up a flyer for a tournament or for new classes, put some general information about your organization on the back of the sheet of paper. You are already paying for the paper and the mailing, get the most out of your expenses by using all the print surface available. Include a "QR" code that links to your web site on all printed materials. That way, mobile device users can easily transition from print to an electronic version of your message.

At Pasadena Roving Archers we have added a PayPal feature to our web site for members to pay their dues. Members find the PayPal feature convenient and now nearly 50% of our membership applications and dues payment come through the web site. We are also looking at introducing an online class reservation and payment system. Our Saturday morning classes are so popular that we regularly have to turn away latecomers who are in the waiting line. By using a reservation system, archery students can be assured of a place in the class and folks won't have to get up early on a Saturday and stand in line, just to be told that the classes are full for the day. There are administrative as well as technical issues that will need to be addressed to implement this program. While better for the students, an online registration system will result in more work for the club's administrative staff.

Facebook

Facebook has a number of features that can be a big help in reaching out to the public. People who "like" a Facebook page will automatically receive messages from you when you update your page. While people really dislike spam, Facebook posts don't seem to have the same stigma. By posting information and reports on Facebook, you will be reminding your fans of your activities and programs.

Facebook pages can be easily updated by minimally trained staff. You will want to limit the number of people who are authorized to post news on your Facebook page but once authorized, the process is very simple. Use Facebook for immediate news about your programs and events as well as for reports about the events once concluded. Try always to include a photograph with each post. Photographs should be sized to seven inches in their maximum dimension at 72 pixels per inch. Photos any larger will take longer to upload and will be resized by Facebook anyway. You may use any photo editing software to crop, adjust and resize photos to fit on the Facebook page.

Limit the number of links you post on Facebook. Only post links that you think will be of specific interest to archers associated with your organization. Links to the official reports of State and National tournaments are appropriate. Links to cute cat videos are not. Also avoid the usual social taboos of religion, politics, and gender issues. Stick to archery and news about your organization.

There are some down sides and cautions to Facebook programming. Once set up, a Facebook page can not be easily edited. When first setting up the page you will be asked to create a Facebook page name, which will be the web name for your page. Pick a simple name or initials that can be easily typed in by the user. Avoid long page names as they are harder to deal with later. You can choose a photograph for the top of your page. These photos need to be not more than 500 pixels wide or Facebook will crop them for you. Pick an image that fits well into the available space. Include a link to your web site in your Facebook page. Fans should be able to link to your site with just a click.

Find at least two page moderators. You will need a backup person in case one of the moderators is locked out. I had that very thing happen to me when my email account was hacked and I lost access to it. That account was the one I used for Facebook and so I lost access to those Facebook pages also. A second moderator could have gotten into Facebook and updated the information. Also, you can't delete a Facebook page. Once up, it is there forever. I have a number of Zombie Facebook pages that I have lost control of but can't kill. Have at least two moderators (better three!) and you will avoid this problem.

Facebook pages should be updated at least weekly. Post news of upcoming events, weather conditions that may affect events and news about your organization. Post reports on all organizational activities including tournaments, classes, and outreach efforts. Always include a photograph in each post. For larger events you may want to crate a Facebook photo album.

Once your Facebook page is up, you will need visitors to "Like" or become "Fans" of you page in order for them to receive your posts on their Facebook home page. Start by emailing your club members including a link to the Facebook page and requesting that they "Like" the page. Put a link to your Facebook page on your web site. Include a link to your Facebook page on every publication, poster and flyer that you produce. Some patience is required here as it takes time to build a Facebook audience. The Facebook page moderator will receive periodic email updates on the number of likes on your page and the projected reach of your information.

Informing the Informed

Web pages and Facebook pages are outgoing messages that are primarily aimed at uninformed audiences and the general public. Once a person responds to one of your posts, they become an informed audience member and you will need a strategy to address their specific communications needs.

People will usually respond to your web page by telephone or by email. On Facebook, responders may post a comment on your wall. Track Facebook comments closely for accuracy and delete derogatory or hateful posts. It is critical that a single person be responsible for each of these media. It is much too difficult to unify a message through multiple responders. Others in the responsibility chain can be CC'd on responses but responses should all come from a single source.

Email Email enquiries should receive a response within 24 hours of receipt. During the business week, emails should receive a reply within the hour. Responding to emails can be a near full time job for a busy program. Don't put emails off for later in the day or to catch up on the weekend. Incoming emails are from informed and interested potential participants. They should be treated with a quick and accurate response.

Generally speaking, most email inquiries will fall into a number of specific categories for which you can prepare a stock response with the potential for customizing the copy to address a particular inquiry. Write your stock responses down in a Word file that you can access, copy, and paste into your email reply. Content of the responses may include registration information, hours, schedule, costs, directions to your facility and any needed special instructions. Always address the person by name when responding by email and make adjustments in the copy of the email to be sure that any specific issues are addressed. Occasionally you will receive an email with a laundry list of questions, most of which are already addressed in your stock response. In responding to such emails, I will copy their questions into my reply and specifically address each question with an individual answer. Include a link to your Facebook page as part of your stock responses.

If you are creating an email list for later distribution, copy the email address of each incoming inquiry into a Word file, Excel file, or other data base file program.

Telephone Addressing the issue of telephone responses poses more difficulties. As soon as you publish your phone number, you will be entered into a wide range of junk call databases. For a commercial business, you are pretty much obligated to answer the phone personally during business hours. You can deal with the junk calls as you wish but they can be wearing during the day. To avoid such junk calls you can list your telephone number as a graphic (a JPEG, for example). Many of the robots scouring the web for telephone numbers are looking for text and this will make your phone number unreadable by the robot.

For a club or recreational program, you can chose to use an automated response to incoming calls and only pick up the calls that have an actual person on the other end of the line. Some guidelines on the telephone line setup:
- Only use a land line for incoming calls. Do not use a cell phone or internet phone service for your main incoming line. Cell and internet services are unreliable and have very poor sound quality.
- Use a hardware type answering machine at your location. Do not use a phone company provided voice mail system. With an answering machine on site, you can screen calls and pick up the ones you want to answer directly. Answering machines have better sound quality than software based voice mail. Any improvement in sound quality is a big help when trying to decipher a return phone number.

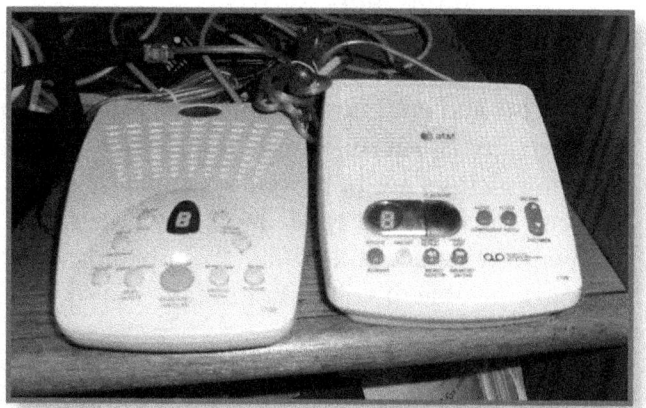

Even old-fashioned telephone answering machines still have their uses.

- Caller ID can be a help in responding to incoming calls.
- When making a return call to a phone message, use a telephone that is setup to receive incoming calls as well. Many people will press a "redial" function on their phone to respond to your call.
- Script out a phone announcement that will answer your most common enquiries. Leave an option at the end for callers to leave a message if you don't pick up. Be sure to specifically request that the caller say their telephone number twice when leaving a message to you so that you can copy it down accurately. Once the script is written, practice reading it aloud a number of times before recording it into the answering machine. A properly designed phone message may answer the caller's questions and require no further response from you or your staff. I've found that of the 30 or more calls we receive per day on our incoming phone line, fewer than four are real calls. The rest are robo-calls and hang ups.
- When you do receive a real phone message, it is important to return the call as soon as possible. During the week, calls should be returned before the end of the business day. Weekend calls can

be returned the same day or on the following Monday. As with email enquiries, people leaving phone messages will often ask expected questions. Have your replies thought out in advance. Encourage your callers to participate in your programs. You'll find that there may be misconceptions about your program or the participants in it. Be prepared with supportive answers and look to address unclear information about your program in your other media.

Newsletters Newsletters are a traditional communications tool for archery clubs and organizations. The audience for a newsletter is the club membership, and is an informed audience. Today, most newsletters are produced for email or online viewing and are not printed out on paper. The Adobe portable document file (PDF) is the easiest and most flexible distribution format.

Newsletters are "old school" but still a good way to communicate with your own members.

Producing a newsletter requires three key skills: the creation of original writing and photography, a copy/photo editor, and the ability to arrange the copy into an attractive visual package for distribution. It may be possible to find one person within your organization who has all of these skills but it is not likely. More typically you will need separate individuals with specific skills, organized under the direction of a newsletter editor. Identifying club members with these skills and keeping them on the job and motivated is a constant struggle for club administration. At Pasadena Roving Archers we have had a number of newsletter editors over the years but we have not been able so far to sustain a consistent publication over a number of years.

The newsletter content can include reports of club events, announcements of upcoming events, a club calendar, member profiles, information about archery topics of interest to the members, tournament score tables and photos of winners, and contact information about the club and its leadership.

You will need to make a policy decision about newsletter distribution. If the newsletter is a benefit for members, then the distribution should be only to the members using an email and an attached PDF file. If the newsletter is for the general public, you can post it on your web site and post a link to the newsletter on your Facebook page. Some clubs send a PDF copy of their newsletter to neighboring clubs for their information. You may also want to share the newsletter with your state archery association, especially if you host state archery tournaments.

Twitter Twitter is a poplar social media network for quick comments and personal messages. In the archery club world, Twitter doesn't serve much of a need and can be a big time waster for the staff. I'd advise against making a big effort to keep up to date on Twitter.

Local News Organizations Local news is another way to get your message out to the general public. From time to time motion pictures and other media events raise the awareness of archery. Your organization may be contacted by local media including television, radio, and print for comments or to come to the range to do a story. The contact person within the club should be media savvy, articulate, and ready to accommodate the needs of production. Have your story line well defined and practice your interview techniques in order to be fluid on camera or on microphone.

You can initiate articles about your events or news worthy achievements. In deciding on press release topics, look for stories that are timely, report on current events, include a photograph with captions and all necessary contact information so that a reporter knows how to reach you for more details. At Pasadena Roving Archers we have been listed in a number of "Best of" features in the local newspa-

Getting TV coverage may expose you to a much wider audience, so make sure the viewers learn how to contact you for more information.

pers. Such listings are usually a result of the news finding you rather than the other way around. If your local paper has a "best of" contest for local organizations, use your influence among your participants to get out the vote for your program.

Social web pages and local activity web sites are another vehicle for reaching the general public. Often the aggregators of these sites search for web sites with activities offered within the locality. You may not have control over the content of these sites, especially if they include a public comment section. Do your best to keep track of where you are listed and verify that the information posted is accurate. Contact the aggregator with factual corrections to keep your listing current.

Caveat Emptor There are many scams that prey on publicity hungry companies. Avoid paying for any service that promises to increase your presence on web search pages such as Google. These Search Engine Optimization (SEO) services are really not worth the money. An archery program has only a local reach and there are better ways to spend your limited marketing dollars.

To Sum Up

The key factors in a media strategy are:
- Identify your audience
- Write clear and compelling copy with a consistent message
- Take photographs that illustrate your points
- Package your information in a form best suited for the chosen media
- Use software that can be easily updated by lay persons
- Be prompt and consistent with responses to email and phone inquiries
- Keep your information up to date
- Don't be bogged down in trivia

Your best public outreach is the quality of your program offerings and services. If you have qualified instructors and run an organized program in a business like manner, the word will get out. Your satisfied customers are your best advertising. Treat people well and they will spread the word for you.

Electronic media make it much easier and less expensive to get your marketing message out to the general public and to your club members. Take the time to create meaningful content and you will reap

Local newspapers are often looking for "local interest" stories to cover. Send them announcemnts of your events and any special news you think might interest them.

the rewards of increased participation and awareness of your programs.

The PRA is a large club, if your club is smaller with fewer resources, downsize these plans, but always with an eye toward being able to expand. Every large club started as a small one.

Why not shoot for the moon? PRA got a notice in Women's Health magazine. They can't print what they don't know.

Chapter 14
Recognition

Archery is an individual sport. Archers compete against themselves and not opponents. However, archery is also a social activity with clubs and teams banding together to train and participate in archery events. Most people appreciate being recognized by their peers for their accomplishments and their contributions. It is important for an archery club or organization to recognize club members who have participated in club activities as well as for personal achievements on the range.

Club/Brand Identification

The first form of recognition is for members to "show their colors" when participating in the sport. Club branded shirts, hats, and jackets should be well-designed and worn by club members at tournaments and other public events. The club's logo forms the basis for the graphics and colors of the shirts. You can go a step farther with embroidery of the member's names on the apparel. It feels good to be identified with a successful group by wearing club gear.

If you are going to commission club apparel, make sure it is of good quality and stylishly designed. Embroidered logos and graphics are more costly than screen-printed artwork but the quality impression of embroidered goods is well worth the extra money. Computer controlled embroidery machines can crate amazingly detailed versions of your supplied artwork. With any custom designed graphic, expect that there will be a set up charge for transferring the design files into control commands for the machines. Once the setup is complete, the same design can be re-ordered at much lower cost per unit for small batches.

You can also have custom embroidered patches made with your logo design to be attached to clothing, gear bags and quivers by the end user. Achievement award patches, tournament themed patches and "service stripe" patches can be made up in advance and distributed as needed.

Badges and pins can be made to promote the club and recognize special efforts by club members. Pins are very popular to display and trade with other archers. Consider making pins of the club logo, the logo of special tournaments, anniversaries and any other important occasion. Every time a pin from your club is displayed, your brand makes another impression with the viewer. These impressions add up to building the recognition of both your club as a group and the individual members of the club.

Club/National Archer Achievement Recognition

Achievement awards are an effective way to recognize individual performances and personal bests. Both USA Archery and the NFAA have achievement award pin or patch programs that you can adopt. The NFAA has award pins and bars for perfect "20" scores at all of the official field distances.

Club branded shirts and caps are a great way to show affiliation with the club and also to get recognition out in your community.

Because PRA has such a busy tournament schedule, the club tracks the member's scores on an annual basis and awards perpetual trophies for the top achievers in may of the shooting categories. First, Second and Third place awards are given annually to the top competitors in all of the contested disciplines. The awards are presented at the annual member's banquet and are very popular with the archers.

Club Volunteer Recognition

Many contributions to the club's activities are the result of the work of volunteers (*see **Chapter 2** The Importance of Volunteers*). Volunteer recognition is a key component is sustaining an all-volunteer staff. The issuing of certificates of appreciation and commendation should take place in a public setting where club members and their families can all enjoy the moment. At PRA, the annual awards banquet is the forum for presenting volunteer commendations.

Archers can earn a bar each time the shoot a 20 at a new distance for them.

USA Archery has an achievement pin program for both young and adult shooters. The JOAD achievement pin program is particularly popular with younger archers. JOAD's proudly display on their quivers the yellow ribbons with the pins attached to it.

There's some administrative work needed to track athlete performance, stage qualifying events, record scores, inventory pins or patches and present the awards. An achievement awards program will have more impact for the club and the athletes if there is an organized structure to the program. Schedule qualifying events on a regular basis so that athletes will prepare for competition in a timely manner. Keep the records and publish the results of qualifying rounds on your web site, news letter or Facebook page. Schedule an awards ceremony on a regular basis, say quarterly. Invite the entire club to participate. Take photographs and publish the awards ceremony report.

Among the possible categories for recognition are instructors and coaches, club officers and committee chairs, tournament chairs, and directors of outreach programs. You may also want to commemorate special member anniversaries and

rewards for longevity of service. The awards themselves can take many forms including certificates, plaques, special trophies, gavels and engraved archery gear. Do whatever you feel is right to truly thank the volunteers for their service to the club and to the community.

As with all presentations, club awards should be publicized to the membership through the club newsletter, web page, Facebook page and the local media. The more ways that you can get the word out about the club, its activities and the accomplishments of its members, the better known your club's brand will be. Successful publicity about your programs will attract more participants to the range and club membership growth over time.

Community Recognition

From time to time your club may be singled out for recognition by the community. Local newspapers and magazines may do a feature article on your club's programs. Some publications produce a "Best of . . ." list for the year and you may be included from time to time. The community government may issue a proclamation honoring a particular anniversary or achievement. You may also receive an award from a community organization for your stewardship of your range property, designating your range as a historical location or thanking you and your membership for contributions to the charitable activities within the city.

What ever the case, if the club receives public recognition, be sure to share the good news with the club members on you Facebook page, your web page and in your newsletter. If you have a permanent club house, post the articles or certificates on your brag wall.

You should also photograph or scan any articles, plaques, or certificates and keep the images as data files in your club's records. Down the road, paper gets lost and you will want to have some way of documenting your club's achievements. In any case, be proud of your accomplishments and don't be shy about letting people know about how you have been recognized.

Chapter 15
Some Thoughts on Coaching Archery

Coaching archery is a business different from teaching archery. A coach's relationship with an athlete is much more personal. Generalities are replaced with specifics. Directions are based on the athlete's individual skills and understandings. Coaching encompasses a wider range of the athlete's life including but not limited to sleep, nutrition, psychological well being, physical conditioning, scheduling, wardrobe, travel and financial issues. While coaching does not lend itself to following a prescribed curriculum, having a plan and a specific set of goals as well as means to achieve them are essential to a successful coaching relationship.

I've been teaching a wide range of disciplines over decades. My athletic coaching experience is much shorter. Like many archery coaches, I came to coaching later in life and found that there was a lot I knew and a lot I needed to know. With the experience, observation reading and discussions with athletes and other coaches I've gathered information that may be useful for you in coaching your own athletes. In putting together this chapter, I'm drawing on the expertise of others as well as my own experience to organize some thoughts and principles that may be applied to your athletic program.

Talent

Archery is primarily a recreational sporting activity. All of the instructional certification materials emphasize inclusiveness in archery programs using an "athletes first, winning second" direction as expressed in the American Sports Education Program materials from Human Kinetics. According to ASEP, the major objectives of (particularly youth)

If you are so inclined, coaching individuals can be very rewarding . . . and challenging.

sports are to " Help the athletes have fun, help the athletes develop as a person and to help athletes become 'winners' in life as well as in sports." As there is no money of any substance as a lure for athletes into the sport of archery, fun must be a key component in any archery development program. Without some element of enjoyment, there is little motivation for athletes to train and to compete.

As I have noted elsewhere, archery is a numbers game. In a high volume archery instruction program you will see thousands of archers per year. From time to time you may find an exceptional individual who has a unique combination of physical abilities, emotional direction, and a drive to excel that can be nurtured through coaching into becoming a successful competitor. Such individuals are one in 10,000. Some of the markers to look for are:

- A strong desire to be successful in archery
- The ability to follow coaching directions quickly and precisely
- A tendency towards Obsessive Compulsive Disorder (OCD)
- The time and willingness to train and practice
- The emotional stability to handle setbacks and disappointments without emotional tumult
- Access to a gymnasium and the willingness to use the gym regularly
- Adequate financial support to provide for equipment, training expenses, travel expenses and sustained time away from work for practice
- Robust family support with time, resources, and emotional support from the other family members.

A top competitive athlete starts with talent. If the talent isn't there, no amount of training will produce top competitive results. At the same time, talent without training and dedicated work will be unfulfilled. Talent alone will only get an athlete so far. After that it is hard work that produces champions. Only time will tell if your 1 in 10,000 athlete will become the 1 in 100,000 champion.

Archery coaches are the talent scouts for the sport. You should be on the lookout for athletic talent at all times. You never know when a first-time archer may have what it takes to go all the way. When you find a talented athlete, nurture that individual's interest in the sport and work to get them into a coaching relationship with someone who can successfully develop their talent into competitive success.

Physical Conditioning

It is important to recognize that archers are athletes. It's easy to think of archery as an aiming sport, but successful archers, no matter what the discipline, have an element of physical conditioning suitable for the task at hand. In teaching and coaching Olympic Recurve archery, the single most common issue I find with beginning and intermediate archers is a lack of physical strength. The NTS shooting form is very specific in its aspects of body positions and movements. The vast majority of beginning archery competitors simply do not have the strength to execute the maneuvers correctly. The mass and draw weight of the bow system crushes their shooting form, they are biomechanically inefficient, and they fatigue quickly.

Archery is a technical sport with a substantial physical component. Archery is both aerobic, in that a sustained effort has to be maintained over a long period of time; and at the same time, archery is anaerobic in that each individual athletic effort is of a very short duration. Devising a training program that addresses both of these issues is one of the first jobs of an archery coach.

Building physical strength takes time and deliberate effort. Coaches should create exercise plans that progressively increase loads, allow for adequate recovery time, and specifically build the strength needed for archery activities. If athletes have access to a gymnasium, you can work with the personal trainers at the gym to guide and supervise an exercise program. If a gym is not available, most archery exercises can be done with the archer's own weight and free weights. The exception to this is the Lat Pull Down exercise; that requires a specific piece of equipment to produce the correct loading and direction. Some type of equipment or apparatus will be required to do this essential exercise. If funds are short, many thrift stores carry a range of weight benches with lat pull down brackets at much reduced prices. (Years ago I worked on a promotional production for Goodwill Industries and their staff said that exercise equipment is one of their top categories of donations from the public.)

On pages 97-101 in Rick McKinney's book,

"The Simple Art of Winning" you'll find a number of useful exercises for archers. If you don't already have a cache of archery specific exercises, Rick's is a good place to start.

The ubiquitous Theraband™ elastic band (*below*) may also be used to create lateral and radial loads for strengthening the rotator cuff and the shoulder joint.

Core strengthening exercises are critical for competitive archery success. You can use balance balls, stretch bands, kettle and dumbbell weights, and even sledgehammers (as weights, not for beating athletes!) to strengthen the core muscles. The archery shot must originate from a stable physical platform. A strong core is essential for success.

As a general guideline to strengthen athletes for archery, use lighter resistance weights and more repetitions when doing an archery workout (a strength-building workout rather than power or speed). Mix the workout exercises with stretching to maintain adequate flexibility and body movement. A key area for stretching is the pectoral muscles in the chest. With most of us spending lots of time in front of a keyboard, there is a tendency for the pectoral muscles to compress and lose their elasticity, pressing the shoulders forward while the back muscles become weak and hyper extended. This condition, called thoracic kyphosis, can be corrected over time by strengthening the back muscles and performing stretches that expand the pectoral muscles. It will be impossible for an athlete to achieve correct back tension and scapular alignment if the pectoral muscles are too tight.

You need to explain to your athletes that the strengthening process will take months to a year or more to achieve the desired results. During the strengthening and conditioning phase of initial training, all archery form work should be performed with very light weight equipment and training aids. The emphasis should be on developing the habits and muscle memories necessary to complete the shot sequence in the correct form. You may find, as I have, that even a pipe bow with a four pound draw weight will tire an athlete quickly when they are practice the shot sequence. You should push your athlete to fatigue but stop the exercise or form work as soon as the athlete is unable to maintain the form. Any practice of bad form will only set back the progress of developing a stable archery shot.

All strengthening and exercises and no shooting makes Johnny/Jill an unhappy archer. Shooting arrows is the prize for all of the work of training. During the strengthening phase, include shooting at a blank bale using the very lightest draw weight equipment possible. A 10-pound draw weight is not too light. Have the archer shoot with their eyes closed while standing two meters/yards from the bale. Emphasize that the archer should focus on how the shot feels. Mental attention should be on the specific portion of the shot sequence that is the subject of the day's workout. Ask the archer. "How does that feel?" Pay attention to the answer and give appropriate directions to the athlete to improve the feel and consistency of the shot.

Use Specific Physical Training (SPT) exercises to further strengthen an athlete's archery muscles. You can also use the 30 second hold as a means of judging the results of the strength building program. Add a stretch band to the loading of the bow for SPT's as a means of stepping up in draw weight. When an athlete can hold a bow plus a stretch band for 30 seconds in good form and with no shaking, they are ready to move up their shooting bow to the next step in draw weight. If the archer is unable to hold the bow at full draw for 30 seconds, start with sets of shorter hold times, say 5, 10, 15 seconds and more until the 30 second hold can be maintained with good form and without shaking.

One of the principles of training is that you should train as you want to compete, because you will compete as you train. Even at these early stages of technical and strength development, the coach should include into the practice process the elements of the shot sequence that will need to be habitual at the time of competition. This is particularly important the "mindset" and the "relaxation and recovery" portion of the shot sequence. If these "non steps" are not practiced consistently, when the pressure of completion is upon the athlete, these critical steps will be left out of the shot sequence producing lower scores. Practice as you want to compete and you will compete as you practice.

The strength phase of training can be long and boring but it is essential for the development of competitive success. Don't short change the process. Don't let athletes move up to draw weights they can't handle with proper form. And don't enter athletes into important tournaments before they are ready to compete.

Training Design and Specificity

There are lots of resources on developing athlete training programs. Look on the USA Archery web site for links to publications from the US Olympic Committee on a wide range of topics. I'm not going to repeat that content here but there are any number of wide scope training principles that can be applied to any athletic endeavor. Here are a few:

The Individual Response Principle states that each athlete will respond differently to the same training stimulus. There are a number of reasons for this range of response: heredity, age, nutrition, general fitness, personal motivation, environmental factors, disease, or injury. Whatever the cause of the differentiation in response, coaches need to monitor and adjust the training process to reflect the individual's physical condition. There is no "one size fits all" category for physical and technical training. The process needs to be customized for each athlete.

Training introduces fatigue into the body. The body reacts to fatigue by adapting and strengthening to meet the loads placed on it. The adaptive changes take time and are subtle at first. Months of training are needed to see progress. Both coaches and athletes need to have patience while the body adapts to the new loads put upon it. Rush the process and you are inviting injury that can set back progress, delay development, and in some cases actually take an athlete out of the sport.

The body will adapt to new loads and if the loading doesn't change it will settle into a state of static fitness. To increase strength, the body needs to have the workload increased incrementally over time. There will be no improvement in fitness/strength without the progressive increase in workload. Also realize that the body does not build muscle during exercise. Exercise fatigues the muscles and tears them down. Muscle is built during rest periods where the body rebuilds the muscles in a stronger form. (It's nice to speculate that if we build muscle when resting, we think we could sleep our way to fitness. I've tried and it doesn't work.)

The rate of physical conditioning is affected by three factors that can be remembered by the acronym FIT: Frequency, Intensity and Time (duration). To make progress, each element must be slowly and steadily increased over time. Frequency refers to the number of sessions per week, month, and year. Intensity refers to the total training load per week, month and year. Time refers to the duration of the training session in hours per week, per month, and per year. Progression also refers to the idea that training starts out in the context of general principles and progresses towards the sport-specific needs. With complex sports such as ours, progression may refer to the development of parts of the process into an integrated whole. Progression may also refer to the transition from quantity of work to the quality of the work.

It is important that the training process and the exercises prescribed for the athlete be specific to the desired results. You should train for the results that you want. Don't expect that strength in one part of the body will automatically transfer to another part of the body. In archery, the required strengths are well defined in the shot sequence. Train your athletes to be strong in the areas where needed.

Include variety in your training regimen. Doing the same thing every day leads to static, rather than dynamic conditioning. Static conditioning works only a limited set of muscles over a limited or zero range of motion creating stiffness and inflexibility. Dynamic conditioning works the entire body over time building strength and flexibility, desirable qualities for an archer. Variety also makes the training process more interesting helping to avoid boredom. The two basic concepts of the Variation Principle are "Work/Rest" and "Hard/Easy." Focus on a different part of the shot sequence with each practice. Shoot long and short distances. Shoot with and without a sight. Vary the draw weight of the bow. Shoot different volumes of arrows. Include other training activities in your training week including gym workouts, yoga, mental training, visualization, aerobic workouts, and mock tournaments. Things that break up the day will improve participation.

Be sure to properly warm up and stretch before any training exertion. Proper warm up will prepare the muscles for work, increase blood flow to the muscles, increase cardiovascular activity and prepare the body for exertion. After the workout, a proper cool down period is also required so that the body can return to its at rest state without cramping or the pooling of fluids. Cool downs should also include lots of hydration to help the body flush away waste products produced during muscular activity. Failing to cool down properly may result in injury and the interruption of the training progression.

Training is a long term process. Strengthening takes place over time and can't be rushed. Plan for the amount of time it will take to get your athlete into condition and work with them to understand how important patience is when building both strength and technical excellence.

Training is also reversible. The loss of conditioning and endurance can be quite rapid. On average it takes three times as long to develop a level of conditioning as it does to lose it. During the season, athletes are constantly challenged with workloads that build and maintain a level of strength and fitness. During the necessary off season recovery time, the coach should provide the athletes with off season maintenance programs using a variety of sporting activities to minimize conditioning loss in preparation for next season's training.

There's lots of specific training information in the USA Archery Level 3 Coach curriculum. Don't just think of taking the Level 3 class, seeing some stuff, and then going back to what you were doing before. The Level 3 course materials, if thoroughly studied and understood, have enough substantial content for a coach to take an archery athlete to the top levels of competition. Really pay attention to the information in the course content and do your best to implement them in your own coaching activities.

Analysis and Synthesis in the Coaching Process

Because archery is a technical sport, there is a lot of detail in the shot sequence for an athlete to learn and execute. Archery is the prototypical OCD sport, so each step of the process must be repeated exactly from one shot to the next. Adaptations must be made for weather conditions and possibly equipment issues but the basic process of archery is "Shoot a 10. Do it again." Shooting a 10 is relatively easy. Doing it again is the hard part.

A coach should have a very clear understanding of the idealized shot. NTS provides us with such a model. If a coach is going to coach NTS archery, they should have an absolutely full understanding and mental image of the idealized shot process. If a coach is going to teach another shooting style or with other equipment, the need to fully understand and picture the idealized shot is no less important. A coach must know what the expected shot sequence looks like in every detail.

When working with athletes, coaches observe the shot process. During the observations coaches may see a number of items/actions by the athlete that are inconsistent with the idealized shooting form. The coach must then prioritize the issues to be revised and then create, "synthesize" a plan of communication and action to direct the athletes toward the desired results. The most serious issues, the ones that may affect the safety of the archer or that will be the most difficult to correct if repeated incorrectly, must be addressed first. An archer is only likely to address one shooting form issue at a time. Giving a ton of notes will just overwhelm the athlete. Prioritize and then direct the practice accordingly.

The coach's process is to analyze what is before you, compare it to the idealized vision of the shot and then synthesize the best method to adjust the issue into compliance with the idealized vision. Sometimes this analysis happens in real time, as the archer is shooting. If so, an immediate adjustment can be made. Sometimes the insight occurs after the action but still in time to tackle corrective action. And sometimes an insight will occur after and event or training session is over and action must be taken at a later date. The point is that the role of coaches is to be acute and informed observers who can provide useful feedback to their athletes in a timely manner.

At some point, it is likely that you will reach a conflict between the ideal and the actual that can not be resolved by additional coaching. At that point an adjustment in the technique will be required in order to produce a repeatable result, sustainable over days of competition. Using the principle of individualized response, the ideal model for one athlete may be different from the idealized model for another athlete. Only time and the coach's experience will develop the necessary vocabulary of movements for each individual athlete. Whatever the adaptations, the process of analysis and synthesis remain the essence of the coach's job.

Using Video and Image Feedback

Imaging technology is ever changing with greater capabilities at lower costs. The development of the camera capabilities of smart phones and tablet computers puts high definition videography in the hands of everyone. Today there is no need to purchase extra equipment in order to add video feedback to a coaching vocabulary. The camera, monitor, and storage are all in one handy package. The ability of a coach to record and immediately play back an action is invaluable when running a training session.

Adding position and motion analysis software allows a level of precision that was not available just a few years ago. Dartfish software is the gold standard in image analysis for sports but the very high cost of a license along with the need to use a more complex computer system puts Dartfish out of the price range for most archery programs and coaches.

Smart phone and tablet users have an option in the Coach's Eye app for iOS and Android. While not as sophisticated as Dartfish, Coach's Eye is an extraordinarily useful tool for a very modest investment.

High speed video is another useful coaching tool. Professional high speed video camera systems cost thousands if not tens of thousands of dollars. An affordable alternative is the Casio EX-FC100 snap camera that includes high speed video with frame rates up to 1000 frames per second. At the time of this writing, the Casio camera is no longer being imported into the US. Used ones can be found on the Internet. The Casio EXILIM High Speed EX-FH25 is still available (has the 1000 fps capability) and the FH20 it replaced is available used. The FH25 is the better part of $500 unfortunately. Nobody else seems to want to put HiSpeed video in our hands; HD yes, but HS no.

As with any technological product, technical offerings and market conditions change on a moment to moment basis. Keep you eye out for new imaging tools that you can adapt for archery. Do your research and you will find a host of affordable video coaching aids.

Details and Fine Tuning of the Archer's Shot

At some point in an archer's training, the archery shot stabilizes and the athlete is not going to make any more major changes in their shooting form. You may encounter an archer who has been shooting for years, has a stable shot sequence and is not likely to disassemble and rebuild the shot for the sake of an idealized vision of the "way things are done."

In broad strokes, there are three essential factors in the shot sequence that are required for archery accuracy. One is a strong bow arm. Two is shooting with back tension to align the forces in the bow

Capturing video images, even high speed video, has never been easier, allowing archers to see themselves as others see them.

along the arrow line. Three is to have a smooth release. Everything in the shot sequence either leads up to or derives from these three actions. Look for any deviation from these principles when analyzing a non-standard shot sequence.

Fine tuning an archer's shot consists of very careful observation of the shot process to detect any small movements and inconsistencies. Many small movements and tics are unconscious to the archer. Using video is a big help in refining very small deviations in the shot sequence. Look at each part of the archer's contact with the bow/arrow system in very close detail. Magnify the image if using video and look for any tics or contrary movements. Use high-speed video to analyze arrow flight and look for contact of the arrow with the bow system during the power stroke and as the arrow leaves the riser. Archery consistency is a matter of fractions of a millimeter from shot to shot. Look very carefully at all aspects of the shot as you refine an archer's shooting form.

Criteria for Evaluating Coaches

(From materials presented by Wade Gilbert, Ph.D. and Catherine Jackson, Ph.D.)

Included in the USA Archery Level 3 Coach Certification curriculum materials are a list of qualities of a successful coach as noted by National Head Coach Kisik Lee in his book "Total Archery." Another instrument for measuring coaching effectiveness is the Coaching Behavior Scale for Sport (CBS-S) in which athletes evaluate a coach's performance along seven different categories of coaching parameters:

Technical Skills Coaches need to fully understand the technical requirements of the sport. Such understanding can include physical training, sport-specific skills, equipment choices and adjustments, and tournament rules.

Competition Strategies Coaches need to know and communicate the appropriate strategies for entering, pursuing, and winning competitions. While this skill is more relevant in team sports, there are competitive strategies that can be employed to improve outcomes in archery tournaments.

Personal Rapport Coaches need to be able to communicate with the athletes both verbally and nonverbally. Empathy for the emotional state of the athlete is essential in such communications. In many cases, the perceived value of empathy is not so much in the clarity of speech but in the attitude of the speaker.

Physical Training and Planning Directing physical training is a fundamental responsibility of coaches. Coaches should not only know what exercises and work loads are appropriate for their sport and athletes but also should monitor and adjust training loads to reflect the response of the athlete's body to stress.

Mental Preparation Archery in particular is a mental game. Once an athlete has reached a level of proficiency, it is the athlete's mental state that will have the greatest influence on his performance. The goal of sports psychology is to create right thinking in sport. Sports psychology training should be integrated into the regular training process and not isolated off in separate training segments.

Goal Setting Goal setting for both the program and the individual athlete is a cooperative process between coaches and the athletes. The Level 3 Coaching curriculum uses the "SMARTER" goals method to analyze an athlete's current state and establish short term, mid term and long term goals in three categories, process, results and outcomes. Using the supplied worksheets and templates in the Level 3 curriculum will help athletes and coaches establish demanding and attainable goals.

Negative Rapport There are times when the personalities of coaches and athletes clash. While short term fixes can some times be implemented, long term resolution of personality conflicts are very rare. In an environment of negative rapport, communications will stop and rebellion may ensue. There is no option but to sever the coach-athlete relationship and find an alternative.

This list of coaching skills is necessarily subjective and, as tested, is based on the opinions of athlete's responses to questions by researchers.

In order to more numerically quantify a coach's effectiveness Cunningham and Dixon have proposed a new model that attempts to evaluate coaching effectiveness along six dimensions of coaching performance:

Athletic Outcomes Coaches, especially high-priced ones in high visibility programs are always subject to evaluation based on the athletic outcomes of their athletes. Athletic outcomes are easily quantified in scores and statistics. Evaluating a coach based on scores is direct and specific.

Academic Outcomes (for students) Coaches working with young athletes who are in school have a responsibility to see that the students are accomplished in the classroom as well as the athletic field. Academic outcomes are quantifiable in class grades and can form a basis for comparison between coaches.

Ethical Behavior There are lots of temptations to cheat in sports. Coaching relationships with athletes are close and personal. There are opportunities for abuse, coercion and criminal misconduct. A coach must keep his/her actions beyond reproach with only the most scrupulous of behaviors and statements.

Fiscal Responsibility Athletic programs often have a budgetary component. Coaches are responsible to create accurate budgets for their programs and administrate those programs with financial discipline. A coach will be held accountable for the way they handle their program's money.

Recruit Quality Recruiting is an activity that is often associated with big time team sports. Recruiting is also a key component for an archery coach. As noted above, talent is the raw material for a coach and an athletic program. The ability of a coach to identify, recruit and nurture talent is an essential coaching skill.

Athlete Satisfaction Because the only reward for an athlete in archery is tournament results, the process of training needs to be satisfying as well as productive. Athlete satisfaction with their performance and their relationship with the coach is essential to sustaining a competitive archery program. Much of athlete satisfaction turns around the relationship with the coach and the other athletes as much as it does with competitive outcomes.

Schemes of this type are valuable in large scale athletic operations where salaries, reputations and athletic outcomes are highly visible and are the subject of public speculation and opinion. For our small sport, where the vast majority of coaches are volunteers and the athletic outcomes have little impact beyond the interests of the athletes and their families involved, there is not much point to doing an extensive study of the effectiveness of archery coaching. However, for a coach or for the director of an archery program, these lists of coaching traits can be a useful tool for understanding your own skills and the skills of your colleagues. Identifying strengths allow a coach to feel confident in their abilities. Working on areas of coaching skills that could be improved is then guided by these models. Not every issue is relevant but reading and reflecting on these topics will only improve your coaching skills.

How you perceive your role as a coach will frame the way you pursue the process of coaching. Because framing is often implied rather than specified, you may find that an approach that appeared to be working for you is not as effective as it could be.

I was introduced to the writing of a Coaching Philosophy statement as an exercise during a Level 3-4 course at the Olympic Training Center in Chula

Serious archers must keep written records . . . serious coaches, too.

Vista, CA in 2005. I found the process of developing a coaching philosophy to be very valuable, both as an intellectual exercise, a source of valuable conversational insights between the coaching candidates and as a marketing tool for describing the framework from which I coach athletes. Writing a Coaching Philosophy statement is now part of the current Level 3 course curriculum and I have included the same exercise as a part of my Level 2 classes since 2006. Putting into words the reasons and motivations for teaching archery has proved to be an important learning and sharing experience among archery instructors and coaches. Once written down, the abstract ideas become concrete and can then be shared with athletes and their parents.

Coaching Priorities: Winning First or Athletes First?

The ASEP curriculum emphasizes athlete centered sports programs over wining focused training. Such an approach includes everyone and can build character (for youth) that extends beyond the scope of athletics. But how many times have you read articles in the news about big time coaches in big time athletic programs and businesses being fired for athletic performances that don't meet expectations.

There's no such big money or big public expectations about the sport of archery but some coaches may find themselves in an environment where winning performance is expected. In such situations, your priorities may have to shift. If you expect your athletes to win, you will need to put 80% of your coaching effort into your best athletes. It's only fair to them and top performers will expect nothing less. Others in your program can receive direction as available but the best athletes deserve the most time and expertise from the coaching staff. This is not a popular or politically correct point of view but it is essential if winning is the goal of an athletic program. Be sure you know what the expectations of your situation are before signing on to coach in a competitive environment. Does winning first work for you? If it doesn't, then pass on the opportunity and seek out a less stressful recreational program.

Expectations of High Performance in the Athlete

In the mid 2000's the United States Olympic Committee issued a directive that all of the sanctioning sports organizations appoint a High Performance Director and develop a high performance plan for excellence in their sport. When I first came to the sport of archery, I was unfamiliar with the term High Performance as applied to sports and assumed that a high performance program was a matter of identifying and implementing best practices within the sport so that athletes could perform at the top level.

It turns out that there's much more to high performance programs than that. In practice, High Performance Directors are primarily statistical mathematicians who analyze the performance data from competitions in order to establish benchmark standards of performance that will win competitions. High performance analysts tabulate and graph the top performances of not only their own athletes but those of the competition, identifying patterns and performance standards that are required to be successful in a sport.

For archery, most of the source data comes from tournament scores. Other information may include demographic data about the competitors, weather and field conditions, the time of day of the competition and the spacing of time between competitions. The analysis of such information is usually closely held by the sponsoring organization in order to preserve a perceived or real competitive advantage.

For archery, most of the needed source data is public information, published in the results portion of the event's write up. Historical information may go back a number of years for larger state, national and international tournaments. It doesn't take a lot of sophisticated math to look at the top finishing results in each category and determine what scores it takes to finish in the top 3, 5 and 10.

For example, if you want to compete in the Men's Freestyle Compound division at the Las Vegas indoor tournament, the top score for the top 20 or so finishers will be a perfect score. An elimination shoot off will require a perfect score to advance. After a few rounds of eliminations, inside out scoring is employed to finally find a winner. As a competitor, every arrow you shoot must be a 10 and if you want to win, eventually those arrows must fall entirely inside the 10 ring. This is the high performance expectation for this tournament. If you can shoot this well, you can be competitive. If you can't, you won't win and will have to train harder to win next time. In either case, there is a well-defined standard of excellence that you either make or loose.

Looking at long distance outdoor tournaments, the winning score is usually 95% of a perfect score for male recurve archers and 97+% for male compound release archers. You can look at the results of top tournaments in local, state, national and international tournaments for the shooting categories in which you or your athletes compete and pretty quickly establish what the performance standards that you will need to achieve in order to win.

Serious students need competition to determine where they stand. It is the proving ground of technique.

These standards are pretty well fixed by the competitive nature of the sport. In your practice sessions, archer-athletes will need to achieve the required standards in order to have any expectations of a podium finish. If the standards are not met in practice, it is up to the archer and the coach to decide whether entering the tournament at all is the right thing to do at that time. You may choose to go to tournaments for the competitive experience. To shoot a personal best or to socialize with other archery friends but if you want to win, you will have to shoot as well as the best competitors to come out on top.

Creating a culture of excellence in a program is an ongoing effort to expect and reward the best performance from each athlete. You can't get excellence in competition if you don't demand excellence in preparation. Sue Enquist, UCLA and USA Softball coach, said that at the beginning of each practice session she asked each athlete how they were feeling. Are you at 100% today? Are you at 70% today? However you are feeling, give me 100% of that. Excellence comes from giving 100% of your available skills and energy each day.

Competition Routines and Mindsets

The NTS shot sequence contains a short, say 4-6 second, pause after setting the hands called mindset where the archer is expected to clear the head of extraneous thoughts and pre-visualize the aspect of the shot process that they are working on at the time. A somewhat longer period of time, about 15-20 seconds, is allotted at the end of the shot sequence for reflection and feedback. That's not much time to get an athlete into a competitive frame of mind. There are lessons from other individual sports, such as track and field, that may be of value in preparing an archery athlete to compete.

An archer, in their relaxed, day to day state, is not mentally or physically prepared to be a competitive athlete. There is a necessary transition from an ordinary state to a competitive state that must be made each time an athlete comes to face competition. A coach needs to define and direct a ritual of preparation that is consistently performed at each tournament in order to prepare the athlete to be ready.

The transition from civilian to competitor starts in the day or days before the event by organizing all of the equipment, uniforms, and supplies that will be needed at the event. A check list should be made and items checked and double checked to be certain that all required materials are in hand and packed.

Traveling to the venue will involve some time and possibly some disruption, whether flying or driving. If you are driving it is possible to take more supplies and equipment than when flying. Be sure to include a shade device, either an umbrella or a pop-up canopy. Also pack chairs and a lounge chair for each archer. The athlete should stay as relaxed as possible while traveling, focused on enjoying the trip.

Once you have arrived at the hotel, unpack your suitcase, hang up the competition uniform, and verify that all of the equipment is in place as packed. If the venue is unfamiliar to you, a pre-competition visit to the field can help to reduce jitters.

The mental preparation to compete starts on the morning of the first day of practice. After showering, the athlete puts on each piece of clothing of the competitive uniform. At each step of adding another layer, the athlete should look in the mirror and really picture themselves as competitors. The morning breakfast should be a combination of slow burning carbohydrates and fats with little protein. The hydration process should begin with lots of fruit juice and plain water.

> "Archers should be polite and friendly as they walk up to collect arrows and walk back to the waiting area but not linger in social conversations. They are there to compete. There will be time to socialize later."

Once the archer arrives at the venue, a resting place needs to be established that is unique for each individual athlete. If the event is outdoors, the shade device should be set up. Each athlete needs to have their own chair or chaise lounge for resting between ends. Chairs should not be shared. The athlete should mentally repeat that "this is my space" and "I am in full control of what happens in this space."

The equipment should be set up and checked in every detail. The archer needs to repeat to themselves that "I am here to compete," "My equipment is the best available and in top working order" and that "I am here to compete at my best." The strapping on of the quiver, arm guard, finger sling, and finger tab should be performed as a ritual and reinforce the mental picture of the athlete, ready to compete.

Stretching and warm up drills should be accompanied by mental images of the athletes succeeding in every aspect of the competition. If your athletes are competing as or with a team, a team member may lead the warm up and mental imaging exercises. If your athlete is competing alone, having a prepared recording of music with verbal prompts can be helpful.

When the archer steps to the shooting line for the first time, they should take a moment to establish their possession of that space. If compliant with the rules, four golf tees should be placed in a rectangular pattern just in front of and just behind the shooting line to establish a box for the archer to shoot from. Additional tees may be used to mark foot positions. Indoors, small tabs of removable tape may be used to mark the floor. This box on the archery field is like a batter's box in baseball. It is the archer's territory. If there is no way to mark the box, archers should mentally picture the space every time they step to the shooing line. Archers should say to themselves "This space is mine. Everything that happens in this space is my doing. I am responsible for all the actions in this box. No one else can enter or intrude into this box while it is in my possession." Each shot is then executed with confidence. If obstacles arrive, the athlete will feel ready to address them and adapt as needed.

Between ends, the athlete should return to their resting chair and sit quietly. They should take the time to re-hydrate and add fuel if needed. Some venues play loud music between ends while athletes are recovering their arrows. If there is some opportunity for silence, athletes can use their own calming music playing on earphones. They should take the time to picture the process of making the next shots but should not brood over past shots that are over and done with. They should not socialize with other archers while the shooting continues. Archers should be polite and friendly as they walk up to collect arrows and walk back to the waiting area but not linger in social conversations. They are there to compete. There will be time to socialize later.

At the end of the competitive day, they should carefully repack their equipment, checking for any damage or wear that they will need to be repaired before the next day of competition. If this is a one day event, they should say their goodbyes. If the competition continues on the next day, have a dinner with a balanced mix of carbohydrates, fats and proteins and get to bed early to be rested for the next day. Repeat the preparation ritual each day of competition until the event is over.

Think of each activity in transitioning from everyday street self to competitive self as a step towards actualizing the competitor meant to be. This transition is not automatic and must be practiced and ritualized as much as learning every step of the shot sequence.

Trusting the Field

There are many variables that may impact athletic performances. Weather, footing, lighting, mental states, physical health, and conditioning can all be score affecting factors at a tournament. Each of these factors need to be addressed and adapted to during the course of completion. There are some elements of the environment that do not change no matter what the conditions. The distance to the target will always be the same. The target will always be the same size. The amount of time allotted for an end will always be the same. Athletes need to trust the field and the rules. No matter what may be changing around you, the field will always be the same. Athletes need to focus on doing what they have trained to do and to expect the same results as in practice. Focus is on the constants in competition, and adapting to the variables.

The Coach's Role in Administrating a Training Program

Keeping records is never fun. It's time consuming, boring, and seldom appreciated. However, it is the coach's job to organize and keep records of the training progress of each of their athletes. Management guru Peter Drucker said that if you can quantify what you measure, you can improve it. Logging athlete's performance numbers and graphing the results is a solid tool for monitoring an athlete's progress. Keep records of training days, arrows shot, scores achieved, miles run, weights lifted, and any other metric that you feel is valuable.

Take the time to go over the records with your athletes from time to time in order to recognize progress and identify training areas that need more work. If the archers are minors, go over the training records with the archers and their parents. Parents will appreciate your thoroughness and being included in the training process (that they are paying for.) In the records they can see the progress of their son or daughter in the sport. Having records can also be of value if there is any question about your coaching program. Dates, times, work loads, and scores are all evidence of the work done.

Thinking Right about Coaching

In objective of sports psychology is to guide athletes to thinking right about their sports and to achieve an optimal level of arousal to perform their best. Athletes need to have access to all of their abilities at the time they are most required, during competition.

There's no such category of psychological study for coaches. Coaches are pretty much on their own to find a path toward the maximum performance of the coaching art. A coach finds reward in the development, growth and performance of their athletes with a lot of frustrations along the way. It can be a struggle for a coach to maintain composure and motivation when things get tough.

As coaches, we direct our archers to focus on the shot process, rather than the arrow results. It is only through executing a consistent process that top scores can be achieved. So as coaches, we need to take our own advice and focus on the process of coaching when times are tough and athletes appear to not be making any progress. It is our job to think right about coaching just as we ask our athletes to think right about sports.

Trust your knowledge and experience. You've done this before or you've seen someone do this before. Trust the value of that knowledge and apply it to your work.

Have a reason for every coaching action that you deliver to an athlete. Really think about the process of athletic preparation and only act out of deliberateness. Don't just wing it, be clear and focused in your directions.

Be eager to learn more about your sport and your coaching skills. Seek out classes, workshops, books, videos and colleagues to learn as much as you can about sports training.

Remember the analysis/synthesis process of coaching. Look at what is before you, compare what you observe to the ideal image and then direct the athlete to move towards the ideal.

Respect your athlete at all times. As their age and maturity permits, involve the athlete in the decision making process. Work together with your athlete to define and then achieve their goals. Trust that you are making a positive difference in their lives.

Appendices

Appendix A
Safety and Orientation Script

Note Your audience is assumed to be standing, presumably near your target butts.

* * *

Hello everybody and welcome to the archery range. My name is <*your name*> and I will be your instructor for today's session.

We have three goals today. The first goal is to teach you the *archery range safety rules* so that you and everybody else on the range can be safe. The second goal is to teach you *basic archery shooting form* so that you can get the arrow from where you are to the target. And the third goal for today is to *have fun*! Does that sound good to you?

To get you off to a good start with your archery shooting form, let's have everyone spread out a bit so that there is enough room around you so you won't bump into your neighbor. Stand with your feet about shoulder-width apart. Check to see that your weight is evenly balanced between your feet and that your feet, hips and shoulders are all squarely aligned. Raise your two arms into a "T" shape with your hands at shoulder height. You have been given two pieces of safety equipment: an arm guard and a finger tab. The arm guard is on your bow arm. Rotate your head so that you are looking at your bow hand. Bring your draw hand up to a position under your chin. Check to see that your bow hand, draw hand and draw elbow are all positioned in a straight line. This is the posture that you will use to begin shooting the bow. Let's all practice getting into this form to a count of 1-2-3. <*Count off 1-2-3 slowly and repeat as necessary.*>

The bowstring is released by relaxing the fingers of your draw hand. When the string is released, you will feel a natural followthrough that takes your draw hand along your jaw line to the back of the neck. Let's practice the release motion by dong the 1-2-3 release drill. <*Count off 1-2-3 slowly and repeat as necessary.*>

Is everyone comfortable with this drill? Are there any questions? <*Answer any questions that arise.*>

As you look at the range you will see three lines on the ground. The line closest to you is the waiting line and you will stand or sit behind the waiting line at all times unless you are actively shooting or retrieving arrows.

The second line that you see is the shooting line. When you hear two blasts on the whistle, you will pick up your bow from the bow rack and go to the shooting line, straddling the line with your feet shoulder-width apart on either side of the line and your toes on an imaginary line perpendicular to the target. Do not touch an arrow at this time.

When everyone is safely on the shooting line, I will sound one blast of the whistle, which is the signal for you to take an arrow from your quiver, nock it on the bow, and commence shooting. When you finish shooting your three arrows, step off of the shooting line, step behind the waiting line, and place your bow on the bow rack.

<Instructor picks up a bow and an arrow to demonstrate all of the subsequent steps>

To shoot those arrows, you must:

Nock an arrow on the bow, holding the bow

straight up and down or resting the bottom tip of the bow on your shoe top. Place the nock of the arrow on the bowstring, orienting the index feather towards you and away from the bow handle. As you fit the nock to the string, listen for a "click" sound that tells you that the arrow nock is firmly seated on the string. The shaft of the arrow sits on the arrow rest. Note that when the arrow is correctly fitted to the bow it sits securely and will not fall off. Do not use your first finger to hold the arrow on to the bow.

Form a scout sign with your draw hand. Your draw hand should grasp the string with the first three fingers by forming a hook grip around the string at the first knuckle joints. Place the draw hand with three fingers under the arrow. Keep the back of the draw hand flat and relaxed. Put a little tension on the string to hold your hands in place on the bow and string.

Place your bow hand on the bow handle with the grip firmly seated in the "V" shape formed by your thumb and first finger. The handle of the bow should rest on the fleshy pad in your palm at the base of the thumb. Your first finger should rest on the front of the bow handle and your thumb should point towards the target when the bow is up in shooting position. Your other fingers should be relaxed and not gripping the bow handle.

Rotate the bow arm elbow outward so that the hinge joint at the elbow is straight up and down when the bow is held out in position. For right-handed archers, this rotation of the elbow is clockwise. For left-handed archers the rotation is counterclockwise. Let's practice this elbow position now. Everybody raise their bow arms to their sides and stick up their thumbs like you are hitchhiking. Rotate your hand so that your thumb is pointing toward the ground. Notice that the point of your elbow has rotated outward. Now, without rotating your elbow, rotate your wrist back until the knuckles on your bow hand are at a 45-degree angle to the ground. If you bend your elbow now, your thumb will point towards your chest. You can say, "Who is the best archer on the range? I'm the best archer on the range!"

Raise both hands together until the arrow is parallel to the ground and just below chin level. The bow arm elbow should be rotated outward (crease now vertical) and the knuckles of the bow hand should be oriented at a 45-degree angle to the ground. The draw arm should be at a height about level with your nose. Rotate your shoulders until they are oriented in a line towards the target.

Draw the bowstring back in a smooth motion until your draw hand comes to rest under your chin. Look at the target and relax the muscles making the hook in your draw hand fingers, releasing the string. Keep your eyes on the target and keep your bow arm up until you hear the arrow hit the target. Let the bow down and rest the bottom tip on the toe of your shoe while you nock another arrow and continue shooting. *<Instructor demonstrates how to shoot an arrow. Shoot only one arrow.>*

When you have shot all of your arrows, step off of the shooting line, walk behind the waiting line and place your bow on the bow rack. *<Now the participants shoot under your direction.>*

Now, let's start out with our first shot. Here are two whistle blasts. Go to the bow rack and pick up your bow. When you get to the shooting line, straddle the line, feet shoulder-width apart with your toes on a line perpendicular to the target the target. Remember to not touch an arrow until I give you the "one whistle" command.

To get you started, I (and the other instructors) will supervise your first shot to be sure that you are safe. Okay, <name of student>, you have the one whistle command, you can nock your arrow and shoot.

<Supervise each archer individually until they can handle the equipment safely. This process will take some time. The more coaches you have, the less time it will take. Do not rush or skip individual supervision. Do not have first-time archers shoot as a group at the beginning.>

When all of the archers have finished shooting, you will hear three whistle blasts, which is the signal for the archers to walk forward to the target line and then recover their arrows. As you move forward towards the target, pick up any arrows you find on the ground and take them with you to the target. Stop at the target line. At each target, the first two archers can approach the target from the side, not the front.

The most dangerous part of the arrow is the nock, not the point. As you pull the arrow out of the target you can poke your neighbor or you can poke yourself. Approach the target from the side to minimize the danger of being accidentally poked by a nock.

To remove an arrow from the target bale, place one hand flat on the target face, around the arrow. With the other hand, preferably your stronger hand, grasp the arrow shaft as close to the point as possible and pull the arrow straight out of the target. Do not bend or wiggle or twist the arrow as you pull on it. When the arrow is removed, place it in your quiver and then pull the next arrow. (If you are using ground quivers, lean each pulled arrow against the target bale as you pull them. When all the arrows are pulled, hold them by the points like a bouquet of flowers and return them to the ground quiver.) At no time should an archer have more than one arrow in their hand except when returning arrows to their ground quiver.

When you have pulled your arrows, walk back behind the waiting line and wait for the next whistle command.

If at any time you hear 5 or more blasts of the whistle, stop what you are doing, put your arrows in your quiver and look to the Range Master for further instructions.

Appendix B
Eight-Meeting Archery Program Instructor Class Syllabus

How to Use this Guide

The goal of the National Training system (NTS) is to maximize the application of biomechanics to the archery shot in order to increase athlete consistency and efficiency while reducing fatigue. This guide is intended to help archery instructors and coaches organize and convey the principles of the NTS method to new archers who have little or no previous experience with archery instruction. You are encouraged to bring your individual experiences, insights, and approaches to the teaching of the NTS method.

Use this course curriculum to help you to teach each of the steps of the archery shot in a sequence of classes designed to help new archers learn and achieve. Taking a cue from the coaching methods of international championship teams, this teaching approach uses string bows and stretch bands as training aids to help students learn the forms and muscle control needed to execute the archery shot. Students will not be expected to actually shoot the bow until the end of the third meeting. Use the anticipation of shooting arrows as a motivator to increase student participation.

Your students will be using lightweight archery equipment in this class along with ultra-lightweight training aids. String bows are simple loops of string, adjusted to your draw length, which can be used for miming the steps of shooting away from the range. Stretch bands add some draw weight and can be used to mimic the entire shot sequence including the release. A "pipe bow" adds the feel of having a bow in your hands and the reality of having a string to position on your face. Unlike a conventional archery bow, a PVC pipe bow may be safely "dry fired" for practice. The use of lightweight training aids allows you and the instructor to monitor and adjust your shooting form without placing your joints and muscles under the risk of injury that might occur when making a change under full bow load. (During the training process, your instructor may need to touch your arms or other parts of the body to bring you into alignment. If you have any concerns about contact by the instructor, please let him/her know and alternative approaches will be worked out.)

Set reasonable goals for achievement with each class. Only a very small percentage of the students will have the motor and mental skills needed to achieve a high level of success as a competitive archer. Do your best to nurture the talented students that you do identify. For the others, archery can be a lifelong recreational activity. Help the archers to have fun and remember that improved self-esteem comes from real success.

To help students to mark their progress, use a *Student Record of Achievement card*. This card is a printed form with places for the archer's name and group. Each class session is signed off on the card by the instructor. Stickers can be used to substitute for a signature. When all the class sessions are completed by the student and signed off by the instructor, give each student a certificate of completion.

To make the most of this instructor's guide, take the time to read through the material before your class begins to become familiar with the flow of the content. There may be a tendency to want to teach too much material too soon. Take your time and cover each topic as it comes up. While you are becoming familiar with this teaching approach, read the section on the lesson you are about to teach just before you meet with the students. Do not read from the guide while giving a lesson. Be sure to include your own personal touches to this material.

Also be aware of safety issues at all times. Use the safety backstop net and whistle commands, and enforce the rules for withdrawing arrows from the target. Also be certain never to be alone with an individual student archer at any time. Always have another adult with you especially if there is a need to discipline a child. Children needing to go to the restroom should go in pairs. Never escort a child to the restroom by yourself.

Meeting 1
Safety and Orientation

The goal of meeting one is to introduce the program, emphasizing three things: *Safety, Shooting Form* and *Having Fun*.

Safety Describe the range layout and the three safety lines: the waiting line, the shooting line and the target line. Explain the use of whistle commands for going through the shooting sequence. Keep the explanations short. More detail can be added as the class progresses. Establish the rules for bow and arrow handling including the use of the bow rack, when arrows can be drawn and when they can be shot.

Shooting Form Establishing good shooting form for the student will be the primary archery goal of this introductory program. The objective is to create a foundation of proper technique that the archer can use to build on towards competition success. Young students may not understand detailed explanations but they are very adept at mimicking demonstrations and modeling behavior. When giving directions to younger children, remember that they are not yet fully body aware. They know about their head, hands, and feet. They will understand best when you direct them to put these body parts in a specific place. The position of arms, legs, and torso will naturally follow the head, hands and feet directions. Even if you don't explain every detail, always use the NTS method shooting form in any of your demonstrations. Kids will learn the shooting form by observation and imitation.

The first day's instruction should be without the use of the bow and arrow. Use a string bow to demonstrate and practice the basic postures of shooting form.

Start with the foot positions on the shooting line. Remember that the body will follow the feet. Direct the students to place their feet on either side of the shooting line with their toes on a line towards the target. Indoors, you can use tape on the floor to indicate the desired line. Outdoors, lines can be drawn with lime, indicated with rope or arrows carefully placed on the ground.

Once the feet are in place, work with the students to ensure that their body is square with their feet and that the student's weight is evenly balanced between the feet. Look carefully at the position of the hips and shoulders to ensure correct alignment. The hips need to be rotated from the bottom forward, tucked under, so that the back is flattened. This maneuver will take some time to learn. Have the archer keep practicing until they can achieve a flat back posture. Look for exaggerated curvature of the lower back or for archers who are sticking out their buttocks. Try to get the archer's posture to be straight in all planes. As the instruction progresses to other topics, keep an eye on posture issues as they can creep up at any time.

In the more advanced stages of learning the NTS, archers will need to lower their center of gravity by dropping the rib cage and tightening their abdominal muscles. Depending on body type, the lowering of the rib cage can also increase string clearance for some archers. Competitive recurve archers will learn to focus their attention on the center of gravity of the body that is located inside the abdomen about 3" below the navel and about 2" inside the front abdominal wall.

For beginners, too much attention on these details will be distracting and boring. As an instructor, an awareness of future refinements will help you to monitor and adjust the archer's form to avoid having to unlearn incorrect form later. At the start, look for exaggerated chest positions and excessive spine curvature. Keeping the torso straight up and down will be a good first step towards a competitive stance.

The "T" stance is a good way to get started with upper body positioning. Have students extend their hands to the side to form a T shape. Again, the body will follow where the hands go. Look for balance and even weight distribution in the torso. Watch for twisting of the hips and shoulders that will put the archers out of alignment.

Work next on the bow hand and bow arm. Have the students hold the hand on their extended bow arm with the knuckles at a 45-degree angle towards the ground and with the fingers loosely curled. <need a photo here> Explain that the bow is held in the hand by the pressure of the string and that the handle is not to be gripped tightly. Have each student make an okay sign with their bow hand while holding their fingers relaxed. Demonstrate that only the first finger should come in contact with the bow handle. Have each student hold an arrow, point down, in their bow hand to simulate the bow handle. Adjust their hands into the proper position as needed. Check often for any tightness in the bow hand fingers.

The NTS method starts students right out with a three-finger draw hand grip on the string with the fingers held under the chin. The objective of this approach is to have students learn the correct form from the beginning and not to create the problem of having to unlearn incorrect techniques later. Start by having each student make a "scout sign" with their draw hand, 1st, 2nd and 3rd fingers up with the thumb holding the tip of the little finger. <need a photo here> In the early stages of learning shooting form, the position of the thumb can be troublesome. By holding the tip of the little finger with the thumb, the thumb is kept out of the way of the face. Also watch for students who include the little finger in their grip of the bowstring.

Use the string bow to indicate the position of the string on the three fingers of the draw hand. Have the students get the feel of the string in the deep hook of their fingers with the line of the string passing along the first joint of the middle finger.

Watch for students with too shallow a string hook and for students who place their thumb on the string behind the arrow and correct these if they occur.

Using the string bow, have the students mime their shot posture. Monitor and adjust each element of the shot form to bring the body into correct alignment. One of the goals of body alignment is to create a straight line between the bow hand, the draw hand and the draw elbow. Use a string or a long dowel measure this relationship and have students adjust their form to bring the hands and arms into alignment.

Fun Games are used to increase the fun factor and provide friendly competition. As the students will not be shooting on day one, ask questions along the way and give prizes for the correct answers. Examples of questions could be; "What is the two whistle command?" "Show me how to hold your bow hand." "Show me your foot position on the shooting line" "When can you draw arrows to shoot?"

A General Note on Games Games are more fun and more effective if you offer small prizes for achievement. For example, use small bags of M&M's, nuts, or Skittles. Keep a batch of prizes handy for any reward opportunity.

Meeting 1 Class Schedule

Introductions and class orientation	5 min
Range orientation and safety rules	10 min
Stretching	10 min
Shooting form demonstration and practice	25 min
Give out handouts and homework	5 min
Cleanup	5 min

Handouts
Student Record of Achievement Card
Class Syllabus
Printed guide to the NTS Method

Homework
Use a piece of string to practice your shooting form.

Meeting 2
More on Shooting Form

Review the basic shooting form and safety rules from Meeting 1.

Introduce the Draw Hand Hook, the Set Position prior to raising the bow.

Use the string bow to demonstrate and practice shooting posture. Introduce *stretch bands* as a tool for modeling the dynamics of the shot process. As the students shift from static poses to dynamic miming, the stretch band can provide a low-resistance simulation of the bow without overtaxing muscles.

Review Start the review of the previous lesson with foot position on the shooting line. Be sure the students feel comfortable at the line with their feet about shoulder-width apart and their toes on a line towards the target. (*Note* An open stance is preferred for outdoor competitive archers but is much too difficult to introduce at this early stage of training. Save the open stance for a time when the upper body positions have been fully mastered.) Have the students rock their bodies slightly left and right until they have a feeling for their feet connecting with the ground. Ask the students to pretend to grasp the ground with their toes. This grasping motion will cause a subconscious re-balancing of the body onto the balls of the feet.

Demonstrate how the body is unbalanced when the weight is resting on the heels. Demonstrate how much more stable the body is when more than half the body weight is resting on the balls of the feet. Have each student position their body so that about 70% of their weight is on the balls of the feet.

Using the string bow, have the archers review and practice the hand positions for both the bow hand and draw hand. Focus on the bow hand position, the bow arm elbow, and the draw hand under the chin. Check each archer to see that there is a straight-line relationship between their bow hand, the draw hand, and their draw elbow.

Introduce the Bow Demonstrate how the bow is brought to the shooting line and how it is held prior to making a shot. Have the archers handle their bows on the shooting line without an arrow. After emphasizing that the bow is never to be dry fired, have the students take a stance and bring the bow to shooting elevation. Let them feel the weight of the bow string and the pressure of the string and bow handle on their hands. Do not let them draw the bow at this time.

With the bows safely back on the bow rack, show the students the parts of the arrow emphasizing the nock and the index feather. Demonstrate nocking the arrow onto the bow string with the arrow nock placed under the nocking point. Show the relationship between the position of the index feather and the string. Be sure to point out how the nock makes a click sound when the string is correctly seated in the nock. Show them how arrow shaft is held by the arrow rest. Point out that the first finger of the bow hand is never to be used to hold the arrow in place. Also demonstrate that, for safety on the shooting line, the bow is to be held in the vertical position at all times during the process of nocking and shooting the arrow. Never permit archers to swing the bow to a horizontal orientation while nocking arrows or finishing a shot.

With bows again in hand, have each student practice nocking an arrow. Look for smooth equipment handling. Make sure the student handles the arrow in such a way that their fingers are not in the way of the nock when attaching the arrow to the string. Be sure the arrow is tight to the string nocking point and that the nock is fully seated. Verify that the arrow shaft is on the arrow rest and not on the shelf of the bow.

With an arrow nocked and the bow in the at-rest position, the students should place their draw fingers on the string and confirm the position of the string and arrow with the fingers of the draw hand. The NTS method has archers starting with the arrow nock placed between the first and second fingers. You may find that it is better to start archers out with three fingers under the arrow until a solid shooting form has developed. Placing the draw hand under the arrow minimizes the chance of pinching the arrow off of the arrow rest. Young archers especially will need some practice to hold their hands in the correct position and to not pinch the arrow nock. The use of a split finger grip can be introduced when the archer transitions into using a bow sight. The use of a finger tab with a spacer between the first and second fingers is strongly recommended when employing the split finger technique.

Have the students make the scout sign with their draw hands to remind them of the proper finger position. Look to see that the string is placed along the first joint of the first and middle finger. Check to see that the tip of the thumb of the draw hand is touching the little fingernail and that the archer is not grabbing the string while making a fist created by bringing the thumb forward. The back of the draw hand should be flat with no bending at the third knuckles (from the tips).

Ask the archers to build a habit of checking and verifying their draw hand position every time they hook and grip before a shot. Any small variation in the relationship between the string, arrow nock, and hand position can have a big impact on consistency.

When the students begin shooting, be sure the draw hand is placed in a consistent position on the bow string.. A solid hook on the string allows the draw fingers to be more relaxed and increases consistency.

Fun A Game Place a number of arrows in a blank target butt. Have the students count the number of arrows of each color fletching in the butt. Give a prize to all students who get the correct answer.

Meeting 2 Class Schedule

Welcome and goals statement	5 min
Stretching	10 min
Bow demonstration, nocking and draw hand set practice	35 min
Give out handouts and homework	5 min
Cleanup	5 min

Handouts List of archery organizations and key vendors with web site addresses
Homework Practice shooting form with a string. Visit the web sites and be prepared to talk to the group about what you learned.

Meeting 3
Still More on Shooting Form

Review NTS shooting form covered to this point. The review period is also a time to help students who have missed a session to catch up.
Reinforce and Introduce Bow Hand Position, Set Position, Set-up, Mindset and First Arrows

With their bows in hand but without arrows, introduce the students to the Hooking and Gripping portion of the shot. During gripping the archer's attention shifts from the draw hand to the bow hand. First have each student find their "life line" on their bow hand. Demonstrate to the students that no part of the bow grip should touch their hand to the outside of the life line. Again have the students make an okay sign with their bow hands and remind them that only the first finger is to come in contact with the bow.

With the lower bow tip resting on their inner calf, have the students place their bow hand on the handle with their knuckles at a 45-degree angle to the bow handle. The pivot point of the bow handle should fit firmly into the U-shape formed by the thumb and first finger. Walk the shooting line and verify that all the archers have the correct bow hand position and that their fingers are relaxed. Look for hands grabbing the handle like a baseball bat and for students using a "Death Grip" on the bow and correct them. Relaxation is the key.

The bow hand will naturally come to a moderately low wrist position as the force of the bow is resisted by the pad at the base of the thumb, known as the pressure point. This position also helps to align the bones in the hand and wrist with the bones of the lower arm. Shifting the burden of holding the bow's draw weight from the muscles to the bones is a fundamental principal in the application of biomechanics to archery shots. Any body misalignment of the skeleton will have to be compensated for by increased muscle strain. The net result of skeletal misalignment is increased muscle fatigue and inconsistent shooting.

The hook and grip phase is also a time to set the rotation of the bow arm in order to place the elbow of the bow arm away from the string. Many people have difficulty separating the movement of their elbow from the movement of their hand. One method to help with this problem is to have the archer extend their bow arm and rotate their bow hand so that the thumb points directly towards the ground. This action will force the bow arm elbow to rotate into the correct position. Then have the archer rotate their bow hand back to the 45-degree position without rotating their bow elbow. The bow arm will now be in the correct position. This action will require some practice as the archers learn to separate the motion of their arm from their hand.

Be vigilant on this point as the lessons continue. Many archers will set the bow arm properly and then rotate the elbow back downward as they raise the bow and begin to take the draw weight of the bow into their arms. When that happens, work with the archers on the transition from set to full draw without an arrow to improve their muscle memory on the elbow position.

Another way to help archers check their bow arm elbow position is to have them extend and then bend their bow arms. If the bow hand moves across the chest, the elbow is in the correct position. If the hand moves upward, the bow arm elbow has rotated downward and needs to be readjusted outward to the correct position.

When working on the bow arm, it is also important to look for archers who have pronated or hyper-extended elbow joints. This phenomenon, more common in girls than boys, is a condition in which the elbow joint bends beyond 180 degrees to form an obtuse angle. People with pronated elbows will have to be instructed to keep their elbows slightly bent to avoid string contact. Some people can do this and others are not able to control the angle of their elbow. Students who have pronated elbows should use a full-length arm guard.

Once the bow and string hands are properly placed, there is a brief time in which the archer prepares to address the target before raising the bow. In this Set position, the bow arm should extend at about a 45-degree angle to the ground. The draw arm should lie across the archer's torso in an "arm in a sling" position and some tension should be placed in the bow string by moving the draw side scapula partially around the rib cage.

Archery is a mental game as much as a physical one. Bringing a positive Mindset to the shooting process improves an archer's consistency and score. Young archers should focus on the process of making a successful archery shot and not the results of that shot. Too much concentration on the target or the score will distract the archer from the task at hand. If the form is correct, the arrow has no choice but to go to the correct place.

The goal of the competitive archer is to shoot the same shot every time. Have the students come to the shooting line without their bows and mime the steps of shooting the arrow with their eyes closed. Talk the students through each step as they practice miming the motions. Develop a script for talking yourself through the shot and repeat it each time you do this exercise. The exercise of visualizing and miming the shot is an activity that should be part of every practice session. In time, the students will be able to repeat the shot sequence with you. Eventually this script will become part of the student's own shot sequence (*see sample*).

A Sample Script

Draw hand down, in, rotate. Hook on the string. Bow hand, wrist down and the pressure point on the base of the thumb. Bow arm elbow rotate outward. Raise my head and look at the target. 1. Raise the bow arm and draw arm together and lock the bow arm. 2. Load the back and 3. Up to anchor. Beat. Transfer to the back and expand. (As you are expanding you may repeat either "bow arm, bow arm, bow arm" to reinforce the need to stabilize the bow arm or "back tension, back tension, back tension" to focus on back tension.)

This is the third meeting and by this time the young archers are dying to shoot arrows. Ideally, the shooting of arrows would be left until after the completion of the study of the shooting form. However, some shooting now will reinforce the topics already learned and will give the archers an emotional boost.

Start by demonstrating the shot. Shoot at a very short distance, about 10 feet, and shoot at a blank backstop. Remind the archers of the whistle commands. Use all of the form elements covered in the previous lessons as well as the form elements to be covered later in your demonstration shot.

Use the two-whistle command to bring the archers to the line but do not allow them to touch an arrow. Give the one-whistle command to each archer individually. Supervise every aspect of their first shot. When you feel that they can shoot safely, have each archer continue shooting until they have finished their allotment of arrows. Use your best judgment as to when to move on to the next archer. Have archers who have finished shooting their arrows return their bows to the bow rack.

Watch for posture issues. Keep the students balanced. Look for good alignment of the bow hand, draw hand and draw elbow. Watch for the correct bow hand position and for the rotation of the bow arm elbow away from the string path. Keep a special eye out for those students who have pronated elbows. Watch to see that all archers rotate their bow arm elbows outward so that the hinge joint is vertical for string clearance. Take action immediately to avoid injury form the bow string striking the bow arm. Always use a long arm guard to avoid injury. Also watch for archers who bend their bow wrists sideways to increase the clearance between the bow string and their arm. Work with a stretch band or string bow to help these students achieve the correct bow arm position.

Introduce the three-whistle command.

Show the archers how to remove arrows from the target. Demonstrate and emphasize the safety rules at the target butt:
- Always approach the target from the side, not the front.
- No more than two archers at the target at any one time.
- An arrow is to be put in the quiver before a second arrow is drawn
- Only one arrow in the hands at a time.

Have the archers shoot no more than two ends on this first day of shooting.

Practice Target Shoot at a blank bale for shooting form. Use the string bow to mold and practice form issues.

Meeting 3 Class Schedule

Welcome and goals statement	5 min
Stretching	5 min
Setup and mindset demonstrations, Shooting their first arrows + Safety at the target butt	40 min
Give out handouts and homework	5 min
Cleanup	5 min

Handouts Parts of the Bow and Arrow Diagram
Homework Study the parts of the bow and your practice shooting form.

Meeting 4
Adding Details

Review NTS Method shooting form to this point. Start by using the string bow and take the archers through the steps they have already learned. By now they should be fairly proficient at the basics. It's time to begin to work on the details. Use positive reinforcement to correct form flaws. Reward students who are doing well and those who make significant improvement.

Expand On Drawing and Anchoring
Several motions need to be accomplished during the Set-up phase of the shot.

Before Drawing Starting with the stretch band, demonstrate how to raise the bow hand and the draw hand together from the setup position to the draw position by raising the arms without raising the shoulders. This is a crucial step in the NTS method. The key to this maneuver is learning how to pivot the arms in the shoulder joint without raising the shoulder blades (scapulae). Keeping the shoulders down is critical for later steps in the shot as lowered shoulders permit the scapula to move as required to shift the draw load from the arms fully to the back. Have the students practice this motion without a bow until they can comfortably separate the motion of the arms in the shoulder socket from the muscles that control the position of the scapula in the back.

When the hands are raised, the arrow should end up parallel to the ground with the bow hand at its final elevation and the draw hand at an elevation about 2" below the jaw. The bow arm may be raised slightly higher than the line of the target during the draw to facilitate setting the draw shoulder in the down position. The draw hand is away from the body and the arrow will be pointing to the left of the target for a right handed archer.

The *Loading* (drawing) phase of the shot uses the lower trapezius muscles of the back to rotate the draw-side scapula around the rib cage to load the muscles controlling the position of the scapula with the draw forces of the bow. This movement of the scapula and shoulder pulls the upper arm into alignment with the forces in the bow. The biceps should not be used (or used minimally) in the loading motion. The draw arm continues to pull on the string until the draw arm elbow and hand come into alignment with the force of the bow string. The

Teaching Archery

draw force on the bow should be through the pressure point on the thumb pad of the bow hand and not up in the webbing between thumb and forefinger. The loading should be accomplished with a minimum of wasted energy or movement.

Watch for rising shoulders as the archers reach full draw. There is a tendency for the bow shoulder to rise as the bow arm takes on more compression load. There is also an element of fear of the bow that some young archers may have to overcome. Raising the bow shoulder is often a symptom of this fear.

On the draw side, bringing the draw arm forward to grasp the string without rotating the torso will often result in the draw arm shoulder raising up. Help the archers to set up the bow properly to avoid torso rotation or forward movement of the draw shoulder.

Another draw issue to look for is archers who begin drawing as they are raising their hands. The act of drawing with the bow moving upward is a common cause of arrows pinching off the arrow rest. Help students to separate the act of raising the bow from the process of loading the back.

When full loading is reached, the bow hand, draw hand and draw elbow should be oriented in a straight line. The shoulders (scapulae) and the bow hand come to alignment along a line passing to the right of the target for right hand archers. This alignment of the shoulders is a key element of the NTS method and is called by Coach Lee "Barrel of the Gun." To check the scapula position with the archer at full draw, place a bow string parallel to the ground and touching the two scapula on the back. The line of the bow string should be pointing along a line that is angled to the right of the line to the target when viewed form above. If the string that you placed on the back is pointing to the left of the line to the target for a right handed archer, the scapulae are not correctly positioned to create proper alignment.

Watch also for archers who lean away from the target at full draw. Some students have a tendency to think that leaning backwards will aid in pulling the bow. Use stretch bands to help young archers practice keeping their spines straight, without leaning, while doing the drawing motion. Other archers feel the mass weight of the bow held by the bow arm at a distance to their bodies and try to re-balance their center of gravity between their feet. Teach the archers that as the bow is raised, they should stand straight wile raising the bow and drawing.

Spend the time necessary with the stretch band for the students to achieve the correct body alignment. Repeat the Set, Set-up and Loading motions until the students can comfortably perform all the movements and positions correctly.

It is very important to keep head and eyes steady and consistent throughout the load and anchor. Archers and coaches should be especially vigilant to see that student's heads do not move as the string is drawn. If head motion is detected, the archer and coach should explore alternative draw hand paths to anchor that will allow the archer to keep the head completely still. One approach to correcting head movement is to have the archer initiate their draw on a path to the collar button of their shirt. Once the chin has been cleared, the draw hand can then be raised to the anchor position without any head movement.

Anchoring occurs when the draw hand is fully in contact with the underside of the jawbone. There should be no air gaps between the top of the draw hand and the underside of the jaw. Look carefully for any gaps and work with the archers to adjust their draw hand and wrist positions until a solid "bone-to-bone" contact is made by the draw hand. The string should be properly positioned on the face and not move during the remainder of the shot sequence.

The *anchor point* is the "touch point" for the drawing hand along the jaw line of the face (bone structure is solid). Additional touch points for the string on the face include the chin, lips, and nose. Work with your students to help them find the best touch points for their facial shape. The guiding principal is to adjust the equipment to the archer and not the archer to the equipment. Ultimately the archers may find that a longer or shorter bow length may be required to achieve the correct string alignment on the face.

The next step is the Transfer, in which any remaining load being held in the draw arm biceps is transferred into the lower back muscles. Using the stretch band, have the students come to full draw and hold their position. On the draw side, have the students move their draw side scapula down and towards the center of their back. This motion will enable the draw arm elbow to reach its final alignment with the draw hand while maintaining the draw hand position under the chin. Young archers will have trouble isolating the muscles of the back that control the scapula. Work with them using low-tension training aids until they have a feel for the correct movement. This step will take some time and will have to be revisited often during subsequent class sessions.

Watch for students who are afraid of the string and so hold the string away from their face. Some beginning archers use the first joint of the thumb to contact their face, rather than the upper part of the first finger and the string. Use the string bow and then the stretch band with these archers to help them confidently move to the under-the-chin anchor position.

Once at anchor, the body does not stop moving. The movement of the muscles becomes much smaller and is internalized rather than being externally visible.

Practice Exercise Have the archers shoot at a blank bale to work on coming to anchor with good body alignment. Use the string bow and stretch band as needed to help archers discover how to control their form. Reward archers for achievement and for improvement.
Practice Target blank bale for shooting form
Fun Game Grouping
Rules Shoot at a target. Before pulling the arrows, take a string and wrap it around the group of arrows. Mark the length of the string. The archer with the shortest string wins.

Meeting 4 Class Schedule

Welcome and goals statement	5 min
Stretching	5 min
Drawing and anchoring demos, Practice shooting form	20 min
Grouping Game	20 min
Give out handouts and homework	5 min
Cleanup	5 min

Handouts None
Homework Purchase a small notebook for recording archery information.

Meeting 5
Adding Even More Details

Review the NTS Method shooting form to this point. Start by using the string bow and take the archers through the steps they have already learned. Use positive reinforcement to correct form flaws. Reward students who are doing well and those who make significant improvement.
Expand on Holding, Aiming and Expansion

In this session, work with the archers to strengthen and refine the position of their back muscles as they transition from the draw to the holding position.

Holding In the *holding position*, the load of holding both the bow's draw weight and the bow's mass weight is held by the bones with the muscles primarily aligning the bones rather than directly holding the bow draw weight. On the draw arm side, the focus is on keeping the draw arm scapula down and moving the draw arm scapula towards the spine. Use the latissimus dorsi muscles to hold the draw shoulder down and the lower trapezius muscles to hold the draw scapula towards the spine.

On the bow arm side, the latissimus dorsi muscle also holds down its scapula. In addition, the lower trapezius muscle acts as a diagonal brace to support the bow arm. Watch each archer carefully for his or her scapula and shoulder positions. Help archers become aware of their shoulder positions and use the string bow as a low-tension method of practicing this technique.

One of the advantages of the NTS method is that the draw weight load is transferred primarily to the bones in the holding position. Achieving the correct skeletal alignment facilitates this transfer and greatly reduces the perceived effort to hold the bow at anchor. Watch carefully at every step of the learning process to see that your students achieve the proper alignment in both the vertical and horizontal planes. When done correctly, the "over the center" mechanical advantage of the NTS method alignment will become obvious and much more comfortable. While it looks as if the moving parts of the archer's body have stopped, large-scale motions are replaced with smaller scale motions from here on.

Aiming Successful archers "feel" their shots more than aim them. The *aiming and expansion phase* of the shot sequence is a very short interval of time. Teach your students to start aiming after the transfer and holding phase is reached. Aiming too early will distract the archer from the feel of the shot and reduce consistency. Watch for students who spend a long time aiming. Even when using a sight, aiming is largely an instinctive process. Archers who take too long to aim will only increase their fatigue and decrease their consistency. Aiming should only take a maximum of 3 seconds. Use a counting system to help archers get their shots off relatively quickly. You don't want young archers to snap shoot but at the same time it is important not to over aim.

When using bows without sights, there will be a tendency for beginning archers to aim by sighting down the arrow. "Arrow shaft aiming" can be identified when archers bring their draw hands up to their eye, rather than under the chin. Placing the nock of the arrow near the eye is dangerous and should be corrected quickly by the instructor. Watch for this phenomenon and help the archers to trust their instinctive ability to aim much as they might when throwing a ball or using a tennis racket. Students may also try to aim by putting the point of the arrow on the center of the target. At close range, the arrow will go high. Teach students to aim off of the center of the target by the distance that the arrow is missing the center and in the opposite direction. <a diagram needed here?>

Expansion Expansion is the final physical process before release. In this phase, the archer expands their upper body by slightly extending the rotation of the shoulders around the rib cage. The movement of the arrow on the bow as the result of expansion is very small, typically about 1-2 millimeters. The focus of the archer is on aiming and the target. Expansion acts as a trigger for the release. Later on, when the archers are shooting with a clicker, this expansion causes just enough additional draw to activate the clicker. In the NTS method, the draw arm does not continue to move backward and the anchor points on the face remain constant. The draw elbow continues to rotate around toward the back. This is something coaches can look for and correct as needed. The position of the draw elbow when the archer is viewed from the back is a clear indication of the presence or absence of back tension and expansion.

Finding the "Natural Point of Aim" All archers' bodies are different but all have a natural point of aim. To find it, have the archers come to the holding position and aim their bows at a vertical line. While holding, have them close their eyes for 5-10 seconds and then open the eyes without releasing the arrow. When they check their alignment to the target they may find that they have drifted a little to the right or left. Have them let down, adjust their feet position and then repeat the exercise until the before and after eyes-closed position is the same. You can also introduce the technique of marking the feet position on the shooting line. Outdoors, golf tees work well for this purpose. Indoors, tape can be placed on the floor to mark the foot position. Marking the foot positions and using those to return to that position every time helps an archer to become more consistently precise with their aiming.

Practice Target Blank bale for shooting form. Vertical line for introduction to aiming. Horizontal line for aiming.

Fun Game Battleship
Rules The game is played on a grid target of 10X10 spaces. The columns are numbered 1-10 across the top. The rows from top to bottom are lettered A-J. On the grid are placed equal numbers of "ships," each in one of two contrasting colors. Some ships take up 2 spaces, some take up 3, some 4, and one is 5 (the battleship).

Divide the group into two equal teams. We find it works best with four on a side. Assign each team a color fleet of ships to shoot at. Shoot 3 ends of 4 arrows (or less) each.

Scoring It is not necessary to land on a ship to score. Any arrow that lands in the grid square occupied by a ship counts. Usual archery rules apply for arrows touching a line. "Friendly fire" also counts. If an archer hits the wrong color ship, the score is for the other team. The instructor should remove all non-scoring arrows first. Then count the number of "hits." All scoring arrows remain in the target until the end of the game. Return all non-scoring arrows to the archers to shoot again. At the end of three ends, count the total number of scoring arrows for each team. The team with the highest score wins. Give each winning team member a prize.

Meeting 5 Class Schedule

Welcome and goals statement	5 min
Stretching	5 min
Transfer/Loading, Holding and Aiming and Expansion demonstrations, Practice shooting form	20 min
Battleship Game	20 min
Give out handouts and homework	5 min
Cleanup	5 min

Handouts Target faces and scoring of 10-ring rounds.

Homework Give the students a print-out of target faces with 3 arrow marks per target. Have the students score the targets. Give a prize to all students who score the targets correctly.

Meeting 6
Completing NTS Form

Review the NTS Method shooting form so far. Start by using the string bow and take the archers through the steps they have already learned. Use positive reinforcement to correct form flaws. Reward students who are doing well and those who make significant improvement.

Expand on the Release/Followthrough, Relaxation and Feedback

During the Release, it is important to minimize tension in any place in the body other than in the muscles that cause expansion. Teach the students to release the string by totally relaxing the drawing hand fingers and allowing the string to push the fingers aside. This is the phenomenon of letting the string go, rather than letting go of the string. Because the string fingers are relaxed, once the string clears, the fingers will return to a naturally curled, relaxed position, much as they were before the release. The path of the draw hand will recoil closely along the neck. When done properly, a natural backward recoil action followthrough will occur of itself.

Use stretch bands to help students learn to relax their draw hand fingers. Relaxing "on command" may be one of the most difficult physical motions in sports. Virtually all other sports motions require the athlete to contract their muscles to accomplish a task. Help your students to lean this skill by having them hold by their sides a bucket or paint can with a metal bail (handle) partially filled with gravel. Let the students practice their release by simply relaxing the fingers while holding on to the handle of the bucket. Helping them to achieve a smooth, relaxed release will require an ongoing effort.

Watch, too, for students who pull their draw hands away from their anchor points just at the moment of release. Typically, this action occurs because the student is afraid of the string. Use the stretch band to help the students understand that, at release, the string moves away from their face and not towards it.

Have the students keep a strong and steady bow arm during the release and followthrough. The bow arm should remain unmoving until the arrow has cleared the bow riser. Teach your students to keep their bow arm "in the shot" until they hear the arrow strike the target. This will build the habit of holding the bow arm still. The bow hand should fall at the wrist with a relaxed motion. When the archers progress to a finger sling, the bow hand will be completely relaxed. Without the finger sling, only the first finger of the bow hand should restrain the bow from flying forward out of the hand.

The *Followthrough* is the extension of proper shot execution and the release of the bow pressure as restrained by the back muscles. When the arrow is released, there is a natural recoil of the body and the equipment. The tension and compression held in the body will become visible as the body moves. As a coach, watch this movement carefully. All of the initial motion should be along the line of the arrow towards the target. Any motion of the body away from that line is a clue that the body is using misaligned forces during the holding and expansion phase. Use this information to monitor and adjust the archer's shooting form until the recoil is in a straight line.

The response to the release of the shot will be the bow moving forward out of the bow hand (until stopped by the sling or first finger) and toward the target. The bow arm is held up stable and strong. The bow hand should be completely relaxed and fall downward naturally. The draw-side scapula will move toward the spine. The drawing hand will be pulled along the face by the continuing action of the back muscles and tend to go behind the neck. If the body alignment is correct, everything should initially move in the same plane or straight line towards or straight away from the target.

Look for archers who have an exaggerated or contrived followthrough. Such artificial movements are often the result of excessive tension in the draw hand. Work with the stretch band to help archers learn to relax their draw hands. Also watch for plucking, with the draw hand moving excessively away from the face, as a sign of tension in the draw hand. Archers and coaches can look at the followthrough as an indicator of how correctly the shot was executed.

The eyes should remain fixed on the target during the followthrough. There is a tendency to want to "watch the arrow fly" when the string is released. This is to be avoided. Check also to see that the archer does not close their eyes at the instant of release.

Relaxation and Feedback These are the natural regenerative steps in repeating the shot sequence during an end. Once the shot is over and the arrow is in the target, it is time for relaxation. The mass weight of the bow is removed from the bow arm by placing the tip of the lower limb on the top of the downrange foot. The shoulders should be down and the arms relaxed. The abdominal and back muscles should be relaxed while the posture remains upright.

Archers should reflect on how the shot felt and not on the specific results of the arrow placement. The arrow grouping should only be used as an indicator of how the shot sequence was executed. When a shot goes well, the archer will know it and when it doesn't the archer will know where to improve. The coach, and eventually the archer, should ask themselves "How did (does) that feel?" The answer to the question will set the direction for the focus of the next shot sequence.

Have the archers relax for a brief amount of time as they prepare for the next shot. Again, counting may help to establish a relaxation rhythm.

Another option is to have the archers use their breathing to relax by taking three full breaths before moving on. Relaxation is the key to long-term consistency and accuracy. Focus the mind on the steps to making a successful shot and avoid self-punishment for poor performance.

The shot sequence repeats itself through the duration of the end. Congratulate the archers on their successes.

Shoot at a blank bale to practice form.
Review natural point of aim and adjust as needed.
Explain basic FITA rules and competition
Practice Target FITA 80 cm target at 10 Yards
Fun Games *Old Maid*
Rules Create a target in grid format with pairs of grids filled with a distinctive pattern. For example, vertical stripes, horizontal stripes, circles, stars, etc. Have one solid black square. The object of the game is to shoot 4 arrows in two pairs of squares without hitting the black square or "Old Maid." As a practical matter most students are challenged shooting a single pair. Give a prize to each student who hits a pair. Play three times.

Game Tournament Shoot a five-end, three-arrow per end tournament, 60-cm target at 10 yards, 10-ring scoring. 150 Points is a perfect score. Give a prize to all archers who shoot 75 or above.

Meeting 6 Class Schedule

Welcome and goals statement	5 min
Stretching	5 min
Release/Followthrough, Relaxation demonstrations, and Practice shooting form	20 min
Old Maid and Tournament games	20 min
Give out handouts and homework	5 min
Cleanup	5 min

Handouts NAA "Spectator's Guide to Archery" "Archery Resource Guide to Pro Shops"
Homework Visit a pro shop near you, if you can.

Meeting 7
Bringing It All Together

Review the NTS Method shooting form. Start by using the string bow and take the archers through the steps they have already learned. Use positive reinforcement to correct form flaws. Reward students who are doing well and those who make significant improvement.

Drill Have students shoot volley rounds at a blank bale using a counted rhythm. Talk the group of students through the shot sequence with everyone releasing their arrow at the same time. Kids love the sound of volley rounds and shooting as a group can help them practice rhythmic shot execution.

Vary the game by using novelty targets. Cardboard illustrations of stars, pumpkins, hearts, turkeys balloons and the like can be purchased inexpensively from party stores and discount shops. Avoid targets that have images of people or are anthropomorphic.

Fun Game *Tournament* Shoot a five-end, three-arrow per end tournament, 40-cm target at 10 yards, 10-ring scoring. 150 Points is a perfect score. Give a prize to all archers who shoot 75 or above.

Meeting 7 Class Schedule

Welcome and goals statement	5 min
Stretching	5 min
Practice shooting rhythm and shooting form	15 min
Tournament game	25 min
Give out handouts and homework	5 min
Cleanup	5 min

Handouts Score cards with the record of the student's tournament score. Be sure to add positive comments on good work. Use stickers and stamps to reward accomplishments.

Meeting 8
Graduation!

Review the NTS Method shooting form. Start by using the string bow and take the archers through the steps they have already learned. By now they should be fairly proficient at the basics. Use positive reinforcement to correct form flaws. Reward students who are doing well and those who make significant improvement.

Practice shooting at a range of distances up to 20 yards if practical.

Fun Game *Tournament* Shoot a six-end, three-arrow per end tournament, 80-cm target, 3 ends at 15-20 yards and 3 ends at 10 yards, 10-ring scoring. 180 Points is a perfect score. Give a prize to all archers who shoot 90 or above.

Graduation Print out, sign and issue Certificates of Completion. If you have a camera, take photos of each archer and include a print with their certificate.

Thank the students for participating and encourage them to seek out an archery club near them to continue with their archery practice.

Meeting 8 Class Schedule

Welcome and goals statement	5 min
Stretching	5 min
Tournament game	35 min
Give out certificates of completion	10 min
Cleanup	5 min

Appendix C
Four-Meeting Archery Fundamentals Class Syllabus

Archery Fundamentals
Student Handout

All archery is fundamentally the same. While adaptations are made to accommodate various styles of equipment, the procedures needed to produce a successful archery shot are consistent in all archery disciplines.

Archery Fundamentals is a class in basic archery shooting form that can be the foundation for success in whichever archery discipline you choose to take: Traditional, Compound, or Olympic Recurve. The emphasis is on helping each student establish the body positions and movements necessary to complete a stable, consistent archery shot. Archery is a discipline of postures and movements that result in predictable arrow flight. Mastering the postures and movements is essential to archery success.

In this class you will learn how to progress through the basic steps to begin your archery experience. During the class the instructor will place significant emphasis on performing all of the steps correctly. You may find that you will be using muscles and alignments that you haven't used before, resulting in the need to strengthen and condition yourself to perform the shot sequence correctly. You should plan on spending some time each week away from the range doing exercises that strengthen your upper body, shoulders, and core muscles.

You will be using lightweight archery equipment in this class along with ultra-lightweight training aids. String bows are simple loops of string, adjusted to your draw length, which can be used for miming the steps of shooting away from the range. Stretch bands add some draw weight and can be used to mimic the entire shot sequence including the release. A "pipe bow" adds the feel of having a bow in your hands and the reality of having a string to position on your face. Unlike a conventional archery bow, a PVC pipe bow may be safely "dry fired" for practice. The use of lightweight training aids allows you and the instructor to monitor and adjust your shooting form without placing your joints and muscles under the risk of injury that might occur when making a change under full bow load. (During the training process, your instructor may need to touch your arms or other parts of the body to bring you into alignment. If you have any concerns about contact by the instructor, please let him/her know and alternative approaches will be worked out.)

Your goals: At the end of the four class sessions, your goal is to have a solid stance, be able to handle the equipment smoothly, build a strong and stable bow arm, work towards a consistent draw holding the bow weight with back tension and execute a smooth release with consistent arrow flight. If you have not yet mastered all of these skills by the end of class, you will have the knowledge to work on them in future practice sessions.

Once you have successfully completed this class and have built up sufficient strength to handle the equipment comfortably, you may choose to take one or more of the specialty classes in the three equipment disciplines of archery.

Meeting 1
Student Handout
Getting Started

Review Basic shooting form and safety rules from the Safety and Orientation class.

Introduce The steps of the Simplified NTS (BEST) Method

The Shot Sequence, Part 1

1. Stance/Posture
   a. Start with a square stance: the feet straddle the shooting line with the toes on a line toward the target's center.
   b. The hips are aligned with the feet and the shoulders are aligned with the hips. There should be no twisting of the torso or leaning back from the target. (The open stance can be taught to students who are learning Olympic-style recurve archery, shot at long distances, outdoors.)
   c. The feet are placed shoulder-width apart with 60% of the body weight on the balls of the feet and 40% of the weight on the heels. If you try to grasp the ground with your toes, your body will automatically pivot forward at the ankles, shifting the body's weight to the balls of the feet. The heels should remain on the ground. Your center of balance will be over or near the front of the feet.
   d. The hips are tucked under, chest down, back straight (no "hollow backs").
   e. The knees are straight and relaxed, not locked.
2. Nock
   a. Place the nock of the arrow on the string, under the nock locator point and with the index fletching correctly oriented consistently.
   b. The index fletch should be pointing towards the archer and away from the bow.
   c. Listen and feel for a "click" of the nock onto the bow string. Be sure the nock is fitted under the nocking point locator on the string.
3. Hook and Grip/Set
   a. Place the draw hand on the bowstring with the fingers forming a hook. The bowstring should sit on the joint of the first finger, just behind the joint on the second finger and in the middle of the pad on the third finger. The pressure of the string on the fingers should be 40% to 30% on Index finger, 50% on middle finger and 10% to 20% on ring finger.
   b. Form a "C" shape with thumb and pinky curling the thumb and little finger under the palm of the draw hand. The back of draw hand is flat with no bending of the fist knuckles.
   c. The draw hand wrist is cocked out (and up) in a natural position such as when carrying a bucket.
   d. Slide your bow hand first into the pivot point of the bow handle and then lower the hand down to the grip. The fleshy pad at the base of the thumb should rest on the rounded portion of the bow grip. The bow should only touch the thumb side of the life line of the palm. The wrist axis should be horizontal.
   e. Rotate the bow arm so that the elbow hinge is vertical and locked. For right-handed archers, this rotation is clockwise. For left-handed archers, the rotation is counterclockwise.
   f. Take a relaxing breath and extend the bow arm towards the target slightly to form a 45 degree angle with the body. The draw arm should fall low across your torso with the elbow bent in a right angle.
   g. Turn your head to face the target (head square to the target).

Meeting 2
Student Handout
Learning the Shot Sequence, Part 2

Review the steps from the previous lesson.

The Shot Sequence, Part 2

4. Set-up (Raise the Bow) (. . . On One)
   a. Imagine that there is a giant clock face surrounding the target. For a right-handed archer in a square stance, the bow hand will be pointed towards the 5:00 o'clock position

before raising the bow. Raise the bow arm to point toward 11 o'clock (right-handed archer) or slightly to the left of the target. Allow the draw arm to follow. Keep the bow vertical with the draw hand, keeping the draw elbow inside of the arrow line and the draw hand not higher than 2" below your jaw line. (The bow will still be pointing to the left of the center of the target.) A short beat of time should be taken after the bow arm is raised to "lock" the bow arm in place by engaging the bow arm triceps muscle. Once locked, the bow arm should not move through the rest of the shot.

b. Rotate the shoulders into a line to the target. The bow hand, bow shoulder and draw shoulder should form a straight line as the bow is brought to shooting height.

c. Simultaneously with the movement of the bow arm, raise the draw arm by pivoting the arm at the shoulder joint to an elevation about 2" below the height of the chin.

d. Position the draw hand elbow so that it is 90 degrees or less from the shoulder and slightly lower than the arrow line.

e. This is the beginning of establishing back tension with about 60% of the draw weight in the back and 40% of the draw weight in the front of the body; the rest of the bow load is borne by the chest, shoulder, and arm muscles.

f. The shoulders must stay down while raising the bow. Some archers may have a habit of raising the shoulders when raising the arms. A lot of practice will be required to separate the shoulder and arm muscles to ensure that the shoulders do not rise up during the Set-up maneuver.

5. Draw (Load) (. . . On Two)
   a. Draw the bow by moving the draw side scapula around the rib cage until the draw hand is about 1" below the jaw. The major motion of the draw is made with the lower trapezius muscle on the draw side. Archers should minimize the use of the draw arm biceps in drawing the bow.
   b. Draw with the force of the bow coming through the fleshy pad at the base of the thumb on the bow hand.
   c. Add more back tension on the lower trapezius bring the force ratio to around 80% back, 20% front (back to chest, shoulder, arm muscles)
   d. The string should now be pulling into the face with the string touching the center of the tip of the nose, just to the side of the mouth and on the side of the chin. Your arrow line should point somewhat towards the target face

6. Anchor (. . . On Three)
   a. Raise the draw hand (straight up) tight into the jaw, maintaining the wrist position, and placing the base joint of the thumb into the pocket formed on the neck by the jawbone and the neck muscle. (don't allow draw hand to move forward as you raise the draw arm).
   b. Keep the draw side elbow as in-line with or slightly above the arrow line to not lose your scapula position.
   c. Make sure to have a solid "bone-on-bone" connection between the jawbone and the bones of the first finger of the draw hand. The thumb of the draw hand should be down below the jaw line and relaxed. Do not use the thumb as a draw hand anchor reference.
   d. Instructors will watch students to be sure that back tension is not lost as the draw hand moves up to anchor.

7. Transfer (. . . On Four)
   a. Take a moment to completely relax the biceps in the draw while increasing the tension in the lower trapezius in the back on the draw side. Hold the scapula in position and bring the draw side elbow to the archer's side of the arrow line.
   b. The draw force should be almost entirely borne by those back muscles at this point.

The above steps can be done to the count of "One, Lock, Two, Three, Beat, Four." Using this four step shot sequence, beginners can be taught to shoot with back tension on even the first day of training. Using numbers instead of the names for the dynamic part of the shot sequence simplifies communications between the instructor and the student. The entire shot sequence can be performed using a metronome and the steps counted out by the instructor. In time the archer will internalize the language and rhythm of the shot sequence.

Introduce the *finger sling*.

Meeting 3
Student Handout
Learning The Shot Sequence, Part 3

Review the steps of the previous two lessons.

Learning The Shot Sequence, Part 3

8. Holding/Expansion/Aim
   a. Holding, when the bow is at full draw and the draw weight of the bow is fully held in the back, is a very important step in the shot sequence. The archer needs to remain calm and near motionless. The forces in the archer must precisely align with the direction of the arrow to ensure a straight flight. Any lateral forces in the archer will translate into errors in the arrow launch and corresponding inconsistencies of arrow flight.
   b. Expansion is a near-invisible motion during which the body feels the force of the bow acting on it in equal proportion on the bow and draw side. The archer resists the force of the bow by expanding the shoulders around the rib cage.
   c. Aiming begins when holding has been reached and expansion has begun. The archer should look at the target and maintain eye focus and control throughout the rest of the shot sequence. The string should be in the line of sight of the archer and aligned with the inside of the sight window on the bow riser. The eyes should be focused on the target throughout the rest of the shot.
9. Release/Followthrough
   a. The release should be a natural consequence of the expansion. As the expansion progresses, the string fingers will lose their grip and the string will go.
   b. Continue to maintain all posture, stance, and head positions, muscle tension and directions as the release happens. If you relax those muscles on release, you will "collapse" and your arrows will hit low and to the side of the point aimed at. The followthrough will happen naturally.
   c. Archers should have full control of their bow arms until the arrows hit the target. Avoid peeking around the bow to watch the arrow flight.
10. Relaxation and Feedback
    a. Once the shot is complete, let the bow down and support it on your toe (or long stabilizer) to eliminate the effort of holding up the weight of the bow.
    b. Reflect on the feel of the shot, with an eye to repeating the good parts and fixing any mistakes.
    c. Take several breaths to re-oxygenate your blood and relax your muscles.
    d. Prepare to shoot the next arrow. Focus your attention on the shot process, not the arrow results. If the process is correct, the results will happen.

Meeting 4
Student Handout
Putting It All Together

Practice shooting using all the steps. Concentrate on shooting form and not arrow results.

Work towards shooting tighter groups. Shooting a tight group means that you are shooting consistently: that each action in your shot sequence is being performed exactly the same way each time. Once you can shoot a group, it is relatively easy to learn to move the group. Look for any inconsistencies in your shot sequence. Look for movement of your bow arm, the smoothness when performing a release, and whether direction and force are maintained in the shot throughout the followthrough. Your instructor should look for any form or posture issues that may cause the bow string to contact you during release and advise you on corrective action.

Work towards a more consistent shot sequence. Shoot one shot at a time, without focusing on the previous or the next shot afterword. Take your time with each shot. Use a metronome for shot pacing.

Have fun!

A Reminder Students are reminded that their enrollment in the Archery Fundamentals class includes an expectation that they will become members of the

Archery Club. In addition to the Saturday Morning Instruction Programs, the club offers many archery opportunities including tournaments, 3-D shoots, gymkhanas, and social activities.

Post-Graduation

The club offers more advanced archery training for archers that want to improve their skills and specialize in a particular form of archery. The "next step" classes are in Traditional Archery, Olympic Style Recurve Archery, and Compound Archery. Please let your instructor know of your interest in these more advanced programs and we will get you signed up.

Advanced competitive coaching is available for members who have their own equipment and are shooting in the recurve and compound styles.

Thank you,
The Club Teaching Staff

Appendix D
Olympic Recurve Archery Class Syllabus

Introduction to Olympic Style Recurve Bow Target Archery
Course Syllabus and Class Outline

Note This class requires that the archer has completed the Archery Fundamentals class.

Olympic Recurve target archery is a highly technical archery discipline. To master the National Training System (NTS) shooting form the archer must learn a series of precisely choreographed movements and postures in order to place the bow and arrow system into the correct alignment to complete the shot successfully. The sport of archery rewards consistency. The Olympic Recurve archer needs to be able to repeat the shot process precisely every time.

In learning to shoot target recurve equipment, great emphasis is placed at the beginning of the training on learning to execute the postures and movements of the shot sequence correctly. Strength training is required simultaneously with shot sequence training in order to build the muscle strength and awareness needed to execute the shot properly. All beginning archery training should be done with very light draw weight equipment until the shooting steps can be executed correctly. Bows in draw weights of 10-15 pounds are not too light to use to begin training. It takes a long time to build up the physical strength in the correct muscles to execute the NTS shot sequence correctly. Using too heavy a draw load will cause the bow to crush the archer's shooting form, making progress impossible and injury probable.

Once the form is mastered, the draw weight of the bow may be increased in small increments, with continuous monitoring and adjustment, until the shooting form and the archer's strength are properly matched.

Meeting 1
Class Content
Stretching and warm up exercises
Introduce additional equipment to the bow: bow sight, stabilizer, finger sling, finger tab with finger separator.
Use mime, string bow, stretch band and pipe bow to work on shooting form.

Stance
Introduce the open stance. Draw a line across the shooting line toward the target. The down range foot is placed with the toes about 3 inches on the archer's side of the line to the target. The up range foot is placed on the line with the ball of the foot directly over the line. The hips remain in near alignment with the feet, open to the target. The torso is rotated so that the shoulders are oriented directly toward the target. Watch for a rotation of the hips that puts the hips in line with the shoulders

when they are rotated. This is to be avoided. The objective of this stance is to create torsion in the core muscles to increase strength and stability. This stance is also more stable in windy conditions.

Posture
The hips should be tilted under the body in a "pelvic thrust" alignment to flatten the back, lower the rib cage and compress the abdominal muscles. The legs should be straight and locked. The weight of the archer should be held on the balls of the feet. Have the archers try to grab the ground with their toes. This grabbing motion will automatically create a leaning forward at the ankles, placing the body weight on the balls of the feet.

Nock the Arrow
The arrow needs to be nocked onto the string and placed on the arrow rest in a consistent fashion. The archer should be certain that the nocks are correctly oriented on the arrow each time an arrow is mounted on the bow. Friction-mounted nocks in general and pin nocks in particular can rotate with respect to the arrow fletching. Verify that the nocks are correctly rotated and that the arrow is consistently mounted on the bow with the fletching in the same orientation for each shot.

Listen for the click of the nock onto the string and for a consistent feel of the pressure of the nock as it is snapped onto the string. Any loose nocks should be discarded.

Be sure the nock is placed on the string in exactly the same place with respect to the nock locator. For recurve bows, if two nock location points are used, they should be tightly spaced on the nock as the string will be straight up and down at full draw. (For compound fingers shooters, the bottom nock locator needs to be placed with additional space below the nock to allow for the angle of the string at full draw.)

Hook and Grip
On the draw hand, form a "C" shape with the thumb, middle fingers bent and pinky finger curling toward the palm. The back of the hand must be flat with no bending of the first knuckles joining the fingers to the hand. The outer two knuckles of the first three fingers of the draw hand are bent into a hook and placed on the bow string.

There are three moves needed on the draw hand when setting the hook and before Set-up.
1. The drawn hand pivots down towards the ground to form an angle that matches the archer's jaw line. At Anchor, the top of the draw hand, along the first finger, must be fully in contact with the jaw from the base of the thumb to the second knuckle of the draw hand.
2. The draw hand pivots at the wrist towards the body so that there is an outward bend of the wrist. The wrist is not straight with the fingers. It is pivoted outwards. This pivot allows the movement of the draw arm such that back tension can be achieved without bending the wrist under full draw load.
3. The draw hand needs to rotate the top of the hand towards the archer's body about 15 degrees to align the finger joints with the string. For right-handed archers, this rotation is counter-clockwise. For left-handed archers, the motion is clockwise.

The string should lie just across the first knuckle crease of the first finger, just behind the first knuckle crease of the middle finger and the pad of the end of the third finger should just rest on the string. 50-60% of the draw weight is taken by the middle finger. 30% of the draw weight is taken by the first finger and 10% or less of the draw weigh is taken by the third finger.

A finger tab with a finger separator should be used. The finger separator should be large enough that the first and second fingers of the draw hand have sufficient clearance with the arrow shaft. Verify that the finger separator is not touching the arrow nock or shaft at any point during the shot sequence. Some trimming and customizing of the finger tab may be required to fit the tab properly to the archer. The preferred finger tab does not use a shelf along the jaw line. The use of a shelf can interfere with the solid contact with the jaw desired at holding. If a shelf is used, be sure that the height of the shelf will permit the proper positioning of the draw hand on the jawbone. Look also to see that no part of the metal of the finger tab sticks up so high as to contact the jaw .

Some grinding of the metal portion of the tab may be required to provide appropriate clearance.

Use the pipe bow to demonstrate how important maintaining proper finger pressure is to the consistency of the shot. The little finger of the draw hand remains loosely curled and may rest gently against the neck at anchor. Additional adjustments of the draw hand wrist angle may be needed in order to achieve solid anchor on the jaw line and back tension while holding.

On the riser grip, the bow hand is placed in the pivot point and then the wrist is dropped so that the force of the bow is resisted by the pressure point on the pad at the base of the thumb. No portion of the bow should contact the bow hand on the outside of the life line on the hand. The fingers of the bow hand should be relaxed and curled. The bow should not be held in a tight grip. The knuckles of the bow hand should be at a 45-degree angle with the ground. The bow thumb should point towards the target with a slight pressure at the base of the thumb on the side of the grip and the thumb tip pointed outward so that the archer can see the thumb nail.

The archer needs to have confidence that the bow will be restrained by the finger sling and not tightly grip the handle of the bow. The last step in this sequence is to rotate the elbow of the bow arm, to move the forearm away of the string. For a right-handed archer, the rotation of the bow arm elbow is counterclockwise. For a left-handed archer the rotation of the bow arm elbow is clockwise. In either case, the line of the hinge joint of the elbow should be vertical.

Set
At the *Set* position, the bow arm extends at a 45-degree angle to the body, with the stabilizer also at 45 degrees to the body. The draw arm rests across the front of the archer's body in a "arm in a sling" position with the forearm and upper arm forming a right angle. The draw shoulder should be rotated partially around the rib cage by pulling on the draw side scapula with the lower trapezius muscle. The shoulders should be down.

The head should be moved into position in two steps. The first step is to raise the head straight up, looking along the shooting line. Rest a beat, take a breath and then simply rotate the head toward the target. Getting the head into the correct position is a critical step to consistency and accuracy. The head should not tilt in any direction. Once the head is in position, the head should not move. The archer needs to learn to bring the string to the face and not the face to the string. As a coach, watch very carefully for any head movement after the Set position is complete.

Mindset
A moment and a breath are taken to relax the body and mind before starting the active portion of the shot. The archer should clear their mind of any distractions and concentrate on the portion of the shot process that will be the focus of the next shot.

Closing Out the Day's Session
Give the archers a written description of the steps of shooting. Have the archers work on their shooting form at home using a mirror for feedback and lightweight training aids (string bows, stretch bands, pipe bows).

Finish the session with Specific Physical Training (SPT) holding the light-drawing bow at full draw with back tension for 30 seconds at a time with a 1-minute rest between holdings. Repeat five (5) sets. Do stretching and warm down exercises.

Meeting 2
Class Content
Stretching and warm up exercises
Use mime, string bow, stretch band and pipe bow to work on shooting form.

In this meeting you will work on the most active part of the shot sequence, the transition from Set to Holding. Holding is the most important part of the shot sequence. Getting the bow and the body into the holding position is a complex series of maneuvers that need much practice to master. The four steps of the sequence are set-up, load, anchor and transfer. In teaching these steps it helpful to assign a number to each step: 1. Set-up, 2. Load, 3. Anchor and 4. Transfer. By using numbers instead of names, you can count out loud the sequence of steps. It is easier for the archer to follow a simple numerical sequence than to hear a description of each step every time they move.

Set-Up

Set-up is the process of raising the bow and arms into position to load (draw) the bow. On the bow arm side, imagine that there is a giant clock face in front of the archers. As the archer starts with the bow hand in the Set position, the bow hand is pointing to the 5:00 o'clock numeral for a right-handed archer. The bow arm is raised using the deltoid muscles along a diagonal path in front of the archer so that the bow hand moves from the 5:00 o'clock position to the 11:00 o'clock position on the imaginary clock face. (Left-handed archers move their bow hands from the 7:00 o'clock position to the 1:00 o'clock position during Set-up.) The objective of this diagonal movement of the bow arm is to create the "barrel of the gun" alignment of the bow hand, bow shoulder, and draw shoulder.

At the top of the bow arm movement there is a small moment of time needed to lock the bow arm in place. The lock is performed by tightening the triceps muscles of the bow arm which activates the latissimus dorsi of the bow arm, bracing the arm into position. (For a right-handed archer there is a slight movement of the bow hand down and to the left as the arm is locked.)

Most inexperienced archers will raise the bow in such a way that there is an angle formed between the bow hand, bow shoulder and draw shoulder, placing the bow in front of rather than to the side of the archer. Use a straight edge, such as a stretched bow string or an alignment stick, to place across the archer's back at the shoulders. The bow hand should touch the string/stick when raised. If the bow hand is in front of the string, work with the archer to bring the bow up to the proper alignment.

For many people, this movement will feel "too much to the left" for a right-handed archer. Keep working until the movement is smooth and consistent. Watch to see that the torsion in the torso of the open stance posture is not lost. (You may find that it is easier to teach the upper body portion of the shot sequence first and introduce the open stance after the four-step shot sequence is fairly well mastered.)

The bow hand should be raised to a point so that the bow is just about on target. Do not raise the bow hand to eye level or above. The objective is to place the bow in a position such that the drawing force is directed through the pressure point on the base of the thumb of the bow hand. Raising the bow up too high changes the lines of force of the draw upward into the pivot point and will make it difficult for the archer to achieve correct hand pressure at holding.

Watch also to see that the student's shoulders stay down during the raising of the bow. Many people subconsciously connect the action of the upper trapezius muscle with the action of the deltoid muscle. Work with your archers to separate the triggering of these two muscles. Have the archer stand facing a mirror and raise their bow arm to a right angle away from their body without raising their bow shoulder. It sometimes helps to use a "scooping" motion of the bow arm to initiate the latissimus dorsi muscles on the bow side, thus holding the shoulder down as the bow arm is raised.

On the draw side, at the Set position, the draw arm is resting across the abdomen in an "arm in a sling" position. The draw hand wrist joint is bent outward so that the draw hand is in something of a claw position. The draw arm is pivoted upward and outward from the draw side shoulder joint until the draw arm is at an elevation about 2 inches below the jaw line. This movement is something like an upward block in martial arts. The forearm of the draw arm should remain parallel with the arrow line (see the photos). At the end of set-up, the arrow will be pointing to the left of the target for a right-handed archer.

Some things to look for on the draw side during Set-up. The draw hand should trace a path along a vertical line parallel to the target side of the archer's body. It should not move toward the target and no deliberate drawing by bending the draw arm elbow should occur. The draw hand and forearm should come up as a unit, pivoting at the draw side shoulder joint. Some opening of the bow will occur during set-up, caused not by pulling on the draw side but by the simple geometry of the separation of the two shoulder joints. Be very vigilant to see that no pulling motion occurs during Set-up.

Work on the bow arm side and the draw arm side separately and then perform both actions together.

It takes a lot of physical strength in the back and a lot of muscular coordination to perform the Set-up correctly. Use light-drawing training aids to get the motion correct before applying any significant bow draw weight. The pipe bow is an ideal tool to teach Set-up.

Now here's the hard part. All of the above needs to be completed to the count of "One, lock."

Loading

The "Two" step is *Loading, aka* the Draw. The term Loading is used because the action of Loading is to move the draw arm using the back muscles, not the draw side biceps, to load the back muscles with the draw weight of the bow. The Loading motion is performed by using the lower trapezius muscles on the draw side to bring the draw side scapula around the rib cage and the draw hand to a position about one inch below the jaw line with the string touching the corner of the chin. The draw force is resisted through the pressure point on the bow hand. The archer should feel the force along a straight line from the draw hand to the pressure point on the bow hand.

The *Formaster*™ is a particularly useful tool for teaching loading. With the *Formaster*™ in place, the biceps are completely eliminated from the loading motion. Archers can use the *Formaster*™ to get the feel of using the correct muscles, as well as using it as a strengthening tool. The draw motion should create an angular movement of the arrow, pivoting around the riser until the arrow is rotated into alignment with the target. One easy way to check the motion of the draw hand is to look at the position of the draw hand wrist. Starting with an outward break in the wrist, the wrist should never break inward during the loading process. If the wrist breaks inward, a linear draw is being used and it will be difficult to achieve proper back tension.

Look for the draw hand to land at a point about one inch below the jaw. The draw movement should never bring the draw hand directly to the jaw as such a motion will cause the archer to raise their head to clear the draw hand. Remember again that the archer should bring the string to the face, not the face to the string. At the completion of loading, the string should be touching the center of the nose, the side of the lips and just to the corner of the chin.

Watch archers from the back during the loading phase to verify that the scapula on the draw side is moving around the rib cage and toward the spine in a downward and sideways motion. Watch to see that the scapula does not lift upward by using the upper trapezius muscles, as such upward motion of the scapula will cause the scapula to lock and prevent proper back tension on the draw side.

All of the above needs to be completed on the count of. "One, Lock, Two." As you work your way through the steps and use the counting system, you will find yourself using the terms "One Move" or "Two Move." Using numbers to describe these four critical steps is much simpler than using names.

Closing Out the Day's Session

Finish the session with Specific Physical Training (SPT) of holding the bow at full draw with back tension for 30 seconds at a time with a 1-minute rest between holdings. Repeat 5 times. Do stretching and warm down exercises.

Meeting 3

Class Content

Do stretching and warm up exercises to start.
Use mime, string bow, stretch band and pipe bow to work on shooting form.

Anchor

The "3" step is *Anchor*. From the end of the Loading position, the draw hand is raised upward, sliding the string along the corner of the chin until the first finger, from the second knuckle to the base of the thumb of the draw hand, is solidly and fully in contact with the jaw bone. The objective of anchor is to produce a consistent and precise relationship between the nock of the arrow and the sighting eye. Emphasis is placed on "bone-to-bone" contact between the bones of the first finger and the jawbone. A downward tilt of the draw hand with respect to the draw arm may be required to align the draw hand and jawbone for full contact. Experiment with finding this correct draw hand angle while miming the shot. Once found, the downward angle of the draw hand needs to be established in the grip and hook stage of the shot cycle.

At anchor, the little finger of the draw hand needs to be gently curved inward and lightly touching the neck. Any change in the little finger position will cause a change in tension of the draw hand fingers, affecting the shot. The base knuckle of the thumb may fit in the pocket of the neck formed by the underside of the jaw and the sternocleidomastoideus muscle that runs from behind the ear to the center of the base of the neck.

Errors to look for include any "gaps" between the top of the draw hand and the jawbone. If a gap opens up, work on the downward angle of the draw hand to match the angle with the angle of the archer's jaw. There is wide variation in jawbone angles. Practice with a pipe bow until the appropriate draw hand wrist angle is identified.

Look for any anchoring attempt using the thumb, rather than the first finger, on the jawbone. Have the archer firmly rub the top of the first finger to raise awareness of its location on the hand and then emphasize full contact of the finger on the jaw. Men may have an advantage in learning this contact because they can feel the roughness of their beard on the draw hand.

Look for any tendency of the archer to bring their draw hand up the side of the jaw, raising the position of the arrow nock. Insist that the draw hand anchor fully under the jawbone.

Look for any loss of back tension or scapula position during the move from load to anchor. It is easy for an archer to loose mental focus when making this move, causing the lower trapezius muscles on the draw hand to relax and the scapula to move away from the spine. Also look for the inadvertent use of the upper trapezius muscles when moving the draw hand up to the anchor position. Archers who activate their upper trapezius muscle will raise the draw side scapula, preventing proper back tension.

Transfer

The "4" step is *Transfer*, which occurs in a small amount of time (aka a beat or count) after anchor in which the archer "transfers" any remaining draw load in the draw side biceps into the lower trapezius muscles of the back, moving the draw side scapula even farther around the rib cage. At the conclusion of transfer, the archer's draw side elbow should be on or inside the arrow line.

Coaches should look for the draw side elbow position and the draw side scapula position to ensure that transfer is complete. Look for and remove any tension in the draw side biceps. It may take some time, especially for very strong archers, to learn to relax the biceps. The only tension on the draw side should be in the digitorum muscles of the forearm needed to maintain the string hook.

Coaches should also look for any movement of the draw hand anchor on the face. The draw hand and the string must stay fixed in the anchor position during transfer. Any movement of the draw hand or the head during transfer indicates that the "transfer" movement is not transferring into the back and is, instead, being caused by additional pulling of the biceps.

The shot sequence leading up to holding can now be executed to the count of, "One, lock, Two, Three, beat, Four."

Closing Out the Day's Session

Finish the session with the Specific Physical Training (SPT) of holding the bow at full draw with back tension for 30 seconds at a time with a 1-minute rest between holdings. Repeat 5 times. Add a second SPT of moving from the 1 position to the 4 position and back again to the 1 position and repeat. Do 5 repetitions per set. Repeat 5 sets.

Do stretching and warm down exercises.

Meeting 4

Class Content

Do stretching and warm up exercises to begin.
Use mime, string bow, stretch band and pipe bow to work on shooting form. Archers should confidently move through the four steps of set-up, load, anchor and transfer using very lightweight equipment (under 6 pounds draw weight). Verify that they can maintain the form while using heavier equipment up to 20 pounds draw weight.

Holding

Holding is the most important position in the NTS shot sequence. All motions and postures of the NTS either lead up to holding or are the result of holding. At the conclusion of the Transfer, the archer should be in the Holding position.

At Holding, two key body alignments must be in place. The first alignment is along a straight line from the bow hand through the draw hand and through the draw elbow. The draw side elbow may be inside the arrow line but it should never be outside the arrow line. A draw side elbow outside the arrow line is a clear indication that the archer has not achieved back tension.

The second body alignment is the "barrel of the gun" alignment of the bow hand, bow scapula and the draw side scapula. The objective of this alignment is to place the compression load of the bow directly in line with the bones of the body, increasing strength and endurance. The "barrel of the gun" line should cross the arrow line.

The most common error in the Holding alignment is failing to place the bow arm in the correct position at Set-up, allowing a hinge point at the bow shoulder joint. This hinge joint places extra strain on the muscles of the bow shoulder reducing endurance and stability. Coaches can use a straight edge to verify the alignment of the bow arm and to provide a reference point for archers to verify their bow arm position.

I find that using the string of a bow provides a convenient and readily available straight edge for verifying body alignment. Simply turn the bow horizontally and place the bowstring along the scapula. Look to see that the bow hand touches the string.

Holding is not a static state but rather a brief period of time in which the motion of the archer is internalized, rather than being visible. The forces of the bow trying to crush the archer are resisted by the bones of the arms and the rib cage. The bones are held in alignment by the muscles, primarily of the back.

Expansion should be felt equally on the bow and draw side. Mental focus should be on imagining the movement of the LAN 2 spot along the shooting line while the aiming eye is focused on the target. During Holding, the position of the draw hand and the position of the string on the face should remain constant. Watch for any movement of the string on the face during Holding and correct the posture until the string position remains fixed.

Practice the sensation of Expansion by standing in a "T" position with your arms outspread and then move your hands backward. You will feel an expansion sensation in your chest and in the distance between the fingertips. This motion is visible when done as a freestanding exercise but invisible when the archer is holding the draw force of the bow.

Holding should last for no more than three seconds while aiming. Any longer than three seconds will cause a loss of concentration and additional stress on the body. If the shot cannot be completed after three seconds of holding, let down and start again. The coach should count the three seconds aloud during practice session to stabilize the rhythm of the holding segment of the shot.

Use a metronome, either a dedicated hardware unit or an application for your smart device, to set the tempo and rhythm of the shot sequence. Start with a tempo of about 52-54 beats per minute. Count aloud the steps of the shot sequence to the tempo of the metronome. Once an archer has found their rhythm, look for instrumental music that is at that same tempo and have the archer listen to the music during practice. Although electronic devices are not permitted in USAA competitions, sufficient practice with a piece of music for tempo will groove the rhythm of the shot sequence.

Release and Followthrough

The *Release* is a natural result of the expansion process. When done correctly, it is the back muscles that cause the string to be released, not the relaxation of the finger muscles in the draw hand. The internal movements of holding change the angle of forces of the string in the draw hand and cause the string to loose subconsciously.

The best way to practice this release is to use an ultra low weight pipe bow as a training aid. The pipe bow can be dry fired so the release can be practiced safely. The key to the practice is to learn to feel the release as a result of back tension and not any opening of the draw hand. Once the release action is mastered, the archer can move up to higher poundage bows, shooting arrows until the release can be successfully executed at the archer's competitive bow draw weight.

The *Followthrough* is a natural reaction to the release of pressure of the bow on release. The internalized forces of Holding now become visible in the explosive expansion of the chest and the movements of both the draw arm and the bow arm. All movements during Followthrough should be either directly towards the target or directly away from the target. Any movement lateral to the arrow line will cause the arrow to veer from its intended flight path.

On the draw side, the draw hand should recoil backward along the jaw line and end up touching the neck just behind the ear. Any loss of contact of the draw hand on the neck is an indication of lateral forces in the archer that need to be corrected before moving onward.

On the bow side, the bow arm needs to remain engaged and firm as the bow is released. Some upward movement of the bow arm may be a natural result of the release of forces in the bow. The bow hand should drop downward in the "Down Spot" maneuver (the first finger of the bow hand pointing towards the ground). The bow should be caught by the finger sling. There should be no gripping of the bow handle at the release.

The head and eyes should remain fixed on the target until the motions of following through are completed. Any movement of the eyes and head on release will lead to an anticipation of the movement and the resulting inconsistency of subsequent shots.

Relaxation and Feedback
At the conclusion of the shot, a short period of time is required for the body to recover and for the mind to clear before starting the next shot. The bow should be rested either with the lower limb on the toe or on the stabilizer resting on the ground, removing the mass weight of the bow from the archer's bow arm. Tensions in the body should be relaxed and the body's joints loosened through some simple movements.

The archer should take two or three complete breaths using both the chest and belly breathing techniques to removed pollutants and re-charge the blood stream with fresh oxygen.

This is a time to "feast or forget." The arrow has been shot and there's nothing an archer can now do about the results of that arrow. The focus should be on the feel of the shot. If the shot felt good, try to recall that feeling and repeat it. If something didn't feel right, focus on the part of the shot sequence that will need to be adjusted to improve the feel.

It is only when the body and mind are fully clear that the archer should begin the shot sequence again.

Relaxation and feedback are skills that should be used consistently during all practice sessions. The breathing, meditation and attentional focus skills should also be rehearsed and practiced away from the range. Top archers put in many hours a week on relaxation, yoga, and breathing exercises. Remember that you can't control the first thought that comes into your mind but you can control the second thought. Maintaining a relaxed and focused state is a skill that can be learned with practice.

Finishing the Class Session
Finish the session with Specific Physical Training (SPT) of holding the bow at full draw with back tension for 30 seconds at a time with a 1-minute rest between holdings. Repeat 5 sets. Add a second SPT of moving from the 1 position to the 4 position and back again to the 1 position and repeat. Do 5 repetitions per set. Repeat 5 sets. Do stretching and warm down exercises.

An archer is not going to learn all the steps of the National Training System in a four-meeting class. Lots of guided practice will be needed to master the techniques and to shoot effectively. Adjustments in the shooting technique will be needed to adapt to the archer's physiology and mental focus. The objective of using the NTS is to produce a repeatable shot that can be executed over and over again with minimal physical fatigue.

It is at this time that the archer must seriously consider purchasing their own, correctly-fitted archery equipment. Archery is a game of consistency and having your own gear is essential to establishing and maintaining consistency. Remember there are only two steps in archery: "Shoot a 10, then do it again." Shooing a 10 isn't that hard. Doing it again and again is the mark of a successful archer.

Appendix E
Compound Archery Class Syllabus

Introduction to Compound Bow Archery Class
Course Syllabus and Class Outline

The compound bow is very popular. According to an Archery Trade Association (ATA) survey of Archery Participation among adults in the United States, over 71% of all archers shoot compound bows at least some of the time and 61% of archers shoot compound bows exclusively.

All archery is fundamentally the same. The steps, movements and postures needed to complete the shot require the same set of muscles and concentration, no matter what the discipline. The Compound Archery class should follow the successful completion of the Archery Fundamentals class. Archers should have developed a stable shooting stance, a strong bow arm, a smooth release and a consistent followthrough.

Meeting 1
Introduction to the Compound Bow
(20 Minutes)

Compound bows have a number of features that make them attractive to archers: a fixed draw length, reduced draw weight at holding, and shorter bow length all contribute to a more consistent, comfortable archery shot for the average archer. Compound bow shooters may be the target of some good natured ribbing from recurve and traditional archers about shooting with "training wheels" and "buying a shot," but shot well, compound bows are just as challenging as other bow types and require the same discipline and attention to detail to shoot successfully.

Compound Bows Have Fixed Draw Lengths
Unlike a recurve or longbow, the compound bow has a fixed draw length. As the bow is drawn, there is a point beyond which the string can no longer be pulled. This stopping point in the draw is called the "wall" and is a distinctive feature of compound bows. (Universal draw length compound bows will be discussed later.)

The draw length is fixed by the geometry of the cams and the length of the string and cable(s). Some cam designs are fixed in draw length. Changing the draw length of the bow requires the replacement of the cam(s). Other cam designs allow for a range of draw length adjustments by the archer using simple tools. Having adjustable draw length bow cams is essential for club archery equipment in an instruction program so that the bows may be more easily fitted to the student archer's draw length.

Compound Bows Have Let-Off
The cam profile of the compound bow has a number of effects on the draw-force curve of the bow system. With a recurve bow, operating within its design limits, the force of the bow is roughly proportional to the length of the draw. As the recurve

bow is drawn back, the amount of force needed to hold the string increases with the amount of the draw distance.

In the compound bow, the draw distance and force needed to draw the bow are not simple with respect to the draw distance. As the compound bow is drawn back, the amount of force needed to hold the string increases quite rapidly and then plateaus at a "peak draw weight." Further drawing of the bow brings results in the force needed to draw dropping down into a "valley" at the bottom of the draw-force curve where the amount of force needed to hold the string is a small fraction of the peak weight. Depending on the design of the bow and the contour of the cams, the amount of force needed to hold the bow at full draw can be 50%-85% less than the draw force needed at peak draw weight. This reduction in draw force is called "let-off" and is a key feature of shooting a compound bow. The reduced holding weight of the compound bow allows the archer to hold the bow for a longer time at full draw and to refine their aiming on the target.

Compound Bows are Shorter

Archery equipment, as with many other high tech products, is subject to fads and style changes. The current trend in compound bow design is to produce bows with parallel (or beyond parallel) limbs. Parallel limb bows offer reduced kickback in the riser as the bow is shot because the motion of the limbs is upward/downward, canceling out the recoil of the bow. Parallel limbs also offer the opportunity for bow designs that have a shorter overall length, resulting in lighter bows. Shorter bow length is desirable for hunting equipment as shorter bows are easier to carry and are less likely to hang up in surrounding brush, nor do they get caught on tree stands.

Compound Bows Have More Consistent Arrow Propelling Force

The combination of a fixed draw length and a predictable draw-force curve result in compound bows having a built-in consistency of arrow-propelling force from shot to shot. Archery is a game of consistency, so eliminating the variable of controlling the arrow-propelling force from each shot is an important advantage of the compound bow.

Compound Bows are Heavier than Recurves

Nothing is free, and the advantages of the compound bow, with its lighter holding weight and consistent propelling force, are offset by the higher mass weight of the bow system when compared to recurve bow equipment. In strength and conditioning, compound bow archers need to strengthen the deltoid muscles of their bow arm in particular to hold up the greater mass of the bow.

Have students draw bows to feel the force-draw curve and let-off.

Introduction and Testing of Release Aid
(20 Minutes)

Most compound bow shooters use a mechanical release aid to draw, hold, and fire the bow. Release aids grasp the string or a "D-loop" with a mechanical caliper that can be opened by the archer to fire the arrow. The use of a release aid eliminates the lateral pressures on an arrow caused by using a finger-style release. As a result, the arrow does not flex and bend around the bow riser (the so-called Archer's Paradox) as it does for a finger shooter using a recurve bow.

Types of Release Aids

There are two general classifications of release aids: finger triggered and triggerless.

Within the triggered category are two general types: the hunter-style release with a wrist strap and a finger-activated trigger, and the T-handle or hand-held release with a finger- or thumb-activated trigger mechanism.<p hoto?>

The wrist strap release with a finger trigger is popular with hunters using compound bows. When fitting a wrist strap release, it is important to get the relationship between draw hand and bow string correctly placed. If the caliper is too far away from the draw hand the bowstring will not be drawn back to its full capacity and there will be a substantial air gap between the bowstring and the face. If the caliper is too close to the hand, the bow string may be drawn too far back along the archer's face, causing the string to rub on the face when released, spoiling the shot.

Achieving a solid anchor on the face is essential in fitting the wrist strap style release aid. Some archers anchor the draw hand between the thumb and first finger along the jaw line, triggering the release with the first finger. Using a finger motion to trigger the release can cause movement of the draw hand and a loss of anchor. In addition, the space between the thumb and first finger is wide and variable, making it difficult to repeat the draw hand anchor in the some position from shot to shot.

An alternative approach to the anchor position for a wrist strap style release is to turn the draw hand over so that the back of the hand is lying on the face. The anchor to the jaw line is made in the gap between the knuckles of the first and second fingers with the second finger resting on the trigger. In this anchor position, the location of the draw hand is more precisely repeatable. The release may then be fired using back tension, rather than a trigger pull move of the finger.

The T-handle triggered release aid is a popular choice among beginning compound shooters and archers who have not yet mastered triggerless releases. The handle is held in the draw hand with the caliper or release hook typically located between the first and second fingers of the draw hand. The thumb is used to trigger the release. Some releases allow the archer to choose between moving the thumb toward the target or away from the target to fire the release. It is preferred to have the trigger move away from the target to fire the release, as this motion makes transitioning to a back tension release easier. The anchor of the draw hand is on the back of the hand with the ridge of the jaw line wedged between the knuckles of the first and second fingers. Resting the thumb on the trigger and increasing back tension will fire the release. Any movement of the thumb directly will move the draw hand on the face, compromising the solidarity of the anchor position. The pad of the thumb should not be put on the trigger; rather, the trigger should rest past the pad.

The handheld triggerless release has been adopted by the majority of top competitive compound bow target archers. Once fitted to the archer, the string is released using progressive tension in the lower trapezius muscles on the draw side. Using the back muscles reduces the likelihood of hand movement and the resulting inconsistencies when firing the bow.

Back tension releases can misfire and can be "punched" by deliberate hand movement during the draw and holding phases of the shot. The archer needs to be able to operate the "safety" on the release and know when to turn off the safety during the shot sequence.

The string loop bow is a convenient and safe tool for setting up a back tension release. The angle of the release cam can be set using a string loop before fine-tuning the adjustment on an actual bow. The use of a string loop allows the archer to practice back tension technique without the risk of misfired arrows.

*Testing Release Aid with Handle
and String Simulator
(Hands-On)*

Archers in the compound class should have the opportunity to try a number of release aid types and set-ups using a string loop. Work on finding a stable anchor position on the jaw line. Practice releasing the aid using back tension. Work to stabilize the archer's draw length with the release aid.

Draw Length

*Measuring and Fitting for Draw Length
(30 Minutes)*

Measure each student's draw length, first using a lightweight recurve bow and a measuring arrow. Refine the measurement using a string bow and a release aid. A universal draw length bow (Genesis) may be used at this point to fine-tune the relationship between the bow string and the face when determining the draw length. Be sure that the archer has full command of back tension on the draw side with the draw side elbow in line with the arrow line. Watch for overdrawing the bow using the biceps with the resulting placement of the string too far back on the face. When the draw length is correct, there should be an absolute minimum of string drag on the side of the face. Adjustments to the wrist strap and caliper-connecting link may be needed to establish the correct string-to-face relationship.

Adjust Cams on Bow to Fit Draw Length

Assuming you have a compound bow with adjustable cams that can be set without the use of a bow press, adjust the draw length of the bow to match the draw length of the archer. Typically the cams may be adjusted by loosening set screws on the cam(s) and rotating the cam to the desired setting and then retightening or reinserting the screws. Settings are marked on the cam plate for reference.

Test the Draw Length with the Release Aid The bow string should be fitted with a D-loop and the draw length should be tested by the archer using the release aid that has been adjusted for them. This needs to be done up close to a butt with an arrow in the bow as dry fires are a distinct possibility. As the archer's shooting form improves, there may be some additional adjustment needed to compensate for draw length changes.

Break (10 Minutes)

Compound Bow Shooting Form
(40 Minutes)

The basic shooting form for compound bows follows the NTS method quite closely with some accommodations. The posture and stance are the same. Archers who plan to shoot long distances outdoors should master the open stance for greater lateral stability in windy conditions.

Nocking the arrow is the same as using a recurve bow, with the correct orientation of the index vane either up, down or sideways depending on the type of arrow rest on the bow. The bow hand position is the same. The release aid is attached to the D-loop and a slight tension of the bow is introduced. At the Set position, the bow arm is at a 45-degree angle to the ground and the draw arm is placed across the lower torso.

In an adaptation of NTS shooting form, the bow shoulders are open to the target at Set and at Set-up as the compound bow cannot be partially opened during setup. The bow hand is raised to target height and the draw arm raises to about 2 inches below the jaw height as with the NTS recurve technique. The bow is drawn using a combination of a rotation of the upper torso into alignment with the target and the movement of the draw arm scapula around the rib cage to bring the draw arm into alignment along the arrow line. Using a low draw may reduce the chance of getting a "bloody nose" caused by an accidental triggering of the release aid and consequent smashing of the draw hand into the face. Keeping the draw low and only raising the draw hand to anchor after the draw is compete is a much safer way to draw the compound bow.

The trigger finger of an index-finger release is kept behind the trigger during draw and anchor. For thumb releases the thumb is kept well clear of the trigger during the same interval.

The draw hand is then brought up to anchor on the underside of the jaw and the string touches the face for reference. When the bow is properly set up, the peep sight should be directly in line with the sighting eye. The sight comes into view and is aligned with the target. (Note It may be best to avoid using a peep sight for this class because of setup issues.)

Some time (a few seconds) may be required for the entire bow system to settle down and stop oscillating.

As the aim is maintained, expansion will fire the bow. The bow arm must remain fully engaged until the followthrough is completed.

Some compound archers use shooting forms that are not in the NTS style. Variations include:

Bent versus Straight Bow Arm The performance of the compound bow is achieved at the trade-off of increased mass weight for reduced holding weight. Some archers are not strong enough in the shoulders to hold up the mass weight of a compound bow a full draw. The bent bow arm engages the biceps of the bow arm to help hold up the mass weight of the bow. The price for using a bent bow arm is reduced draw length with the accompanying loss in power stroke and arrow velocity. Because of the fixed draw length of the compound bow, the use of a bent bow arm does not cause an inconsistency in power stroke as one would find if using a bent bow arm with a recurve bow.

Archers learning the compound bow should engage in enough physical conditioning to strengthen the deltoid muscles of the bow arm to permit a straight bow arm posture. At one time, vertical compound bow limbs produces considerable recoil in the compound bow. A bent bow arm was more effective in reducing the shock load of the recoil on the bow arm shoulder joint. Modern parallel limb bows have virtually no bow recoil so the bent bow arm is no longer needed as a shock absorber. Archers new to the compound bow should be discouraged from using a bent bow arm. Do the strength conditioning first to ensure that a straight bow arm can be maintained.

Raising the bow high above the sight line to the target, with the draw hand equally high, and then drawing downward to anchor is a popular set-up and draw technique that is often used by archers who are over-bowed and lack the strength to draw the bow properly. Such a set-up and draw can lead to bloody noses. It is better to lower the draw weight of the bow and work on a low set-up and draw until the archer's strength is built up enough to handle a higher draw weight.

Leaning Back at Full Draw Leaning back is again a symptom of a lack of strength, especially in the archer's bow arm. This lack of strength is aggravated by the tendency of the body to bring the center of gravity of the body to a place equally between both feet. As the bow is raised, the center of gravity of the archer/bow system shifts to the target side of the body. The natural reaction of the body to restore balance is to lean away from the bow to bring the center of gravity of the system to a position between the feet. Archers need to learn that at full draw there will be an increase in weight supported by the target side foot and to maintain their upright posture with this imbalance in the feet. Beginning archers can widen their stance to compensate for the lack of bow arm strength and the related leaning back posture. In time, as strength is built up, the stance can be narrowed.

Things to Watch For When A Release Aid is Used Hunter-style and thumb-triggered releases create a real temptation to simply fire the bow with the trigger finger (or thumb) rather than using back tension. As easy as this technique sounds, the interaction of the muscles in the hand will cause the draw hand to move on the face when activating the trigger. Such hand movement will cause inconsistencies in arrow performance. Archers should work on using back tension techniques to fire the release aid, no matter what the triggering style of the release design.

Blank Bale Shooting to Test Shooting Form and Release Aid Technique

Archers should practice handling the compound bow, nocking arrows and firing the bows at short range on a blank bale to get the feel of shooting the equipment. The feel of the compound bow system is very different from that of a recurve bow and some time should be spent becoming comfortable and facile with the gear before shooting at longer distances at a target.

You may want to start beginning compound archers out with a universal draw length bow for their first shots. The universal bow has the form factor of a compound bow while shooting more like a recurve bow. The bow has a constant draw weight, neither rising like a recurve nor letting off like a true compound bow. There is no wall with a universal length bow so using a release aid is difficult without punching the release to fire. These bows are best used with a finger release rather than a T-handle release aid. The light mass weight and the consistent draw weight make the universal draw length bow a candidate for transitioning from recurve to compound.

Homework

Strength Exercises for the Bow Arm Archers should do deltoid muscle exercises, raising the arms to a "T" shape while holding a 2-4 pound weight in each hand. Archers may use a commercially made dumbbell, An inexpensive alternative is to use a milk jug with water in it. Each pint of water adds 1 pound to the mass weight, up to a maximum of 8 pounds per gallon jug. Do three sets of 20 reps each to start building to five sets of 30 reps per set as the deltoids become stronger. These exercises should be done in front of a mirror so that the archer can be certain that only the deltoid muscles are used to raise the arms. The shoulders must stay down during the entire exercise. (Many people have subconsciously connected the action of the deltoid and upper trapezius muscles causing a raising of the shoulders as the arms are raised. It will take considerable conscious work to de-couple these two muscle groups in order to keep the shoulders down during the shot cycle.)

Archers with access to exercise equipment should do lat pull downs and "D" handle lower trapezius back muscle exercises.

Obtain a small notebook for recording sight settings and practice results.

Meeting 2
Explanation of different sight types
(10 Minutes)

Adjustable Sight with a "Scope" Target compound shooters competing in the Freestyle/Compound Unlimited and Freestyle Limited categories typically use a sighting system that incorporates an X-Y adjustable mechanism for windage and elevation coupled with a telescopic lens sight aperture (aka "scope") to visually align the sight with the target. Looking through a peep sight mounted in the string, the archer sees a magnified view of the target. Common magnifications range from 2 to 6 times with 4X being the most popular. Centering indicators can include a printed ring on the lens, crosshairs, and/or a fiber optic sight pin. The magnifying lens is mounted in a ring and attached to the sight mechanism with a threaded rod. Archers may add a lens shade to reduce glare in backlit target situations.

The X-Y mechanism consists of horizontal and vertical adjustments made with a rotating screw mechanism and a calibrated scale for recording and repeating sight settings. There are computer, tablet and smart phone apps for recording sight settings and calculating intermediate settings from a sample of range tested marks. Archers will need to keep a record of their sight settings, either on paper or in a smart device, for use on the range. Be aware that some shooting rules forbid electronic devices being used on shooting lines.

Hunting-type Bow Sights with Fixed Pins A popular alternative to the scope type target sight is the pin sight with a number of fixed sighting pins, adjusted to align the bow for different shooting distances. In use, the archer looks through a peep sight in the string and aligns the appropriate pin with the target.

During a practice session, the archer adjusts the vertical position of the individual pins to correspond with known distances. Typically pins may be set at 20, 30, 40, 50, and 60 yards. Once the pins are set, the archer must then use their own judgment to place the target on the fixed pin or an estimated distance between two pins or beyond the pins as they are; no adjustments are allowed. The windage adjustment is done to the entire group of pins. The bow/arrow system needs to be properly tuned for left/right arrow alignment.

The manufacture of sights is a vey competitive business and there are lots of sighting options from which archers may choose. In addition to the pin design, there are adjustable options for both elevation and windage in many designs.

Peep Sights Peep sights are small sighting holes that are installed in the bow string to align the string with the eye while aiming. Target peep sights tend to have a relatively small hole in them to see through. Hunter-type peep sights tend to be larger to let more light through in dim lighting conditions. In installing the peep sight, it is necessary that the peep sight end up oriented such that the archer can look through it at full draw position. The string may twist as the bow is drawn, bringing the peep sight into alignment (or not). Some archers use a peep sight that includes an elastic band or tubing that rotates the string bringing the peep sight automatically into alignment at full draw. There are also peep sights that are designed to be useable no matter what twist the string may take. In any case, it is essential that the peep sight come into comfortable and consistent alignment with the sighting eye without any unnecessary fumbling by the archer.

To test this, have archers close their eyes and draw their bow and anchor while addressing a mid-range target. When they reopen their eyes, the aiming eye should be looking right through the hole in the peep.

Explanation of stabilizer types and uses
(15 Minutes)

Stabilizers are fitted to both compound and recurve bows to improve consistency from shot to shot. Specifically a front stabilizer increases the moment of inertia in the bow system reducing the tendency of the bow to twist in the bow hand due to wind and other disturbances. Second, the stabilizer acts as a balance device, shifting the center of gravity (COG) of the bow system forward, often with the intent of biasing the COG in front of the bow hand to bring the top of the bow away from the archer at the release. Third, many stabilizer systems include some form of shock dampening to reduce vibration in the bow and the potential for recoil shock to be transmitted into the bow hand.

Target compound bows are often fitted with a

long front stabilizer for all of the above reasons. A long stabilizer has more leverage on the bow system, increasing the moment of inertia with a lower mass than a short stabilizer. Weights added at the end of the stabilizer allow the archer to adjust the amount of front COG bias to one that feels comfortable and produces the most consistent results.

Competitive recurve and compound bow risers are typically asymmetrical when viewed along the vertical axis of the bow. Adding a bow sight to the offset in the sight window in the riser further creates a left/right imbalance in the bow system. For compound bows, an offset weight on the bow hand side of the riser is often used to balance the bow system in the left/right orientation. Such offset weights are fitted to a shorter lever arm (essentially a V-bar) projecting from the side of the riser on the opposite side of the sight window. (For right-handed archers, the offset weight is on the left hand side of the bow. For left-handed archers, the offset weight projects to the right side of the bow.) Offset weights primarily affect the feel of the bow and rarely have a significant impact on the physics of the arrow flight.

Whether competing in the various bowhunter classes or stalking game in the field, the users of compound bows configured for hunting have different priorities in choosing their set-ups. Compound bows designed for hunting have become shorter and shorter as manufacturers work to improve or maintain performance while reducing the bow size for easier field handling in brush and foliage. Stabilizers for hunting bows are correspondingly shorter for the same reason. Current trends in bowhunter stabilizers include built -n shock dampening and the use of large-diameter weight discs at the end of the stabilizer for balance and increased inertia. The NFAA rules for the bowhunter classes limit the length of any single front stabilizer to 12 inches. No side balancing weights are permitted.

Stabilizer systems may be enhanced with shock dampening accessories, either built-in or added on to reduce noise and bow hand recoil shock. The trend towards parallel limbs in compound bows has virtually eliminated hand shock in compound bows so additional shock dampening is rarely required.

Shooting at short distances
(40 Minutes)

After the equipment is properly set up and fitted to the archer, archers should shoot at close distances to get a feel for the equipment and make any necessary adjustments to the set-up. Under the instructor's guidance, archers should focus on consistency of shooting form, maintaining body alignment, holding a firm bow arm and working on a smooth release technique. The instructor should watch for a stable shooting form and for any evidence that the archer is over bowed. Any struggling of the archer to bring the bow through its peak draw weight should be addressed immediately. Adaptations include lowering the draw weight by adjusting the limb bolts or, if necessary, changing to a lighter draw weight bow until the archer has built up the needed strength to handle heavier equipment.

As the short-distance practice session continues, have the archer get a 20-yard sight setting for both elevation and windage and write the sight setting down.

Break (10 Minutes)

Move to middle distances
(40 Minutes)

After the break, move back to middle distances and get sight settings for 30, 35, and 40 yards. Make any necessary adjustments in the arrow rest position to insure that the arrows all land on a vertical line as the archer shoots at each distance. If the arrows trail off to the right at longer distances, move the arrow rest to the left and try again. If the arrows trail off to the left, move the rest to the right. The goal is for arrows shot at any distance to fall in the center of the target without any additional sight adjustment for windage.

If you are shooting on a Field Range, explain the colors and markings on the range distance markers. All distances on the shooting position markers are in yards except for the birdie target, where the distances are marked in feet.

NFAA Field Rounds
Adults use the white stakes/markers
Young Adults use the white stakes/markers
Youth use the adult stakes/markers up to 50 yards.
Targets over 50 yards will use the blue stakes/markers
Cub use the black stakes/markers

NFAA Hunter Rounds
Adult use the red stakes/markers
Young adult use the red stakes/markers
Youth use the adult stakes/markers up to 50 yards.
Targets over 50 yards will use the blue stakes/markers
Cub use the black stakes/markers

NFAA Animal Round (paper targets, not 3-D)
Adult use the yellow stakes/markers
Young adult use the yellow stakes/markers
Youth use the adult stakes/markers up to 50 yards.
Targets over 50 yards will use the blue stakes/markers
Cub use the black stakes/markers

Homework
Go to fieldarchery.com and download the rules for NFAA field archery.
Continue with strengthening exercises.

Meeting 3
Discuss issues in choosing a compound bow
(15 Minutes)

Hunting Bow or Target Bow? What is the intended use of the bow? If the goal is to compete, then a target bow is usually chosen for length, stability, and ease of shooting. Archers wanting to compete in the bowhunter class may want to purchase bowhunting style equipment. Hunters will want to purchase gear that is suitable for the terrain or tree stand that they will be using.

Draw Weight The draw weights of compound bows are adjustable within a wide range by adjusting the limb bolts (rotating them in to raise and rotating them out to lower the draw weights). For target archers, the least amount of draw weight that will produce consistent results is optimum. Target bows are shot dozens, if not hundreds of times, in a single session. Excessively high draw weight in a target bow will lead to early fatigue and inconsistent results.

Hunting bows typically have a higher draw weight than target bows in order to increase the kinetic energy of the arrow for game penetration. Hunters typically shoot a very small number of arrows in a session so fatigue from repeated drawing of the bow is not an issue. In hunting, it only takes one arrow.

Bow Length Axle-to-axle (ATA) distance is a measure of the bow's physical length. Hunters prefer bows with short axle-to-axle distances for improved maneuverability in outdoor brush and tree stands. Short bows are lighter in weight and easier to handle. Target archers usually prefer longer ATA length bows for stability and a smoother draw.

Riser Configuration Bow risers are designed in a variety of layouts that place the handle at, behind, or in front of the limb bolts. Deflex designs with the bow handle closer to the target than the limb bolts are more stable and are thought to be more "forgiving" of errors in technique. Reflex designs with the handle farther away from the target than the limb bolts are less stable but provide for a longer power stroke (distance arrow is on the string during launch) with resulting higher arrow speeds. Archers should choose the riser design with which they feel most comfortable and which produces the most consistent results over time.

Basic Bow Design There is constant competition between manufacturers of bows to come up with new designs that may appeal to the buying public. The current trend in bow design is to use shorter limbs, configured in a parallel or near-parallel alignment. As the bow is drawn, the limbs move towards each other, rather than moving away from the target as in a recurve bow. The primary advantages of these parallel limb designs are a shorter axle-to-axle bow length and the reduction in bow hand shock by cancelation of recoil by the two limbs moving in opposite directions from each other.

Compound bows may be fitted with double or single cams. Double cams are a more traditional design and are often preferred by compound finger shooters. Double-cam bows need careful setup to insure that the two cams are synchronized, starting and finishing their rotation at the same time. Setup includes adjusting the length of the cable to synchronize the cam motion, a time-consuming and tedious process.

Single-cam bows use a computer-designed single cam coupled with an idler wheel to handle the string. Single-cam bows are simpler to set up as there is no synchronization required.

Whichever cam type is chosen, for beginners and intermediate compound archers, it is preferable that the draw length of the bow be able to be adjusted without the need for a bow press. For beginning youths, bows with a draw length adjustment range of up to 10 inches are preferred.

Demonstrate the use of the computer for recording and calculating sight settings (15 Minutes)

There are a number of computer programs and smart device applications for logging, calculating, and displaying sight settings. Archers provide some measurements and specifications as inputs to the program and the computer then calculates the sight settings (and often the arrow speeds and other factors).

The arrows are measured for weight, length, and fletching. The bow is measured for brace height and draw length. A measurement of how far the peep sight is above the arrow shaft at full draw is needed (it takes two people to make this measurement) as well as a measurement of the distance between the peep sight and the bow sight aperture or pins. Some programs want you to enter the type of cams on the bow.

Archers then need to shoot and record at least two sight settings at different distances. Usually settings for 20 yards and 60 yards will do. All of the above information is entered into the computer and the computer calculates all the sight settings, typically in 1-yard increments (and will also do metric values). Depending on the device, the sight settings can be printed out for field use or displayed on a mobile device. Some programs will also print out a sight tape that can be attached to the vertical frame of an adjustable sight for quick reference.

Note It would be good if possible to bring a laptop computer and a printer to the range so that students can enter their sight settings and get a printout for their particular bow setup.

Shoot at shorter distances to warm up (15 Minutes)

Break (10 Minutes)

Shoot at longer distance up to 60 yards and record sight settings (40 Minutes)

Shoot a 5-target field round with distances from 20 to 60 yards including a walk-up (30 Minutes)

Homework

Look up web site with "Choosing a Compound Bow" http://www.hungry-for-hunting.com/best-compound-bow.html Print out and read.
Visit web sites for PSE, Hoyt, Martin, Matthews. Look for bow alternatives.
Visit a pro shop and try one or more bows.
Compare the difference between the Genesis universal draw length bow and a true compound bow.

Meeting 4

Discuss the issues of using the Easton Arrow Chart for arrow shaft selection (20 Minutes)

The arrow is the most important part of the bow and arrow system. The arrow is the object that must react to the thrust created by the bow and fly to the target. The speed of the arrow, its reaction to the bow and its flight characteristics are influenced by a number of factors of construction and configuration.

Arrow shafts are constructed of wood, fiberglass, aluminum, carbon fiber and variations of these materials. For compound bows, aluminum, aluminum/carbon, and carbon fiber are the most common materials of choice by far. Shaft sizes include dimensions of weight, shaft diameter, shaft wall thickness and shaft length as well as the shaft's "spine." Arrow spine is a measure of its resilience, typically measured by its resistance to being bent or flexed.

Static arrow spine is measured on a jig. An arrow shaft to be tested is placed on supports 28 inches apart. A 1.94-pound weight is hung from the middle of the shaft and the deflection from straight is measured in thousandths of an inch. For example, if an arrow shaft deflected 1/2 inch, the arrow spine would be .500. For marketing purposes, the arrow spine is often stated as a 3- or 4-digit number with the decimal place removed. A .500 spine arrow shaft would be specified as a 500 shaft. Remember, the lower the number, the stiffer the arrow, with a resulting smaller deflection in the spine test.

Arrows shot from recurve bows are more sensitive to arrow spine for proper flight than an equivalent compound bow.

Shaft weight is an outcome of the construction of the arrow. In principle, lighter arrows will fly faster than otherwise equivalent heavier arrows. Long distance target archers may want to use lighter arrows to allow for consistent form, but some choose slightly heavier arrows to resist movement caused by wind. Indoor competitors often use heavier arrows since the distance is short and the extra weight provides extra stability. Hunters may want to use heavier arrows to increase kinetic energy for greater game penetration.

Arrow diameter is also a factor for target archers shooting outdoors. A smaller diameter arrow will offer less surface area to the wind. Indoor target archers, where wind is not a factor and distances are short, may want a larger diameter arrow to increase the possibility of contacting an inner scoring ring. (Watch out for "inside out" scoring in the shoot-off!)

The dynamic spine of an arrow is the arrow spine reaction as exhibited by the shaft's behavior, not just a static measurement. Dynamic spine can be affected by adjusting the weight of the arrow point. A heavier point weakens the arrow flight characteristics and a lighter point will stiffen the arrow response. Top archers may fine-tune their bow-arrow systems by changing point weights.

Fletching and nocks have a lesser impact on spine but fletching does affect arrow flight and aerodynamics. For compound bows, using the least amount of fletching as possible will reduce drag. Archers using broadhead arrow points will need larger fletching on the arrows to offset the aerodynamic impact of the wing-like broadhead point.

Once archers' draw lengths and draw weights are determined, they can then use an arrow chart, provided by the manufacturer, to see a recommendation for arrow spine. On-line calculators that automate the charts are also available. As an exercise, students should measure their own draw weight and draw length and then use an arrow chart to determine what arrow spines, arrow types, and arrow sizes are recommended.

Shoot at a short distance to warm up and refine your shooting form (15 Minutes)

Shoot ultra short distances and distances over 60 yards to get sight settings and understand parallax (35 Minutes)

In general, as an archer moves away from the target, the sight is lowered to increase the departure angle of the arrow for longer flight, but there is a paradox in the sight settings when shooting at very close distances. The first principle to understand is that the line of sight of the archer is different and separated from the line of flight of the arrow. The archer sees in a perfectly straight line with no deflection for distance. In addition, the archer's eye is about four inches above the nock of the arrow for archers shooting with a release or with an under-the-chin anchor point. Because of this the arrow leaves the bow ascending. The arrow travels a curved path, rising up to the line of sight at fairly close range, rising far above the line of sight and then dropping down to the line of sight at the target. As the arrow climbs, there is a unique distance where the arrow crosses the sight line on its upward trajectory. There is a second unique distance at which the arrow again crosses the sight line on its downward trajectory. Barebow shooters will know these distances at being "point on."

When shooting at very short distances, the arrow is still climbing when it hits the target. The differential between the line of sight and line of the arrow flight is known as parallax. The sight settings must be adjusted to compensate for parallax at very short distances. As a result, the sight is dropped when moving closer, rather than being raised. Archers should practice shooting at close range and log their sight settings to see this phenomenon as well as to improve their scores.

Break (10 Minutes)

Shoot a 7-target field round with ultra short and longer distances (40 Minutes)

Appendix F
Traditional Archery Class Syllabus

Introduction to an Instinctive Way of Shooting

Note These materials were originally developed by Robert Storts of Pasadena Roving Archers and edited by Van Webster

Meeting 1
Review Basic shooting form and safety rules from beginner session

Introduction to Instinctive Shooting
Instinctive shooting is the art of shooting a bow without the assistance of any kind of aiming device, aiming system, or release aid. The arrow is not used for reference, nor is any part of the bow used for sighting purposes. The archer simply concentrates his vision on the spot he wishes to hit, and the brain directs the hands and eyes to point the arrow correctly. The process is much like casting a fishing lure—you focus only on the target, and the brain instinctively coordinates hand and arm movement to achieve the goal.

Instinctive shooting is the least complicated and most basic method of aiming a bow and has a long history. English longbow men aimed their arrows instinctively, as did their predecessors, the feared bow horsemen of Asia, the Mongol, and the Huns. For centuries, Native American Indians used their instinctive shooting ability to feed, clothe, and protect their families.

Prior to the advent of the compound bow in the 1970s, most hunting bows were aimed and shot by the instinctive method. With the compound bow, however, came a different approach to aiming. Because the compound bow's mechanical let-off made it possible for an archer to hold at full draw for extended periods, the compound bow lent itself well to the use of sights and various aiming accouterments. Within a few years, instinctive shooting all but disappeared as archers enthusiastically adopted sophisticated sighting systems.

Today, however, with the resurgence and growing popularity of the bare recurve and longbow, instinctive shooting has resurfaced as a favored technique for hunting and target bows. Historically, the recurve and longbow were aimed and shot instinctively, so it is natural that many devotees of this equipment wish to shoot in the same manner.

And in practical terms, instinctive shooting is well matched to traditional equipment; recurves and longbows increase in poundage as they are drawn and can be difficult to shoot using complicated aiming systems that require the shooter to remain at full draw for several seconds. Archers using traditional recurves and longbows are therefore the most likely candidates for instinctive shooting. Instinctive archers can draw and shoot more quickly than archers using sighting systems and the style also allows more versatility when hunting in tight spots.

Basics

1. Stance
One should stand in such a way as to support your upper body and allow your bow arm and shoulders to be in line with the target. One may have to bend their knees because of uneven ground, and uphill and downhill shooting is not uncommon. One may even have to kneel to make a shot. The stance should provide a stable platform for the shot. The archer should feel balanced and rooted into the ground.

2. Nock
The arrow should be consistently nocked onto the string in the same position on the string and with the same fletching orientation for each shot. The archer should listen and feel for a "click" as the nock snaps onto the string.

3. Concentration is focused on the target
Aiming Throughout the draw, anchor and release, keep your eyes and concentration focused on the target. Intense and uninterrupted concentration on a single spot is what instinctive shooting is all about, and its importance cannot be overemphasized. The more complete your concentration, the better you will shoot. You can practice this skill during your daily routine by picking out the smallest spot on everything you see: a small water spot on your office desk, a cracked taillight on a vehicle in traffic, a small bird high in a tree. Through practice, some shooters develop the ability to assume an almost trance-like concentration prior to and during the shot.

Handouts
Parts of the Longbow and Arrow Diagram

Meeting 2
Review Basic Shooting Form Steps from Week One, then Work on Steps 4 & 5 (Predraw and Draw)

4. Drawing
Begin the draw, keeping the back of the string hand relaxed, while keeping your eyes and concentration focused on the target

A stiff-arm swing draw is best for instinctive shooting, because it ensures a consistent shoulder position, which is crucial to accurate shooting.

When shooting a traditional recurve bow, hold the bow with a straight wrist grip. Position the bow arm to the front and outside of the forward leg, pointing straight toward the ground with the elbow in a locked position. Continue by swinging the bow up and drawing with a single motion, keeping the elbow and wrist of your bow arm straight.

When shooting a longbow, hold the bow with a heel-down hand position. In starting position, with the bow hand to the front and outside of the forward leg, the elbow should form a natural curve. Place the string in the outermost joint of the three drawing fingers, so they feel relaxed and secure, then while keep your eyes and concentration focused on the target, swing the bow up and draw with a single motion, keeping your elbow and wrist straight.

With both kinds of bows, bend your knees slightly as you draw; this will focus and intensify your concentration, and provide better alignment with your target, Make sure to draw using the muscles of your upper back, not the arm and shoulder; at full draw you should feel your upper back muscles under tension.

5. Holding
Holding occurs with the bow held with a straight wrist grip, and with the bow arm to the front and side of the forward leg. The bow arm elbow is locked.

Canting With instinctive shooting, the bow is slanted, or canted, to the right (for right-handed archers) or left (for left-handed archers) as you shoot. Canting the bow brings the eye closer and more in line with the arrow and rotates the upper part of the bow out of the line of sight just enough to give you a clearer picture of your target. Most recurve bows have a cut-out in the riser to allow a clean sight window. Pushing the bow and pulling the bow string simultaneously to your anchor point while maintaining proper back tension is primary to all bow shooting and is the single-most important ingredient in developing consistent archery proficiency. The bow hand pushes toward the target as the bow arm pulls back, and this constant force must be maintained throughout the shot. Without it, consistent accuracy is difficult to achieve.

Maintain your concentration on the target during holding.

Homework
Practice shooting form.

Meeting 3

Review Steps from Week Two then Work on Step 6 Anchor (corner of the mouth). Work on Back Tension

6. Anchoring

String and Hand Alignment Proper full draw position places the string hand, head, and bow hand in straight alignment. As you reach your anchor point, tilt your head slightly, bringing your eye directly over the arrow. Most instinctive shooters anchor with their middle fingers at the corner of their mouths, but some anchor at a tooth, feeling that this anchor point is less likely to move than the corner of the mouth. Take care not to use your cheek or chin to help hold the draw; the anchor point is a reference point only. The draw is held entirely with the upper back muscles.

Maintain your focus on the target while anchoring.

7. Arrow Position

It is crucial that the arrow be as close as possible to the line between the eye and the bow hand. For this reason, instinctive shooters generally shoot "off the shelf" with no arrow rest. This puts the arrow as close as possible to the bow hand.

In some cases your bow may be equipped with an arrow rest. You may have to adapt the shot process to compensate for the additional arrow elevation above the bow hand when an arrow rest is used. The goal is to have the arrow become an extension of the pointing hand. Finding this relationship between the arrow and the bow hand is an integral part of the hand/eye coordination effort.

A good technique for finding the correct grip of a longbow is to point the bow hand at the target, with the forefinger extended, and place the bow between the thumb and forefinger. Historically, longbows are shot with the heel of the bow hand down on the handle. Because the arrow and hand are not pointed together, as they are with the straight wrist grip (Recurve bow grip), shooting the longbow is somewhat more difficult than shooting the recurve bow. Longbow shooting requires more practice but can be mastered with time.

Explain the relationship between arrow weight and stiffness (spine) to bow draw weight (a very basic introduction to tuning) and the influence of arrow specifications on arrow flight, especially over longer distances.

Measure the students' draw lengths

Shoot a Lighter Draw Weight

Heavy-draw-weight bows add to physical tension and increase the likelihood of a bad shot. With too heavy a draw weight bow, you may not be able to keep your eyes and concentration focused on the target. A heavy bow will also crush your shooting form, making proper alignment impossible.

Handouts
Easton Arrow Chart

Homework
Pick out the correct arrow size for a 25# recurve bow at the student's draw length.

Purchase a small notebook for recording archery information

Meeting 4

Review Steps from Week Three, Work on Steps 8,9& 10 (Push, Release, and Followthrough

8. Push

Push the bow hand toward the target while using your back muscles to pull your string hand back to the anchor point. Maintain this tension throughout the draw. Keeping your knees slightly bent can improve your concentration and focus.

9. Release

Done correctly, the release is a simple matter of relaxing of the fingers. If the bow is drawn correctly with the bow hand pushed toward the target and the string hand pulled back with the upper back muscles, the release will almost certainly be clean. Maintain your focus on the target during the release.

At release, your bow arm should spring slightly forward and remain pointed at the target, and the release hand should move slightly backward. This followthrough must be maintained until the arrow hits the target. Without a correct followthrough, the bow arm may drop before the release, affecting the shot.

Don't shoot too quickly. Many archers think that instinctive shooting means drawing and releasing quickly, and that it is incorrect to take your time. Allow your shot to develop its own rhythm and speed. Although it's true that an instinctive shooter usually begins to shoot somewhat more quickly as his/her skills develop, speed is a result of experience, not a goal in itself. With instinctive shooting, the shot is made when your intuition says, "Now is the time."

10. Followthrough

After you shoot, you should keep both your bow arm and your concentration on the target until your arrow reaches the target. This is called following through. There are two reasons for doing this: one is to let your arrow clear your bow's arrow rest and the second is so you can focus on the arrow (flight of the arrow). As you focus and observe the flight of your arrow and imprint its flight trajectory in your mind, you now have reference point from which you can make corrections.

Demonstrate shooting at a blank bale.

Review natural point of aim and adjust as needed.

Shoot longer distances, up to 40 yards.

Explain basic competition.

Show scoring on target.

Homework

Visit a Pro Shop. Buy a finger tab or glove.

Meeting 5

Review all the Steps

Shoot a 5-target match, with each target at different distances including a very short one. Use Field Targets and Field Scoring; 100 points is a perfect score.

Handouts

Field round scorecard

Appendix G
Two-Hour Training/Practice Schedule

The following are some guidelines for scheduling the activities during a typical two-hour archery training session for an Olympic style recurve archer. Archers training in other shooting styles may use the same general blockings of time with adjustments in the content as appropriate for their shooting style. Recreational archers should try to put in at least two at-the-range training sessions a week to develop and solidify their shooting form. Archers wanting to compete should try to get the range at least four or more times per week.

Elite archers train six days per week. A typical at-the-range training session for an advanced archer will last four hours and roughly double the times listed below. On some days there are morning and afternoon shooting sessions. On other days the shooting session is supplemented with strength training, aerobic training and/or mental training.

Archers who are in school or have day jobs will need to maximize their training opportunities by splitting their training schedule around their other obligations. Weekend training is supplemented with early morning and late afternoon and evening sessions. Form work can be done at any time where there is relative quiet and a mirror for feedback.

The most important single step any archer can take to increase their training opportunities is to turn off the television, computer, tablet or smart phone. Time spent looking at a screen is time not spent improving your archery form.

10 Minutes Stretching Work the entire body, upper and lower. Take the time to let the muscles and joints warm up. Do not bounce when you stretch. Come to the muscle's limit and hold for a count of 10. Then move just an eighth of an inch further and hold for another count of 10. Over time, this method will do much to increase your flexibility.

15 Minutes Form Work Form work should include feedback from a coach, a fellow archer, and/or a mirror. Photographs and videos should also be used.

Start with a form strap or string bow. Go through the entire shot sequence.

Use a stretch band next, focusing on the dynamics of the shot sequence. Make sure that each muscle group is properly engaged.

Use a lightweight bow or an elastic string on a conventional bow to refine the feel of the shot. Focus on hand positions and maintaining the correct tensions/relaxations in the muscles.

20 Minutes Blank Bale Shooting Shoot at a distance of 5 yards or less at a blank bale. Put your focus on the feel and process of the shot. Shoot with your eyes closed if safe to help concentrate on the feel of the shot. Use video recordings for feedback. Work with the coach to refine technique.

60 Minutes 50-80 Yard (70 Meters Preferred) Shooting Shoot some sighting-in ends and then shoot a simulated tournament. Tournament variations can include elements of a FITA round, an Olympic elimination round, the "Gold Game" and variations. Shoot with a timer if possible. Keep the mental focus on the process and feel of the shot.

10 Minutes Specific Physical Training (SPT) Now that your muscles are warmed up, do several variations of the SPT exercises. In practice the amount of SPT should be varied in an ascending and resting sequence over time. On the first day, start with three sets of three reps each. The next day increase to four sets and on the next increase to five sets. Take a day of rest and then do four sets. Take a day of rest and start over with three reps of each exercise but with a higher load, using a heavier bow or adding the elastic band to your existing bow. Over time you can increase the loading, duration of the hold and number of reps to increase strength. A stretching and SPT routine should be included in your daily exercise even if you are not able to come to the range.

For compound archers, in stead of SPT exercises, take the time each session to strengthen the upper body muscles, especially those muscles that support the shoulder. Holding a weight in the "T" position for 30 seconds at a time will go a long way toward strengthening the deltoid muscles in the shoulder. Use the same rhythm of exercise and rest as with SPTs, increasing the weight of the load progressively over time.

10 Minutes of Stretching Stretching after exercise is just as important as stretching before exercise.

Off-Range Form Work Include form work with the form strap/string bow and stretch band in your daily exercise routine. Do your form work in front of a mirror to monitor and adjust your progress. Focus on the feel of the shot and on using the correct muscles.

General Aerobic Conditioning Try to do 45 minutes to 1 hour of aerobic conditioning at least there times a week. Aerobic conditioning will build your endurance and mental strength.

Strength Training If you belong to a gym, work with the trainers at the gym to develop a strength training routine that builds the muscles you need in archery. Also, be sure to build your "core" strength. Strengthening the abdominal muscles allows you to connect the lower body to the upper body. Core strength is essential to stance stability.

The above schedule is a broadly based blocking of time allotments. Individual variations may be made to accommodate a particular archer's needs. Additional variation in specific tasks can be introduced when multiple training sessions are held per week. Shooting practice completions, shooting with time limitations, shooting for speed, shooting under stress and shooting off to practice for windy conditions are all possible variations of activities during a training session.

Looking at a training week, roughly 50% of the athlete's time will be spent shooting and 50% will be spent doing something else. Aerobic conditioning, strength training, flexibility training, mental skills, yoga, visualization and a host of other athletic training activities can be worked into a more complex training schedule.

Archers shooting in other disciplines such as compound and traditional instinctive archery can use the same time allotments for training sessions as noted above with the specific activities tailored to meet the needs of their shooting style. The key is to provide a structure to the training session, include a variety of activities, and monitor and adjust the athlete for maximum performance.

Appendix H
Camp Archery Program Equipment List

**Camp Archery Program
Equipment and Supplies Check List**
*Part Numbers are from Lancaster Archery
(1.800.829.7408)*

Equipment
- ☐ Target Butts/Bales (Youth Target MT109)
- ☐ Rope and Stakes for back stays
- ☐ Arrow Curtain and Stand (if indoors) (10´x 30´AIM300)
- ☐ Bows (we use a 5-to-1 ratio for RH to LH bows)
- ☐ Polaris-R54" 3880023 14 pound 7-10 years old
- ☐ Polaris-R 62" 388003 14 pound 11 years old to adult
- ☐ Arrows Select Easton Jazz Aluminum arrows 1716 Youth 28½" 1916 Adult 30"
- ☐ Extra Arrows
- ☐ Arrow/Quiver Rack (home-built)
- ☐ Finger Tabs (Cartel *Pro II Finger Tab* 1760009 RH and LH)
- ☐ Arm Guards (X Spot *Junior Arm Guard* 8560063)
- ☐ Quivers Ground/Hip (Neet NY-615 3300015)
- ☐ Bow Rack at range (home-built)
- ☐ Bow Rack for storage (home-built)
- ☐ Post Stringer (home-built) Use 2.5" X 6" Lag Screws with at 3" piece of ½" hose covering the bolt

Materials
- ☐ Target Faces 80 cm minimum size 3050063
- ☐ Target Pins (for holding target faces on butts/bales-use Bar-B-Q skewers or make pins out of heavy wire)
- ☐ Line markers options (buy at sporting goods store or home improvement store)
  - Sports Field white line marker (buy at soccer store)
  - Exterior Sports Line Paint
  - Rope and Stakes
  - Sidewalk Chalk
  - Painter's Tape (low tack, no residue)
  - Soccer Cones

Supplies
- ☐ Feathers in all the colors on your arrows (Trueflight Feathers 3" 5200003)
- ☐ Fletching Glue (Loctite *GO-2* glue—buy at Target store)
- ☐ Nock Sets (brass rings w/ black plastic inserts) (Saunders *Nok* sets 3890017)
- ☐ Bowstring Wax (Brownell Wax Stick 1600029)
- ☐ Extra Arrow Nocks (American *BJ Nock* ¼" 30060001)
- ☐ Extra Arrow Rests (LH and RH—Hoyt *Hunter Rest* 2560084)

Tools
- ☐ Bow Square
- ☐ Nocking Point Pliers

- ☐ Set of Allen Wrenches (SAE)
- ☐ Set of all three above (*Archer's Tuning Kit* # GT114)
- ☐ Fletching Jig (Straight Fletch #1750)
- ☐ Screwdrivers: Phillips and Flat headed (hardware store)
- ☐ Utility Knife (hardware store)
- ☐ String Jig (*The Bowstring Maker Wood String Jig* # BSM)
- ☐ Spring Clamps (hardware store)
- ☐ Tool Box (hardware store)
- ☐ Saunders *Bow Stringer*

Appendix I
The National Training System

Archery Training and the Shot Cycle
National Training System (NTS)

Note This description of the National Training system (NTS) is based on class notes from a presentation by Coach Lee at the Olympic Training Center in Chula Vista, CA. As the steps of NTS have never been published in outline form as of this writing, this is as close an approximation to the authorized version as possible. Shooting form techniques are constantly under development. Variations in updates to this description are likely in the future. (Some wags have said that "NTS" stands for Never The Same.)

NTS is specifically designed for recurve target archers shooting outdoors at long distances. Archers using other types of equipment and shooting in a range of conditions will need to make adaptations to their shooting form to accommodate the need for consistency. Additional adaptations may be required for body type, physiology and physical strength. Think of this list as a reference for training, not a set of rigid rules.

Steps
Stance
Posture
Nock
Hook/Grip
Set
Mindset
Setup
Load (Draw)
Anchor
Transfer
Holding
Expansion
Aim
Release
Followthrough
Relaxation and Feedback.

1. **Stance** Use only the open stance and teach open stance from the beginning.

    Place the ball of the back foot on the line to the target. Place the front foot so that the toe is about 2 inches open to the line to the target. The feet should be near parallel and splay out slightly so that lines drawn through the center line of

The open foot stance is preferred for Olympic Style Recurve shooters, shooting outdoors and at long distances. In this image the dark line represents the shooting line and the light line represents the target plane line from the archer to the target face. The toe of the down range foot is about 2-3" behind the target plane line. The ball of the up range foot is on the target plane line.

the feet will intersect in a "V" shape about four feet behind the archer. The loading on the feet is 60% on the balls of the feet and 40% on the heels. Use a gripping motion of the toes to establish foot balance. The knees are straight, not locked.

Concept Note The target plane is a vertical plane from the archer to the center of the target along the arrow line when at full draw.

2. **Posture** The tailbone is tucked in, the abdominal muscles are compressed and the rib cage is down. The back is flat. The shoulders are down and the head is straight up. No leaning back and no tilting.

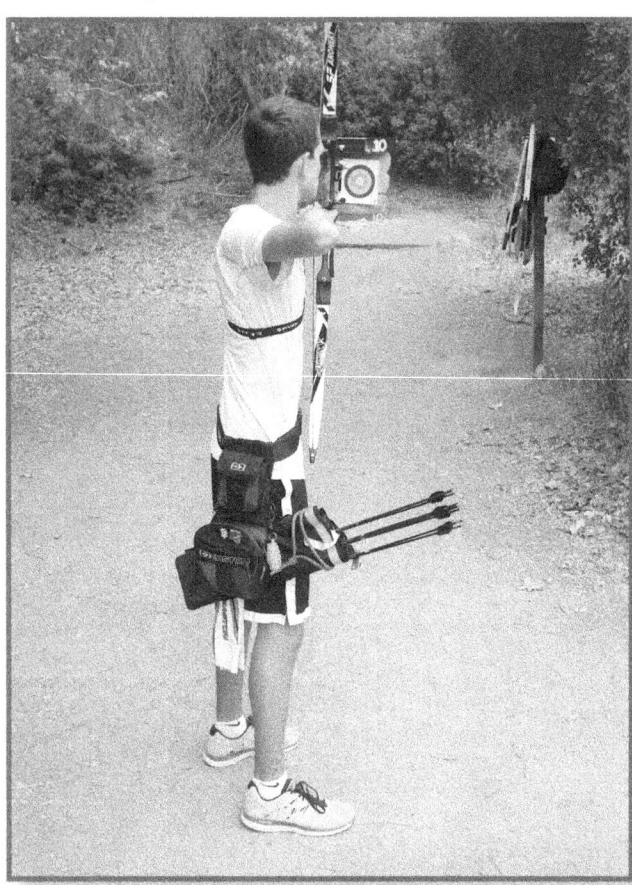

The archer's posture should be upright with the rib cage perpendicular to the ground. The hips should be tucked under the body and the back should be flat. About 60-70% of the archer's body weight should be on the balls of the feet. Note the clearance of the bowstring to the chest.

3. **Nock** Nock the arrow for consistency each time. Feel for a consistent nock pressure/click. Be sure the index fletching is correctly oriented. On a recurve bow, the two nocking points should be spaced at just the width of the nock as the string is vertical in the hands when at full draw. (For compound-fingers archers, an additional space is required between the knocks to compensate for the string angle at full draw.)

4a. **Hook** The Hook is the first point of contact between the archer and the bow system. Hook onto the string first and then set the grip on the riser. Hook the string with the string position just to the outside of the first joint of the first finger; just to the inside of the first joint on the middle finger; and just the pad of the third finger on the string. The loading on the fingers should be 40% first finger, 50% middle finger and 10% on the third finger. It is important to visually check the hook on the string each time.

The thumb and little finger are curved into the hand to form a "C" shape. The back of the draw hand is flat. The finger spacer should be large enough to avoid pinching the arrow at full draw. The fingers should remain parallel when viewed from the bow side of the hand at full draw. The first finger should not curl down with the pressure of the string.

The draw hand wrist is turned out to place the draw elbow behind the arrow line throughout the shot sequence. There may be a slight to moderate tilt down of the draw wrist to accom-

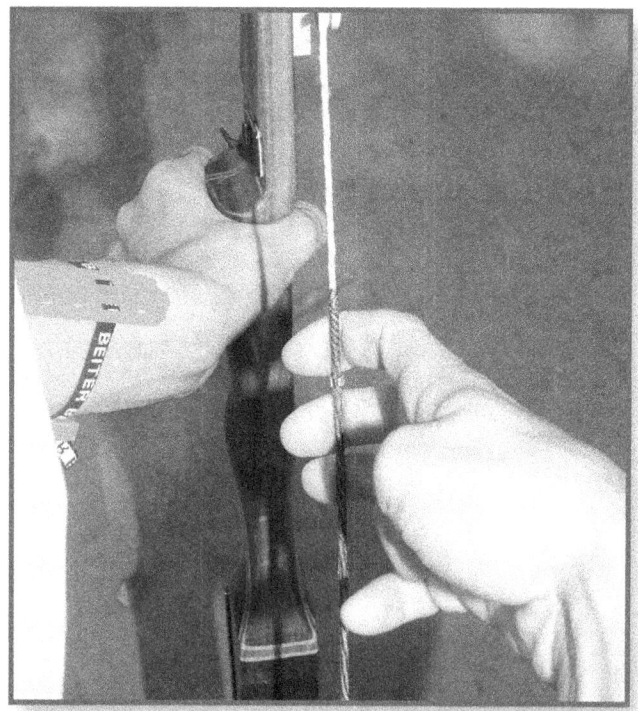

The draw hand should be positioned so that the string crosses the first finger at the first knuckle joint, just behind the first knuckle joint of the middle finger and the pad of the third finger should just rest on the string for balance and location. The thumb and little finger should be curled into a "C" shape.

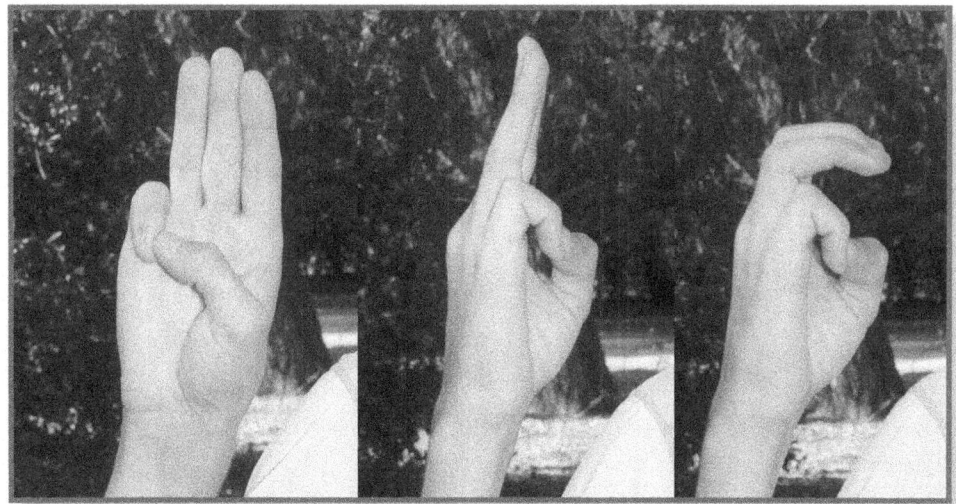

Draw Hand Shape *In this sequence of photos, beginning archers are asked to make a "Scout Sign" shape with their draw hand with three fingers up and the thumb and little fingers touching each other (left). Note that the back of the draw hand is flat (middle). The beginning archer is then asked to form a hook using the first two knuckles of the draw hand while keeping the rest of the draw hand flat (right). The archer then hooks onto the bow string with the hook formed by the three fingers. For first time archers, the draw hand position on the string is below the arrow. When a bow sight is introduced the draw fingers are then split with the first finger above the arrow and the other two below the arrow.*

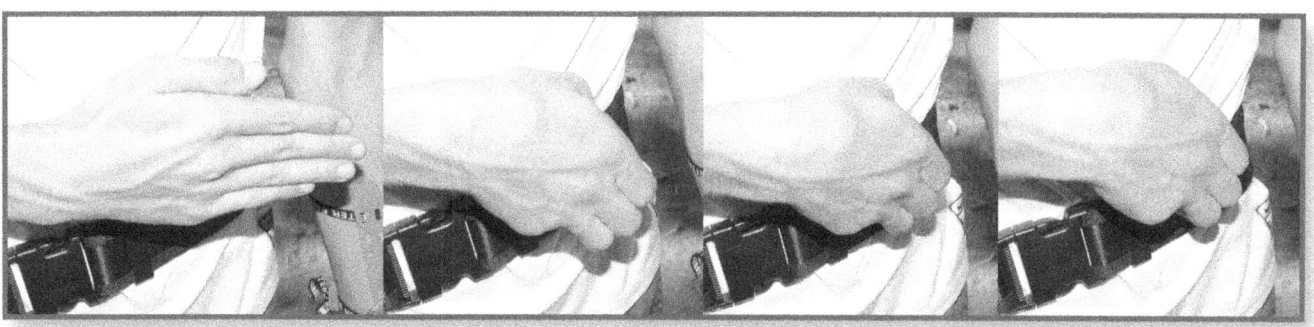

Draw Hand Position Start (left), Down middle left), In (middle right), Rotate (right). Once the fingers are correctly hooked, there are three motions necessary to put the draw hand into the correct position to anchor properly. (Middle Left) The draw hand tilts down at the wrist until the angle of the tilt matches the angle of the archer's jaw line. There can be wide variation in this tilt as faces differ in shape. (Middle Right) The draw hand is then tilted inward, towards the body creating an outward break in the wrist. This inward angle is needed to permit the forearm of the draw side to correctly align when back tension is applied. (Right) The bow hand is then rotated at the wrist about 15 degrees. For right handed archers, this rotation is counter clockwise. Of left handed archers the rotation is clockwise. The rotation of the draw hand permits the optimum alignment of the fingers of the bow string.

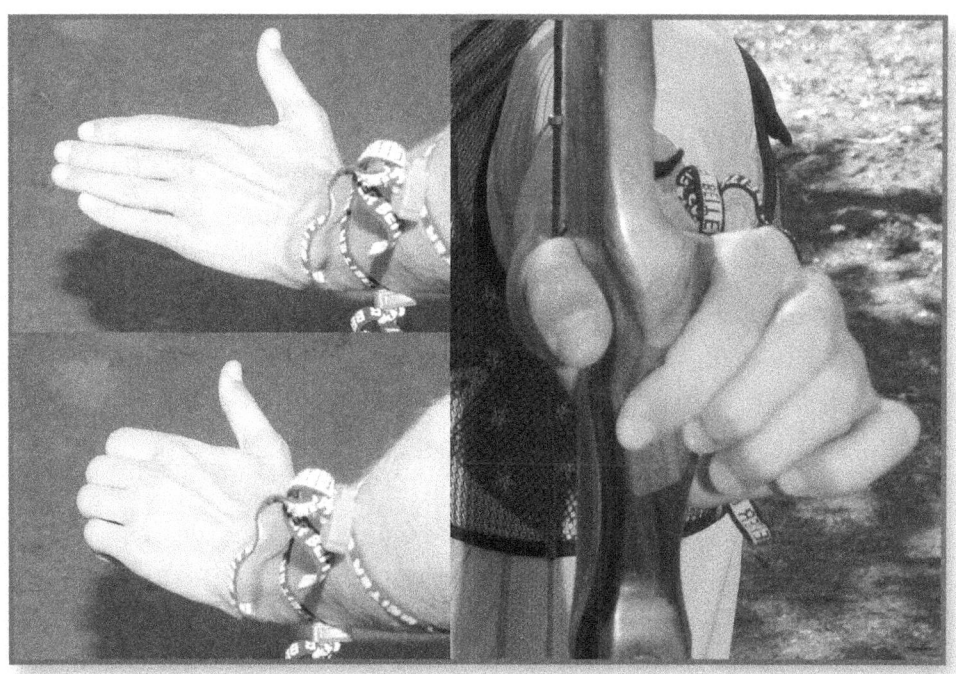

Set Bow Band *(left top) The bow hand position starts with the bow hand extended and a "V" shape formed between the thumb and first finger. (left bottom) The fingers drop down into a natural curl and the bow handle is placed in the "V" between the thumb and hand. (right) The bow hand shown here looking back at the archer shows that the knuckles of the bow hand form an angle of about 45 degrees with the bow handle and that only the first finger of the bow hand wraps around the grip. For more advanced archers, a finger sling will restrain the bow upon release and none of the fingers grip the bow handle.*

modate the angle of the archer's jaw line while at anchor.

Once the draw hand position on the string is established, the position must not change during the entire shot sequence.

4b. ***Grip*** The Grip on the bow riser is the second point of contact between the archer and the bow system. Place the "V" of the bow hand deeply into the pivot point and then drop the wrist to bring the pressure point at the base of the thumb into contact with the bow grip. The wrist joint is horizontal. The knuckles are at a 45-degree angle to the ground. The little finger of the bow hand should be located behind the plunger. The first finger is pressed lightly on the front of the bow riser. The three other fingers should be lightly curled under and away from the riser.

The thumb of the bow hand should press lightly on the side of the riser from the base joint with the thumb tip pointed away from the riser such that the archer can see the thumb nail on the bow hand at full draw.

5. ***Set*** The bow arm is placed down and outward at a 45-degree angle to the body with some tension in the bow arm triceps. The bow is to the left of the target plane and the shoulders are still somewhat open to the target.

On the draw side, the upper arm is close to the body and the forearm lies across the front of the body, approximately level and in front of the stomach. The draw arm elbow is behind the arrow line. Initiate a slight rotation of the draw shoulder to create tension in the core of the body. The shoulders are down and level. A last visual check of the bow/hand relationship is made.

6. ***Mindset*** The head is turned toward the target. A deep cleansing breath is taken. The shot process is visualized or mentally rehearsed. The eyes should be focused on the aiming point on the target. Once turned toward the target, the head should not move until the completion of the shot.

7. ***Set-Up*** The primary goal of Set-Up is to establish the "Barrel of the Gun" alignment of the bow arm and shoulders. The preferred way to raise the bow is to rotate the upper torso to bring the bow and draw shoulders into an alignment

Set *At the "set" position, the bow arm extends away from the body at a 30 – 45 degree angle. The draw arm is placed in front of the body with a near right angle formed by the upper an lower arms (I call this the "broken arm position" as if the arm was in a sling.) The shoulders are down, the head is turned towards the target and there is some movement of the draw shoulder around the rib cage to put about 2-3" of tension on the bow.*

with the bow hand while coiling the torso to create additional tension in the core. This core "wringing," prepares the body to draw the bow. The turning action of the rib cage should pivot around the spine and not either of the shoulder joints.

Upon raising the bow, the bow hand should be in alignment with the target plane and the barrel of the gun should be set and locked with additional triceps tension. There may be a small downward movement of the shoulders to set the bow arm. The bow arm braces the bow using the back muscles. The bow hand should be raised to a height that puts the sight aperture just above the aiming point. (About 12 o'clock in the white ring.) Once set, the bow hand should not move or change elevation during the rest of the shot sequence.

On the draw side, the draw arm is raised by pivoting at the draw shoulder joint directly upward without initiating any additional pulling of the draw arm. The draw hand must remain in its fixed position on the string, wrist bent outward, and the draw elbow should be behind the

Setup I ask archers to perform set up to the count of "One, Lock." Simultaneously, the bow arm is raised, pivoting somewhat to the left for a right handed archer, and locked by engaging the triceps on the bow arm. The draw arm pivots only from the ball joint at the top of the humerous, bringing the forearm up to a level about equal in height to the chin or a bit below. The draw hand retains its shape and orientation form set and the arrow will be pointing to the left of the target for a right-handed archer. The shoulders should stay down during the set up phase. Note that a partial draw of the bow occurs, not because of any pulling of the draw arm but because the geometry of the skeleton causes a separation of the hands as the bow is raised.

arrow line. The draw hand should be raised to an elevation below the chin height. The arrow will now be pointing to the left of the target for a right-handed archer.

Note FITA/World Archery rules limit the excursion of the archer and any of their equipment to within a 1-meter boundary to avoid any interference between archers on the shooting line.

The Set-Up will produce an opening of the bow, caused by the separation of the arm pivot points of the two shoulder joints. This opening motion should be nearly effortless as it is the body's alignment that does the work and not pulling with the muscles.

At the conclusion of set-up, the loading in the muscles should be 60% in the back and 40% in the front and draw hand muscles.

8. *Load* (Draw) The draw hand is brought to a position under the chin by traveling in a straight line from the Set-Up hand position. Load the back (lower trapezius muscles) by moving the draw side scapula towards the spine. The mental focus should be on moving the LAN2 spot on the back of the upper draw arm along a path parallel to the shooting line. The draw elbow, as viewed from the rear moves upward and toward the body along a 45-degree angle track. The pulling motion should be against the pressure point on the bow grip and not along a line through the arrow rest on the bow riser. The bow string should land on the face at the center of the nose, the side of the lips and on the side of the jaw.

At the conclusion of the Load step, the loading in the muscles should be 80% in the back and 20% in the front and draw hand.

Load (Draw) The Load or Draw is done on the count of "Two." Leading the motion with the draw side scapula, the draw hand moves on a straight line form the set position to a location about 1" below the jaw line. The arrow line will rotate around a pivot point formed by the bow hand and bow riser and come into alignment with the line to the target. The bow string should land on the face wit the string on the center of the nose, the side of the mouth and just to the side of the jaw.

9. *Anchor* Move the draw hand upward, sliding the string along the face until the first finger of the draw hand is firmly pressed under the jaw. The hand position should be such that the first finger has full, "bone to bone" contact with the jawbone. Some adjusting of the downward tilt of the draw hand may be necessary at the Hook step to insure that the angle of the top of the draw hand matches the angle of the jaw line. Once the anchor is set, the draw hand does not move on the face during the rest of the shot sequence until release. Some slight sliding of the string on the face may be permitted during loading.

Anchor Anchor is completed on the count of "Three." In a simple motion, the draw hand is raised to its anchor position just below the jaw line. the bow string will slide along the face, guiding the position of the draw hand. The draw hand should have full contact with the jaw bone along the top of the first finger from the second joint to the base of the thumb.

10. **Transfer** The Transfer is the final shifting of the muscle loading from the draw side biceps into the back. The archer focuses on the LAN2 spot and presses it even further along a line parallel to the shooting line. The mental focus transfers from the forearm to the upper arm at the LAN 2 spot. There should be no movement of the draw hand on the jaw. The archer should feel increased pressure of the string on the face. The draw arm elbow should be fully behind the arrow line when viewed from above.

    The Transfer step makes the final commitment to the shot. The load should now be 90% in the back and 10% in the draw hand muscles. Transfer should complete the loading of the bow's draw weight onto the skeletal structure. The draw weight of the bow should now be held in compression in the bones of the archer and the load on any muscles is reduced. The goal is to use the muscles to align the body in order to direct the forces of the bow into the bones. With the exception of the digitorum muscles on the draw hand side, the muscles are primarily tasked with skeletal alignment and not holding the draw weight of the bow.

11. **Holding** Holding is the most important step in the shot cycle. All actions before holding and all actions after lead to or result from maintaining this step. At holding, secure the "barrel of the gun" (BOTG) by fully engaging the triceps of the bow arm. A triangle is formed between the BOTG, the arrow line and the humerus of the draw arm. There should be a feeling of inflation from inside the body. While holding, the rib cage is in a state of compression from the loading on both the bow arm and draw arm scapula. Holding cannot be reached if the step of transfer is not completed. Archers should work on rhythm and timing to make all of the motions smooth and consistent.

    In Holding, the draw side scapula is lower than the bow side scapula. This scapula position requires a combination of a downward motion combined with a scapula rotation. Archers should not "squeeze the back" as such a motion locks the upper part of the scapula, preventing expansion. At holding, an archer, viewing themselves straight on in a mirror, should be able to see their draw side scapula. Keeping the scapula down reduces pain in the back.

    While Holding, there should be a slight reduction in heart rate as the muscle load is reduced. The process of Holding should feel calming to the archer. The mental attention

Transfer Transfer is completed to the count of "Four" In transfer, any remaining tension in the draw arm biceps is transferred into the lower trapesius muscles securing the draw side scapula. There may be some small amount of visible motion of the draw arm elbow as the scapula moves around the rib cage and into place.

Holding At holding, the apparent movement seems to stop as the actual movement becomes invisible due to the forces of the bow acting on the body. **Alignment Draw Side** (middle) At holding on the draw side, the alignment of the bow hand, draw hand and draw elbow should form a straight line along or slightly inside of the arrow line. **Alignment Bow Arm** (Right) At holding the body alignment on the bow side form a straight line from the bow hand through the bow shoulder and to the draw shoulder.

should shift to the target while the mental focus is on continuing pressure at the LAN 2 spot to hold along the target line. The loading in the body should be 90+% in the back and less than 10% in the hands. The clicker should be about 2 mm from the end of the arrow point.

12. *Expansion* Expansion is an invisible motion that uses the principle of ratio of movement to move the arrow the final 2 mm to release the clicker. It is accomplished by focusing on the LAN 2 spot while holding the draw force of the bow. As the scapulae move minutely towards the spine, the shoulders move ever so slightly to cause the overall diameter of the archer to increase to its maximum size. The spine does not move during holding and expansion.

Check points for expansion include no movement of the draw hand on the face, a firm bow arm with the triceps fully engaged and an open chest caused by the contraction of the back muscles. The breath should be let out about 50% and then held during expansion.

13. *Aiming* Aiming is a subconscious process of centering the aiming spot in the sight ring. The key factor in aiming is eye control, focusing on the aiming spot continuously until the followthrough is complete. Aiming should take a maximum of three seconds before the string is released. Any longer than three seconds of expansion will cause the archer to lose concentration. If the arrow is not released in three seconds, the shot should be let down and re-started.

It is important to have a consistent string picture with respect to the sight ring. The string should sit just to the inside of the sight ring.

In windy conditions, the archer will aim off to the right or left as appropriate to compensate for the wind drift of the arrow.

Expansion Expansion is the slight additional angular motion of the draw side scapula toward the spine and the resulting slight expansion of the draw by about 1 to 2 millimeters, enough to dislodge the clicker.

Aiming Aiming takes place only after expansion begins and should last for no more than three seconds. In the sight picture, the ring of the sight is centered around the "gold" of the target while the image of the string is placed on the bow side of the sight ring, tangential to the sight ring. The position of the bow string in the sight picture is critical as it forms the "rear sight" of the aiming process. (This photo is an illustration, photographed without an arrow.)

14. **Release** The release is caused by expansion and the relaxation of the digitorum muscles in the forearm of the draw hand. At release, the string pushes the fingers out of the way of the string while the draw hand drags across the face towards the back of the neck. The archer should not open the fingers. Some stretching and dragging of the skin of the neck may be observed during this movement.

    The bow arm must stay stable and firmly in position at release. At the moment of release, the bow will jump forward from the bow hand, being caught by the finger sling.

    Release Expansion will cause the release of the string to happen. Some archers may choose to "relax the draw hand" to release the string. Relaxation on command is very difficult. The bow arm remains fixed at the release.

15. **Followthrough** The principle of Followthrough is to finish with control. The primary factors are to maintain the tension in the muscles and the directions of movement that have been established in the shot process. The invisible forces of expansion now become visible in the movement of the archer's body. As with all other aspects of the shot cycle, consistency is essential in the followthrough.

    The draw side elbow is seen to move downward and to the rear along a line parallel to the shooting line at an angle of 45 degrees when viewed from the back. The bow hand does a "sit" movement by pivoting at the wrist to additionally throw the bow forward. The movement of the draw hand rearward and the "sit" motion of the bow hand forward happen simultaneously in "synchronization" in order to balance the dynamic forces of the movement of the mass weights of each side of the body to maintain balance in the archer's stance.

    The eyes maintain focus on the target during Followthrough and should not re-focus to follow the flight path of the arrow. The eyes may only relax when the Followthrough is complete.

    Followthrough The followthrough is a natural continuation of the direction and forces in the body as released by the removal of the pressure of the bow. The draw hand remains at or in near contact with the face, ending up behind the neck. The bow hand moves toward the target as it pivots at the wrist in a downward motion. The bow is captured by the finger sling.

16. **Relaxation and Feedback** At the completion of the shot, the bow should be rested on the foot and the archer should relax the tensions in the muscles and the mind by taking a few deep breaths. The results of the shot process should be analyzed based on how the shot felt and not just on the arrow position in the target. This is the time to make tactical decisions about the next shot. Should adjustments be made in the shot process to compensate for external conditions such as wind or equipment issues? If the shot felt good, do it again. If the shot felt bad, make an adjustment and try again.

Summary

The shot cycle is presented in steps for easier understanding and to provide focus points for training. In application, the steps need to flow from one to the next in a smooth, dance-like manner. There will be pauses in the movements, especially to change directions of movement, but the overall execution should be a fluid process.

Additional Notes

Classic Misdirections of Shooting Technique

1. Emphasis on having too deep a hook on the draw hand. A hook on the bottom finger moves the hand away from the jaw.
2. Not taking the Set-up to establish the Barrel of the Gun. Get some distance on the draw to set BOTG.
3. Lengthening the draw by pulling straight back and/or leaning back and losing the brace of the bow.
4. Posture – If you "stand tall" you get a hollow back.
5. Open stance vs. square stance – Pick only one stance and stick to it from the beginning. Open stance should be taught. The hips must be parallel with the feet and not rotate during Set-up.
6. Continuous Movement leads to push-pull technique and bypasses holding.
7. The Release – focus on the movement, not the muscles.

Sales Points for the NTS

Uses BEST technique
Is not the Korean system
16 interdependent steps all linked together
Innovated in sports science
Based on new discoveries, 20th century technique
Proven success
Works for all archers
Reduces injuries and makes archers stronger
The holding position braces the bow
Changing directions is like a change of gear
The focus is on movement, not muscles
Maintaining the form is the result of the desire of the archer
Issues in form are fixed using training aids
Biomechanics makes people stronger
The archery world is improving
Teaches proper technique from the beginning

Principles of Biomechanics
(from "Total Archery" p 69-82)

1. Biomechanics is, "The science that examines the internal and external forces acting on the human body and the effect produced by these forces."

    The goals of using biomechanics are:
    a. Performance
    b. Technique
    c. Equipment
    d. Training methods
    e. Coaching techniques
    f. Reduction of injury

    The tools of biomechanics are:
    a. Newtonian mechanics
    b. Motion analysis systems
    c. High-speed video
    d. Force measurement devices
    e. Electromyography (EMG)
    f. Digital video and computer analysis
    g. Delayed video playback
    h. Heart rate monitors
    i. Insole systems

2. Newton's laws of motion
    a. *First Law of Motion (Inertia)* Every object persists in its state of rest or in uniform motion in a straight line unless it is compelled to change that state by forces impressed upon it.
    b. *Second Law of Motion (Acceleration)* The rate of change of momentum is proportional to the force applied and takes place in the direction of the straight line in which the force acts.
    c. *Third Law of Motion (Action and Reaction)* For every force applied by the body to an object, the object applies an equal force back against the body, or mutual actions of any two bodies are always in equal and opposite directions.

3. *Principle of Horizontal and Vertical Force* The horizontal and vertical forces act on planes at mutual right angles. The summation of these forces is a vector addition of the components in the horizontal and vertical planes.

4. *Principle of Eye Control* The eye must remain focused on the aiming point throughout the shot cycle until the followthrough is complete.

5. *Principle of Followthrough* The archer must keep

the direction and tension of forces in effect during the followthrough for consistency and control.
6. *Principle of Relaxation* The skill must be executed in a seemingly relaxed and effortless manner. Western archers typically have 50%-70% tension in their body during a shot. Korean archers have 10%-30 % tension. Shooting in a relaxed manner conserves energy and reduces fatigue.

Appendix J
A Glossary of National Training System (NTS) Terms

The National Training System uses a number of terms that are not intuitively understood. The following is a personal glossary of terms that may help the archer or coach better understand the nomenclature.

Archery Terms

"American Thumb" A position of the thumb on the grip hand that uses a slight pressure with the base of the thumb on the side of the grip while turning the tip of the thumb outward so that the thumb nail is visible to the archer at full draw.

Arrow Line Arrow line is a line along the shaft of the arrow at full draw as projected toward and away from the target. The arrow line will pivot around the riser in an angular motion at the draw/loading phase of the shot sequence.

Barrel of the Gun (BOTG) An alignment of the bow hand, bow shoulder and draw shoulder into a straight line for maximum strength and control.

Biomechanics The study of the action and effects of internal and external forces on the body.

Energy Ratio Energy ratio is the ratio between the energy expended and the resulting output. In archery the goal is to use low bodily energy to produce a high output of performance.

Eye Control The archer should focus the eye on the target through the completion of the shot. Also called eye followthrough.

Flat Back This is used to describe the archery posture in which the spine is vertical and flat, without curvature. Flat back is the opposite of hollow back.

Followthrough Followthrough is the principle of continuing the motion of the body through the shot to improve control. In archery, the archer should maintain the tension focus in the body and continue with the directions of movement that have been established in the shot cycle to produce a natural followthrough.

Hollow Back A posture in which the lower spine is bent into a "C" shape and the buttocks protrude. Hollow back is a common postural error and results in an unstable torso and increased lower back pain.

Horse Stance The horse stance is a posture similar to the posture of the rider on a horse. This stance is often a basic stance for martial arts. In archery the stance is executed without using the bent knees of the martial arts version.

Motion, Angular Rotation around a central line or point.

Motion, Linear Movement along a straight line in the same direction and at the same speed.

Newton's Laws of Motion
1st – Law of Inertia Resistance to a change in state. Bodies at rest will stay at rest and bodies in motion will stay in motion until acted upon by a force.
2nd – Law of Acceleration A force applied to a body causes an acceleration of the movement of that body in a magnitude proportional to that force.
3rd – Law of Reaction For every action there is an equal and opposite reaction.

Power Zone Located in the core of the body about 2 inches below the navel and about 3 inches inside the body.

Pressure Point The pressure point is at the base of the bow hand thumb where the pad of the thumb presses directly on the bow grip.

Ratio of Motion The principle that a short motion on a short lever arm will produce a larger motion across a fulcrum on a large lever arm. This term is used to describe the results of angular motion during expansion that sets off the clicker.

Summation of Force The method of adding vectors to find the resulting component value of magnitude and direction. In archery the summation of force is used to analyze actions on the horizontal and vertical planes.

Synchronizing The simultaneous movement of the draw hand and bow hands during followthrough. The purpose of synchronization is to match the forces in the body going towards and away from the target to maintain body balance.

Target Plane Target plane is a vertical plane through the center of the target along the arrow line when an archer is at full draw.

Vector Any quantity that has a magnitude and a direction can be described by a vector, typically a directed line segment.

Archers at the Olympic Training Center in Chula Vista, CA use pipe bows, lightweight bows, and elastic bands for form training. The archer with the pipe bow has added an elastic band to increase the draw weight. Note how the angle of the string on the pipe bow allows for good facial contact.

Appendix K
Making and Using PVC Pipe Bows as Archery Training Aids

When working with new archers it is important to get their form right before moving students up to higher draw weight bows. Current teaching techniques start archers out with form straps or string bows to get posture and body positioning correct. Dynamic movements can be practiced under load with an elastic band, strengthening the body and raising awareness of the correct muscle uses.

Archers should then progress to very light draw weight bows to get the feel of the archery shot well in hand before moving up to a heaver bow. Ultra light draw weight bows were available some years back and were commonly called "banana bows." The lightest draw weight bows available commercially now are typically 15 to 18 pounds. Ideally, a bow with a draw weight of under 10 pounds should be used to transition from training aids to drawing a "real" bow. While it is possible to custom order ultra light draw weight bows, such bows will be as costly as a conventional bow and often require a long waiting time for delivery.

An alternative to the expensive custom training bow is the "pipe bow" made out of PVC water pipe. For about US$3.00 in materials and 15-20 minutes of labor, you can build an effective archery training aid that can be dry fired or can cast an arrow a short distance. Here's how you make one.

At a home improvement store, purchase one piece of ½-inch inside diameter (1.2 cm) PVC pipe for each bow that you want to make. PVC pipe comes in 10′ (3 m) lengths. You will be cutting a piece 62 inches to 70 inches (155 cm to 175 cm) long from the pipe so there will be some waste. You can use the scraps of leftover pipe to make target or paper tuning frames for your range. Also purchase some tubular foam insulation for ½-inch pipe, normally used to insulate water pipes. The tubular insulation comes in 8-10′ (2.5-3 m) lengths, so one piece of insulation will be enough material to make the handles for 6-10 bows.

You'll also need some 1-inch (2.5 cm) wide cloth-backed tape for reinforcement. I use gaffer's tape, common in the video and film business, because it is strong and doesn't get gummy over time. You may want some spray adhesive glue, often used to paste targets onto cardboard backing, to secure the handles in place. For a string, I use ½--inch (3 mm) diameter nylon cord, available at sporting goods stores that carry camping and outdoor equipment.

Start the process of making your bow by gently bending an entire piece of the ½-inch pipe to determine in which direction it prefers to bend. All pipes have inconsistencies in manufacture that make the pipe bend more easily in one direction. Once you have determined which way the

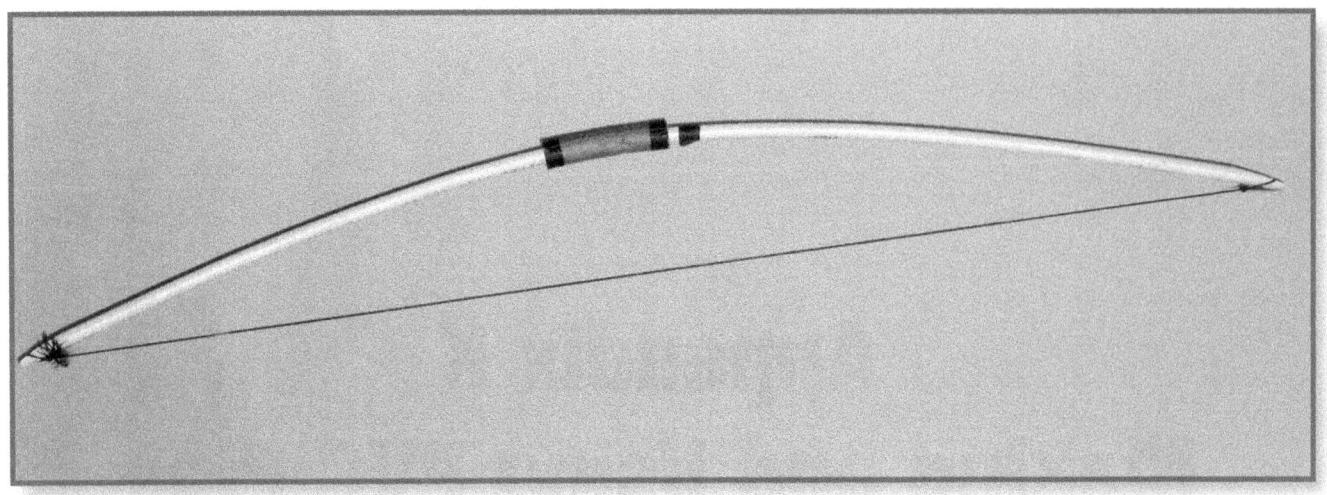

The pipe bow is a piece of half-inch inside diameter plastic pipe cut to a length of 66-70 inches and fitted with a simple handle. It has a draw weight of less than 10 pounds and is a useful tool for shooting form work.

pipe likes to bend, mark the end of the pipe to align your string cuts.

Next cut the pipe to length. The length should be the same as the length of the bow the archer will eventually be using. The goal in choosing the length of the pipe is to replicate the angle of the string as it meets the face at full draw. Cut the pipe to 62"-70" length as desired. Also note that the shorter the pipe, the higher the draw weight of the bow.

If you are working with compound archers, you can make 60-inch (150 cm) bows that will have a higher draw weight but will be more consistent with the shorter axle-to-axle length of a compound bow. You can get two 60-inch bows out of a single 10′ piece of PVC pipe, reducing your cost even further.

Using the marks on the bow as a guide, cut each end of the bow at about a 15-degree angle to form a tapered tip (see photos). I use a band saw for these cuts, but the plastic can be easily cut using hand or power saws. Clean up the feathered ends of the cut with some light sandpaper.

Next, cut the string grooves using a rotary hand grinder such as a MotoTool. I use a conical

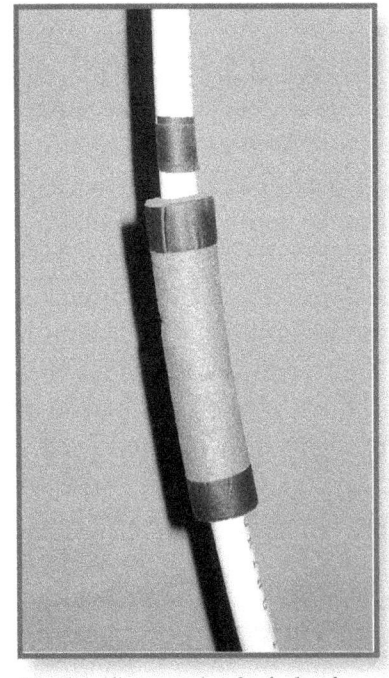

The handle is made of tubular foam insulation, reinforced with tape top and bottom. A second ring of tape can be wrapped around the pipe to indicate the top half of the bow.

cutting tool and form a notch plus a groove for the string to ride in. You can also use a small-diameter rat tail file to do the same job by hand. Smooth all of the edges that come into contact with the string to minimize wear.

Cut a 9-inch (24 cm) long piece of the insulating foam and slide it onto the pipe. You may want to use some spray adhesive or double stick tape to hold the insulation in place. Reinforce the ends of the insulation by wrapping a band of 1-inch (2.5 cm) cloth tape around the insulation.

Cut a 6-foot (2 m) long piece of ⅛ inch cord and tie a loop at one end. Thread the loop on the bow and bend the bow to the desired brace height. Tie a second loop at the other end of the string at the desired length and you are ready to go. There is no need to include a nocking point.

In practice, pipe bows are great for refining shooting form, correcting problems, and as an intermediate step in the daily warm-up process. I find that young archers really like to work with pipe bows as they are easy to use and rather "cool." They are strong enough to cast an arrow into a target up to five yards/meters away.

Compound archers can attach their release aids to the string of the pipe bow and work on their shooting form consistent with the way they shoot. Pipe bows are a great way to set the trigger point for back tension releases, as they can be dry fired without fear of damage.

For fun, stage a clout shoot using only pipe bows shot at a target laying flat on the ground about 25 yards/meters away. The person who gets their arrow closest to the center of the target wins. Pipe bows can also be used for public shoots and community outreach pro-

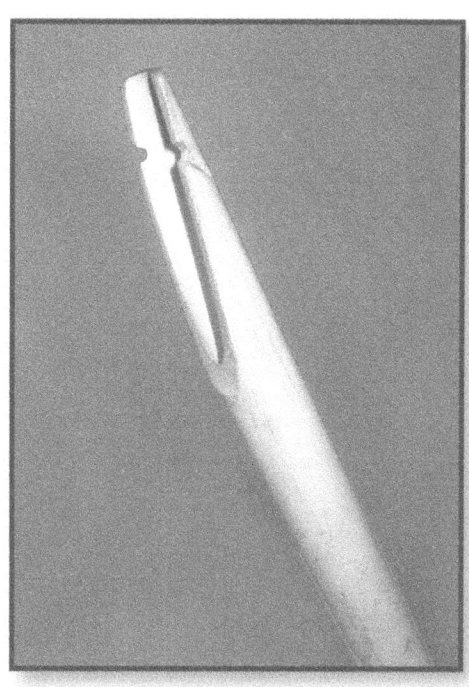

Each end of the pipe is cut at a diagonal and then notched to hold the string. Use a bit of sandpaper to smooth the edges and remove any feathering.

grams. Some people even sell pipe bows as novelty items at craft and outdoor fairs.

Do not leave your pipe bows strung up when not in use. PVC pipe is only moderately elastic and will take a set curve if bent over time, reducing its effectiveness. A pipe bow may only last a training season before having to be replaced but at such a low cost, the expense to your program will be minimal. Pipe bows are a fun, inexpensive and very effective training tool that you can easily add to your archery training program.

Have fun!

Appendix L
Archery, a Numbers Game

Target archery is certainly a game of numbers. Arrows are shot, scores are kept and winners are declared based on the resulting scores. But what of the larger numbers picture? Who is shooting archery and why? Who is the audience for an archery club or instruction program? And, by extension, who are the potential customers for archery equipment at archery pro shops and on-line retailers?

These are important questions because the answers can influence the direction that an organization may choose to pursue to attract and retain archers.

The Archery Trade Association (ATA) asked a polling company, Responsive Management, to find some answers. The results of their survey of "Archery Participation Among Adult United States Residents in 2012" are available as a PDF download from the ATA web site and are very revealing. According to the report, 8% of the US population identifies themselves as archers, albeit with 57% of archers participating in the sport only 1 to 5 days per year. Only 13% of the 8% participate in archery more than 30 days in a year. That translates into a little over 3 million archers in the US who make archery a regular part of their lives.

The Myth of Hunting

I, along with many others, bought into the myth that the dominant demographic in archery was hunters. Not entirely so, according to the survey. 55% of all archers identified themselves at "Target Archery Only Participants." Archers who were both target archers and bowhunters made up an additional 35% of the total archery participants. Only 10% of the archers surveyed indicated that bowhunting was their sole archery activity. Put another way, 55% of all archers are target archers only and 45% of archers are bowhunters at least some of the time.

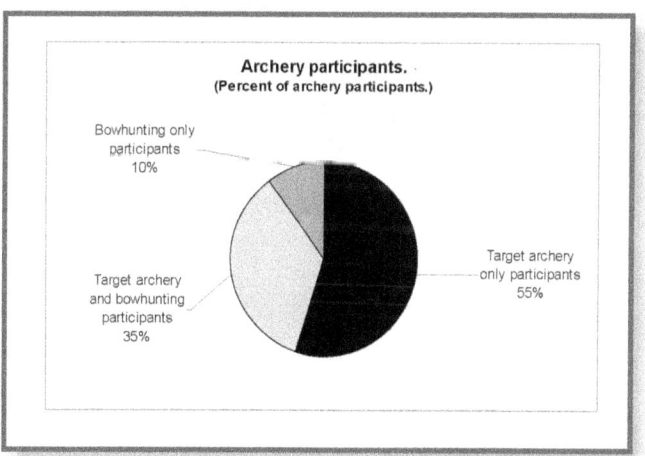

What kind of gear do archers shoot? 75% of archery participants shoot compound bows. No distinction was made in the survey between target and hunting style compound bows. Second in popularity are crossbows with 29% market penetration. Crossbows are the fastest growing segment of the archery equipment sales business. This growth in sales is attributed to newer and more inclusive state fish and game regulations on the use of crossbows for hunting.

14% of respondents shot recurve bows. Again, no distinction was made between target, traditional, and hunting style recurve bows. No distinction

Teaching Archery

Type of Archery Equipment (All Possible Combinations; Groups Are Mutually Exclusive)	Percentage in Each Mutually Exclusive Group (All Groups Shown)	Compound Total	Crossbow Total	Recurve Total
Compound Only	61.1	61.1		
Crossbow Only	18.3		18.3	
Recurve Only	7.3			7.3
Compound and Crossbow (no Recurve)	6.9	6.9	6.9	
Compound and Recurve (no Crossbow)	3.1	3.1		3.1
Crossbow and Recurve (no Compound)	0.0		0.0	0.0
Compound, Crossbow, and Recurve	3.9	3.9	3.9	3.9
Totals	100.0	75.0	29.1	14.4

was made about the use of longbows in the survey.

Many archers owned and shot more than one type of bow.

Of interest here is again the dominance of the compound bow and the relatively small participation of recurve shooters. Recurve only shooters are less than 10% of the total number of compound shooters.

Gender distribution is also interesting.

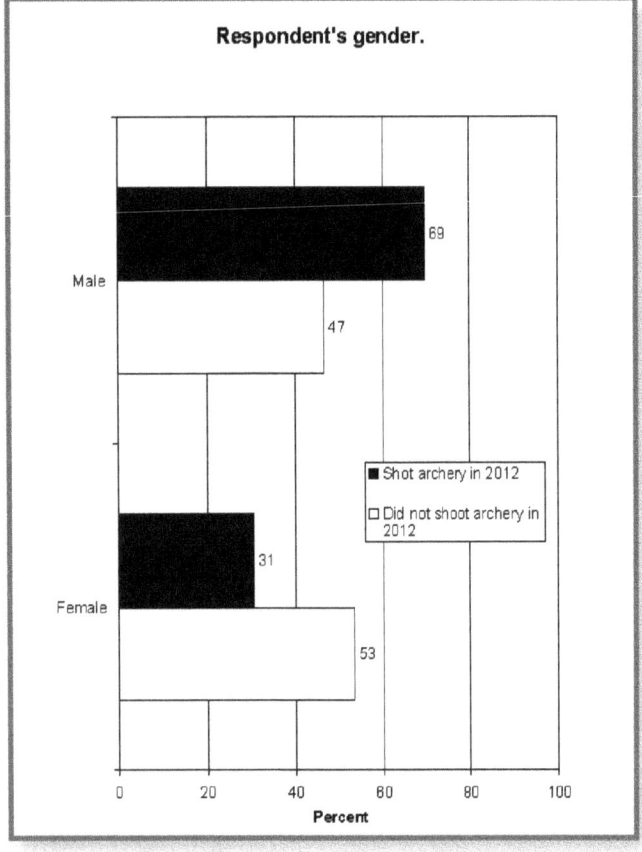

Of archers who shot in 2012, 31% were female and 69% were male. These numbers are consistent with the participation figures we see at Pasadena Roving Archers. There are a very high percentage of our participants who are adult women. At PRA, nearly half of these women shoot longbows with the remainder primarily shooting recurve. There are only a small number of women who shoot compound bows at the PRA range.

In the target-archery-only category, participation by women increases to 41% of the total. More intriguing is that among target-archery-only participants, the mean number of days shooting is only 6.3 days per year, hardly a commitment to the sport. Add in bowhunter/target archer participants and the mean number of days of archery shooting jumps to over 30 days for participants. Here's where the myth of hunting may have some substantiation. Bowhunters are more dedicated to the sport of archery and show it by participating in the sport for a greater number of days. According to the survey, target-only-archers are, on average, not particularly dedicated to coming out to shoot.

The survey indicates that archers primarily shoot at home or at a friend's private property. An overwhelming 72% of respondents shoot at home and not at an organized range or public park. Only 16% of participants shot at a private club or facility and another 15% shot on public land but not at an organized facility. These numbers reflect the convenience of backyard shooting, the near zero cost of range use, and a strong desire of archers to be independent and not be subject to externally applied regulations. Schools, parks and recreation centers added up to less than 10% of archery shooting sites for participating adults. Children were not polled in this survey and I'm sure the attendance figures for school, park and recreation center use would be higher for children.

For club organizers and pro shop management who want to attract archers to their facilities, there is a strong bias in the archery public against organized shooting that will have to be addressed in your programs. Clubs and shops located in urban areas will find a higher percentage of their market open to an organized shooting opportunity where backyard shooting becomes impractical or illegal by city regulation.

The ATA report from Responsive Management provides a wealth of information for the professional and organizational archery community. The

	Subgroup 1: Target Archery Only Participants	Subgroup 2: Target Archery and Bowhunting Participants	Subgroup 3: Bowhunting Only Participants	All Archery Participants (All Three Subgroups)
Gender				
Percent Male	59	82	84	69
Percent Female	41	18	16	31
Residence				
Percent Urban and Suburban	45	26	30	37
Percent Rural	54	74	70	62
Mean Age*	37.33	39.63	36.75	38.07
Equipment				
Percent Compound Only	45	61	63	56
Percent Crossbow Only	18	9	14	12
Percent Recurve Only	18	5	6	9
Percent Compound and Crossbow	4	9	5	7
Percent Compound and Recurve	3	10	5	7
Percent Crossbow and Recurve	0	0	1	0
Percent All Equipment	4	4	4	4
Participation Length				
Mean Number of Days	6.73	30.05	11.69	16
Median Number of Days	3	15	2	4

*Note that only people 18 years old and older were interviewed. Mean age is among adults.

report itself is academically dry and does not make for easy reading. With some effort, shop owners and club organizers can mine the information in the report and combine it with their own experience in their local market to come up with a strategy for attracting an audience to their products and services. Here are some ideas to explore:

Women are making up a higher and higher percentage of the archery market, especially in the target-archery-only category. Is your facility attractive to women? Or does it just feel like a man cave? Are the facilities clean and de-cluttered? Is there equipment available in sizes and draw weights suitable for smaller archers? Are there female staff members to help with customer contacts?

Women are often in charge of the children's activities. Is your facility kid friendly? Are there clean rest rooms and visitor seating available? Are there dead animals tacked to the walls? Lots of urban parents in particular are turned off by flagrant displays of hunting. Keep the trophies in the hunting equipment area and away from the range and target equipment racks.

Is there enough beginner and intermediate level gear in stock? Even adult beginners need very light draw weight equipment. Too heavy a bow will crush the beginning archer's shooting form. Is there enough equipment in children's sizes? Is the staff attuned to the needs of children and beginning archers?

Look at your local market. Nationwide, target archery dominates archery participation. Are your inventory and display areas balanced to reflect the local market conditions? As a hunter, a store owner may prefer to stock and promote hunting equipment. However, if hunting equipment is only what you stock, then hunting equipment is all you will sell. Target archers may try out your facility, find it doesn't meet their interests and go elsewhere, go on-line or simply quit in frustration. On-line retailers have made a profitable business out of meeting the needs of archers who can't find what they want at the local pro shop.

If the dominant location for archery participation nationwide is in private backyards, what can you do to attract archers to your facilities? Tournaments, leagues and competitions are the usual response and are a good place to start. Tournaments, however, don't address the social component of archery. Lots of shooters just like to hang out and fling a few arrows. Look to BBQs, Pot Luck suppers, Pizza days and craft fairs as additional ways to attract the public to your facility.

Many clubs are finding that archery classes and not tournaments are becoming a greater source of

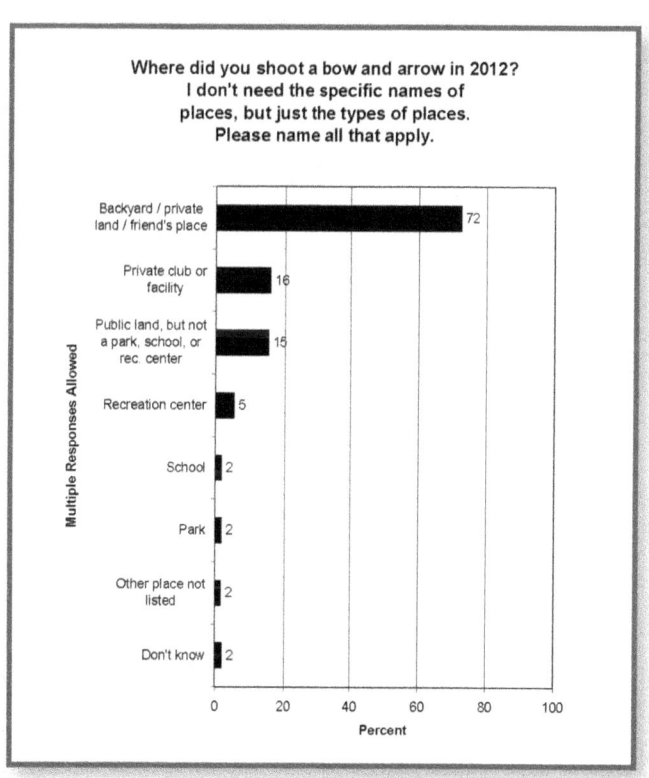

public participation and income. Offering a well-run, regularly scheduled archery instruction program is becoming the best way to attract new club members (and new customers for pro shops). Tournaments attract the same people to every event. Classes attract new participants to the sport. But remember, archery is a numbers game. To make classes work to grow memberships and businesses, you will need to see a high volume of first-timers to find the "archery addicts" who will stay with the sport.

Demonstrations, workshops and clinics from manufacturers can be a source of special event activities. There's a growing interest in traditional longbows and bow making. Hold a bow-making workshop at your facility. Look for events that will appeal to the general public. You will attract archers and you will attract potential archers who are just looking for a new experience.

Recreational archery is the foundation of the archery sport. It is through participation in archery that people learn the game and appreciate the skills needed to compete successfully. In big-time team and individual sports, it is the recreational athlete that develops a passion for the sport and becomes the fan base for the sport's showcase events. Recreational archery is essential to both the business and competitive health of the sport.

A lot of emphasis in the archery instructor training programs is placed on learning to teach the skills needed to develop competitive archers, and competitive recurve archers in particular. While it is very important to get a new archer off to a strong start, the overwhelming number of archery students will never compete, let alone at a top level. The survey shows that a majority of archers are compound archers with recurve archery coming in a distant third in participation after crossbows. The recurve bow is a terrific place to start for beginners as the recurve bow is easy to fit to the archer and can be operated without complex appliances. But people starting out with recurve gear may want to move in another direction when purchasing their own equipment. According to the ATA survey, 75% of archers shoot compound bows. At Pasadena Roving Archers we have also found a strong interest among our members and participants in shooting longbows.

Our experience at PRA also reflects industry figures about archery participation and competition. About 3% of people who take an introductory (free) archery class with us stay with the sport long enough to purchase equipment and join the club. The vast majority of first-timers come to the range, have a fun experience and then move on to other interests. 3% of that 3% have an interest in competitive target archery and commit to training one or more days a week. 1% to 3% of the 3% of the 3% have the talent, skill, motivation and resources needed to become a competitive target archer at the national level.

These percentages mean that you will have to work your way thorough 10,000-20,000 participants to find that one competitive archer. Does your program generate the kind of traffic that will see 10,000 archers in a year? Not many do, but it takes those kinds of numbers to identify and nurture true competitive talent. And what of the other 9,999 participants? These people are your real market. If you can build and maintain an archery program that serves the needs of 300 repeat archers per year, you can provide a valuable service to your community, your organization, your business and the sport of archery.

About the Author

Van Webster is a USA Archery Level 4-NTS Coach, a Level 3 Coach Leader, and was Head of Instruction at Pasadena Roving Archers in Pasadena, CA. Van teaches archery coach and instruction certification courses, as well as serving as an on camera spokesperson for PRA and the sport of archery. He has taught archery skills to principle actors in major motion pictures. His articles on archery have appeared in *Archery Focus* magazine.

Van Webster is president of Webster Communications, a presentation service company with clients in the entertainment, financial services, and sporting goods industries. Van was the founding chair of the Audio Recording Engineering Certificate program at UCLA Extension and served as a senior faculty member at UCLA Extension for more than 20 years. He also teaches fine art landscape photography with the Wandering Around Outdoors Photographic Workshops. He is active doing astronomy public outreach with the Los Angeles Astronomical society and the Local Group Astronomy Club of the Santa Clarita Valley. Van also plays guitar in a rock band a couple of times per month.

Van has a BA in Fine Arts from Claremont McKenna College and Masters Program credits in architectural design from California State Polytechnic University in San Luis Obispo, CA.

Van Webster lives in Los Angeles, CA

*Photo and Rear Cover photo
by Gary Spiers*

The Watching Arrows Fly Catalog

The Watching Arrows Fly Coaching Library

Still More on Coaching Archery (2014)
by Steve Ruis
More in the series–for all coaches.

Larry Wise on Coaching Archery (2014)
by Larry Wise
For compound and bowhunting coaches.

Archery Coaching How To's (2013)
by Steve Ruis
For those coaching out of their area of experise and beginning-to-intermediate coaches.

Even More on Coaching Archery (2013)
by Steve Ruis
Even more coaching advice for all coaches.

More on Coaching Archery (2010)
by Steve Ruis
More coaching advice for all coaches.

Coaching Archery (2008)
by Steve Ruis
For beginning-to-intermediate coaches.

All Titles Available on Amazon.com

General Archery Titles

ProActive Archery (2012)
by Tom Dorigatti
For compound archers wanting to be really good.

Professional Archery Technique (2009)
by Kirk Ethridge
Third Edition
Primarily for compound and 3-D archers.

Why You Suck at Archery (2012)
by Steve Ruis
Written for archers who want to learn why they aren't getting better and how they can.

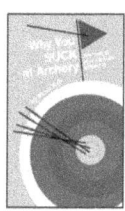

Winning Archery (2012)
by Steve Ruis
You learned how to shoot, now learn how to win .

Shooting Arrows (2012)
by Steve Ruis
Written to help adults cope with their new sport.

Confessions of an Archery Mom (2011)
by Lorretta Sinclair
Stories of an Archery Mom coping with three boys, all outstanding archers.

Archery 4 Kids (2010)
by Steve Ruis
Written for 8 to 14-year old beginners.

A Parent's Guide to Archery (2010)
by Steve Ruis
Written to help parents who have children in archery.

ArcheryFocus magazine

Has What You Need to Know to Become a Better Archer or Coach

Available OnLine at
www.archeryfocus.com

Where to Start? Try This!

There are lots of books about archery—about archery form, archery execution, archery equipment, even archery history; but there weren't any books in print on archery coaching . . . until now. Finally there is a book on coaching for beginning to intermediate archery coaches. In **Coaching Archery** you will learn not *what* to teach (which you can get that from those other books) but *how* to teach it and much more you won't get from certification courses. Topics include:
- tips on running programs
- the styles of archery
- the mental side of archery
- an exploration of archery coaching styles
- helping with equipment
- coaching at tournaments
- plus, advice on becoming a better coach from some top coaches

There are even seven whole pages of resources for coaches! If you are a archery coach looking to increase your coaching skills, this is the book for you!

128 pages • ISBN 978-0-9821471-0-8 • US $19.95

For Beginning Coaches!

An Archery Book for Kids!

Do you know kids just getting started in archery? There is so much to learn and, until now, it all had to be learned on the fly! Now there is a book for kids just getting started that will help them get a good start in the sport they are coming to love. Written for an 8-14-year old target audience, this book can be enjoyed by kids of all ages. Chapters include:
- Bows!
- Arrows and A Lot More
- Shooting
- Getting Your Own Gear
- Competing
- plus helpful Appendices

Each chapter has questions kids most often ask about the topic of that chapter plus answers! Kids learn from one of the most experienced and knowledgable coaches around, Steve Ruis, who is the editor of Archery Focus magazine as well as the authour of A Parent's Guide to Archery, Coaching Archery, Precision Archery (with Claudia Stevenson and other authors).

130 pages • ISBN 978-0-9821471-7-7 • US $14.95

Available at Better Bookstores and Online

Everything You Need to Know to Become a Better Archer!!

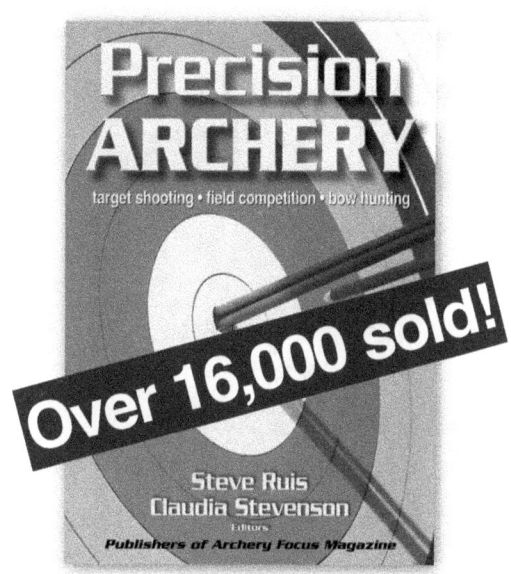

Written by your favorite **Archery Focus** authors—Rick McKinney, Don Rabska, Larry Wise, Ty Pelfrey, Dr. Lisa Franseen, Annette Musta, and others—**Precision Archery** covers every aspect of target archery. You'll find instruction on how to compete, how to perfect your form, and up-to-the minute advice on
- bow purchase, initial setup, and tuning
- fitness training to get and keep a competitive edge
- mental preparation and learning how to win
- how to adjust for wind, rain, and other adverse conditions
- the fine art of barebow
- how to work with a coach
- putting your shot together and taking it apart
- how to check out new equipment and work it into your shot

Nothing is left out, even the spirit of archery is addressed! If you are looking to take your game to the next level, this is the book for you!

216 pages • ISBN 0-7360-4634-8 • US $19.95

Available at Better Pro Shops and Archery Retailers!

Want to Know What It Takes to Win?

Are you . . . ?
An archer who is just starting to compete who
wants to get a head start on learning how to win.

Are you . . . ?
An archer who has been competing for a year or so and
is frustrated because you are not making more progress.

Are you . . . ?
An archer who has competed for quite a while but
never seems to get to those top three spots.

Then . . .

Winning Archery is the book for you! If you have read all of the "how to shoot" books and attended the shooter's schools but still find something is missing, **Winning Archery** addresses all the things you need to know outside of how to shoot that have been keeping you off of the Winner's Stand.

166 pages • ISBN 978-0-9821471-6-0 • US $19.95

Available at Amazon.com!

New In The The WAF Coaching Library!

LARRY WISE ON COACHING ARCHERY

Larry Wise, one of the premier archery coaches in the United States, is sharing his coaching wisdom, especially for coaches of compound-release archers but also bowhunters. So, if you coach or want to "self coach" yourself, there is now a new addition to the coaching literature just for you.

The **Watching Arrows Fly Coaching Library** is a effort to supply archery coaches with a literature, not just on the shooting of arrows out of bows but on how to coach people to do that better.

The Watching Arrows Fly Coaching Library

Larry Wise on Coaching Archery (Jan 2014)
Archery Coaching How To's (2013)
Even More on Coaching Archery (2013)
More on Coaching Archery (2010)
Coaching Archery (2008)

Available from Better Book Stores and Online Booksellers like Amazon.com

Now Available!

The **AER Recreational Archery Curriculum** takes beginning recurve, compound, and traditional archers from their first arrow all the way up to competing in major archery competitions. Detailed, step-by-step instructions tell beginning archers how to become intermediate level archers and then how to advance to expert levels. Each instruction includes an evaluation device so archers and coaches can track progress.

The Complete Archer's Guide is provided for student-archers of all ages who wish to be able to see and read about what they will be learning but is not required for participation in a program using this curriculum. **The Coach's Guide** inludes the entire Complete Archer's Guide with copious annotations and extensive appendices on what to teach and when and how to teach it.

The Curriculum is entirely flexible so Coaches and Archers can adapt it to their needs by changing the order of instructions or even replacing or augmenting them. Additional support is being provided to both Coaches and Archers at *www.ArcheryEducationResources.com*. All programs need to do to adopt and use this curriculum is to purchase one copy of the Coach's Guide. Get your copy today!

All of this is included in here!

Available from Amazon.com Now! and ArcheryEducationResources.com Soon!

More Now in The WAF Coaching Library!

Archery Coaching How To's

For Begining-to-Intermediate Coaches and Coaches Working Outside their Own Specialty

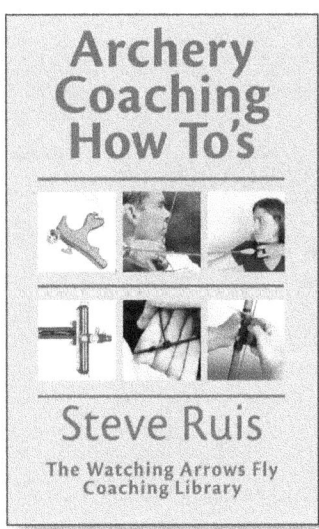

For archers there are all kinds of "how to" books available in print and on the Internet, but for coaches there is hardly anything. Even the coach training courses focus on *what* to teach instead of *how* to teach it. So where should coaches go for ideas as to *how* to introduce various pieces of archery equipment or new elements of form and execution, especially when those are outside of their core expertise? There really wasn't anything available, so I wrote this book. *Steve Ruis*

The **Watching Arrows Fly Coaching Library** is a effort to supply archery coaches with a literature, not just on the shooting of arrows out of bows but on how to coach people to do that better.

The Watching Arrows Fly Coaching Library

Larry Wise on Coaching Archery (Jan 2014)
Archery Coaching How To's (2013)
Even More on Coaching Archery (2013)
More on Coaching Archery (2010)
Coaching Archery (2008)

Available from Better Book Stores and Online Booksellers like Amazon.com

www.ingramcontent.com/pod-product-compliance
Lightning Source LLC
Chambersburg PA
CBHW080538170426
43195CB00016B/2605